MARGARET RUTHERFORD

Margaret Rutherford

DREADNOUGHT WITH GOOD MANNERS

A Biography by

ANDY MERRIMAN

First published in Great Britain
2009 by Aurum Press Ltd
7 Greenland Street
London NW1 0ND
www.aurumpress.co.uk

Frontispiece image courtesy of the Dawn Langley Simmons
collection, Duke University

A catalogue record for this book is available from
the British Library.

ISBN 978 1 84513 445 7

5 7 9 10 8 6 4

2009 2011 2013 2012 2010

Typeset in Garamond by SX Composing DTP, Rayleigh, Essex
Printed in Great Britain by Clays Ltd, St Ives plc

CONTENTS

Preface

'ALTHOUGH YOU'VE NEVER tried to be a glamour girl,' breathy BBC journalist Wendy Jones asked Margaret Rutherford in a radio interview in 1964, 'would you say your face is your fortune?'

After a beat – Rutherford's timing was always impeccable – the actress replied, 'Oh well . . . yes . . . I suppose I have to admit that my five chins may have something to do with it, and all the wrinkles that I have.'

It was, of course, her physiognomy and startling physicality that always drew attention to her performances. Indeed, no character actress has generated such an outpouring of descriptive pronouncements. It seems that Margaret Rutherford's very appearance gave journalists and critics licence to unleash unfettered metaphors and similes: she was depicted variously as a 'spaniel-jowled actress', a 'splendidly padded windmill', a 'dreadnought with good manners' and a 'glorious galleon in full sail firing salvos at all who crossed her bow'. One critic was even quoted as saying, 'If you hung the face of Margaret Rutherford on the side of the Notre Dame Cathedral she would make all the other gargoyles look like Audrey Hepburn. It is quite the ugliest old ragbag of a face you have ever seen.'

Rutherford herself was philosophical about the looks that the Good Lord had bestowed on her: 'If you have a face like mine, the thing is to learn to live with it and come to terms with it. This, I think, I have managed, and it has, after all, been rather good to me. The Americans called my face "an English muffin". It's true the nose is rather insignificant, one half of my mouth does not seem to work and would benefit by a little stretching; the lips have little body to them.'

A glamour girl she wasn't. A great actress she was.

Although Margaret Rutherford didn't make her first professional appearance until she was 33 and had to wait for nearly a decade for her West End debut in *Hervey House* at His Majesty's Theatre, Haymarket, like vintage champagne, when finally uncorked she came fizzing out of the bottle effervescent and inebriating.

She subsequently graced the theatre and the silver screen for over thirty years, and remains one of Britain's most popular actresses. She appeared in over forty films and was the highest earning British actress at MGM. In the late 1950s, she was voted one of the top ten box office stars of all time by the Motion Picture Herald Fame Poll, and in 1963 was awarded an Oscar for her role as supporting actress in *The VIPs*. She was much loved as Agatha Christie's famous sleuth, Miss Marple, in a quartet of films in the 1960s. It is also providential that she reprised on film a number of her celebrated stage appearances, which have thus been saved for posterity: her performances in *Aunt Clara*, *The Happiest Days of Your Life*, *The Importance of Being Earnest* and, of course, perhaps her most celebrated incarnation, as Madam Arcati in *Blithe Spirit*.

Margaret Rutherford's appeal has always been universal, as friend and writer Eric Keown recognised half a century ago: 'Most well known actresses fan a glow in only a particular section of the community. Some seem born to be the pin-up girls of the fifth-form study and it is easy to think of some clearly destined for the walls of the cavalry mess, and again of others whose natural gallery, if anywhere, would be the library of the Athenaeum. But Margaret Rutherford's gently rugged features know no vetoes. She appeals to all ages. Her comic genius dissolves elder statesmen and barrow boys, lorgnetted dowagers and the sternest critics in pretty frocks.'

She was formidable and yet sympathetic, fierce and yet human, and her background in elocution imbued the delivery of her dialogue with meticulousness and zest. She had the capacity in her repertoire for taking the character to its limit without overdoing it, and always used great judgement and consideration in tackling a part.

The drama critic and journalist J.C. Trewin remarked, 'When you have seen any performance by Margaret Rutherford you are certain to remember it. Those penetrating eyes, that quick, spring-heeled voice, remain in mind. She is, in the best sense of the word, an attacking comedienne, one with a flash bulb effect. Immediately she appears you realise that she has the gift, so vital to an actress, of establishing her character at once; there is no need for her to mess about, to play herself in.'

Inevitably Rutherford wished to be an actress in the grand tradition. 'How I would love to have been a great traditional actress like Bernhardt, Duse or Ellen Terry. There have been so many parts I yearned to play . . . there is a twinge of regret that I was typed for scatty types so often and therefore have not had the chance to tackle some of the serious major roles that I would have liked.' And yet acting for her could be a wondrous divertissement: 'All I wish to do is to take a back seat, to retire behind the personality of the part I am playing. There is a wonderful escapism in acting. When you are sick of yourself or of the futilities of life, it is marvellously refreshing to partake of the nature and life-blood of another being and forget yourself completely.'

And there was, indeed, much in her personal life from which to escape. Throughout her life, Margaret Rutherford was haunted by the spectre of mental illness, the suicide of her mother and a murder in her family which was kept secret. Hers was an existence shrouded in mystery and deceit. Rutherford herself suffered from manic depression – nowadays known as bipolar disorder – which at different times necessitated medication, institutionalisation and electroconvulsive therapy. She required regular rest cures from her self-diagnosed bouts of melancholia. Invariably she would recover temporarily, and to paraphrase one of her favourite creations, Miss Muriel Whitchurch in *The Happiest Days of Your Life*, take stock, 'and then into the fray like giant refreshed'.

The line between eccentricity and madness can be narrowly drawn, but Miss Rutherford always refused to play characters that she thought were of unsound mind. On the other hand, many of her characters over the years were described as 'inimitable', 'quirky', 'whimsical' and, most frequently, 'dotty'. In regard to the eccentric label, both on and offstage, Rutherford stated, 'I hope I am an individual. I suppose an eccentric is a super individual. Perhaps an eccentric is just off centre. But that contradicts a belief of mine that we have got to be centrifugal – diversified.' The irony was, of course, that Margaret Rutherford created the most hilarious eccentric onstage and bested any other actress in that role. Her sense of fashion offstage did nothing to diminish the eccentric persona, for she favoured billowing cloaks, colourful dress patterns and loud costume jewellery. But this was no affectation – she was merely being herself.

Rutherford did discover some happiness in her personal life, marrying late to actor Stringer Davis, whom she had known previously for fifteen years. She later ensured, through contractual obligation, that he appeared in most of her theatrical and film productions. Although not exactly a union of convenience – he cared for her devotedly for over 25 years throughout the vicissitudes of her life – there was a suggestion that Stringer was not rampantly heterosexual. Writer Matthew Sweet described it delicately as the existence of 'a touch of lavender in the marriage'.

Throughout her life, Rutherford was attracted to gentle, effete men, professionally, socially and romantically. The lack of a father figure or male role model during her formative years, other than uncles and cousins, may have had an effect on her somewhat quixotic choices of suitors.

Margaret Rutherford was the tenderest of friends with a most generous nature, and was drawn to people whom she perceived as being different and in need of protection. A somewhat naïve collector of waifs and strays, she befriended a mercurial Jordanian Prince and lavished gifts and kindness on a number of 'hangers-on'. Her relationship with Dawn Langley Simmons, a transsexual who claimed to be adopted by the actress and wrote a self-serving biography of 'Mother Rutherford', was based on a major deceit.

Margaret Rutherford may have been unsophisticated and unworldly but she possessed a strong moral creed, born from her religious beliefs. Selflessly loyal, an enthusiastic charity worker and unlikely prison visitor, she knew what was right and what was wrong. Her close friend, actor and writer Robert Morley, said, 'Margaret Rutherford was everyone's Maiden Aunt . . . a woman of enormous integrity who acted naturally – once she found out where the laughs were she never let up. She was like a bulldog in a way. She fastened her teeth into a script and she never varied and was always frightfully funny.'

ONE

Murder at Matlock

'A man's dying is more the survivors' affair than his own.'

THOMAS MANN

A TRAGIC EVENT IN the Rutherford family history which was to torment the actress throughout her life actually occurred nearly a decade before Margaret's birth: a grisly murder, far more bloody than any she was to investigate in her later guise as Agatha Christie's Miss Marple and committed by a man in the throes of a psychotic breakdown. The perpetrator was her father, William Benn, and the victim was his own father, Margaret's grandfather, Rev. Julius Benn.

The Reverend Benn, who was born in 1826, was originally a schoolmaster before joining the London City Mission. He became involved in the institution of reformatories and then took charge of the first such school in England. In 1868 he became pastor of Old Gravel Lane Congregational Meeting House in Wapping, East London, and it was reported in a tribute following his death that 'his labours on behalf of the poor and vicious in that district were unremitting'.

His wife, Ann, bore him eight children, the eldest of which was Sir John Williams Benn, grandfather of veteran politician Tony Benn, MP. William Rutherford Benn was born in 1855 and was, according to Tony's brother, David, 'in some way, the most civilised and educated of all the Benns'. He spoke several languages, was an accomplished poet and worked as a journalist and, in the words of the 1891 census, 'translator of languages'. In her somewhat hazy auto-biography,* Margaret romantically described him as 'a traveller in silks in India'.

William Rutherford Benn and Florence Nicholson were married at All Saints Church, Wandsworth, on 16 December 1882. Only one member of the Nicholson family attended: Florence's sister, Bessie, who acted as bridesmaid. Both Florence's parents were dead and another sister had drowned herself some years before.

The honeymoon and first few weeks of marriage were by no means a period of wedded bliss. William fell ill with depression, and there is some suggestion that this was caused by his failure to consummate the union. Exactly a month after the wedding, William was admitted to the Bethnal House Lunatic Asylum. Medical reports at the time described him as suffering from 'depression alternating with unusual excitement and irritability'.

Within a few weeks his condition had improved, and the attending doctors advised that he could be discharged. The family felt that he should not return to Florence, but that 'a rest cure in the country' would be beneficial. With the necessary paperwork completed, William's father, Julius, decided that the two of them should take a trip to the picturesque spa town of Matlock, Derbyshire.

On 27 February 1883, father and son arrived at their destination and took apartments at a Mrs Marchant's house in the Chesterfield Road, Matlock Bridge. 'Both men were abstemious – nothing in William Benn's conduct betrayed that he was in the slightest degree of unsound mind,' reported the *Derby Daily Telegraph*. 'He and his father were on the most affectionate terms and appeared to be very attached to each other. They were in the habit of taking long walks with each

* She mistakenly calls him Ernest Rutherford; she must have been thinking of her cousin.

other and appeared to enjoy local sights. All went most happily until Sunday morning, the 4th March.'

Suspicions were aroused by noises emanating from their room and the fact that neither of the gentlemen had appeared for breakfast or lunch. 'Mrs Marchant, accompanied by her husband, entered the Benns' room to find William Benn, his night shirt covered in blood, pointing to his father, who lay on the bed quite dead.'

It was assumed that the blow had been struck while the reverend was asleep, as there were no signs of a struggle. The deadly weapon, an earthenware chamber pot, was stained with blood, but had not been broken or chipped by the force of the blow.

Within two days the story had reached the national newspapers. An article in *The Times* on the 6 March reported, 'On Sunday morning a scuffle was heard in their room, and the door being opened, the father was found dead with his skull battered in, and the son with his throat cut. The young man now lies in the infirmary at Derby. He appears to be quite unconcerned and it is stated that he acknowledged having killed his father. The wound to his throat, which appears to have been self-inflicted, is not serious, and the doctors at the infirmary stated last night that there was no danger of fatal consequences, but that in a short time the patient will be fit to be moved. Yesterday afternoon . . . an inquest was opened and adjourned. It is stated that the son William Benn has been for some time in a lunatic asylum and has only recently been set free; and that his father had intended again to place him again under restraint in the hands of some responsible person at Matlock.'

William made what seems to have been another desperate attempt to commit suicide several days later in Derby infirmary. While Police Constable Alexander was putting on his boots prior to being relieved of his duty, William threw himself through the window. Despite falling over twenty feet and suffering back injuries and cuts, he was not seriously injured, and was recaptured.

Following the arrest, William's devoted brother, John, who in 1892 would become the Liberal Member of Parliament for Tower Hamlets, hurried to Matlock for the inquest in an attempt to convince the coroner that William was insane. However, the jury decided unanimously that Julius Benn was 'wilfully murdered by his son, William Rutherford Benn'. William was committed to the mercy of the Derbyshire Assizes where, if found guilty, he would be sentenced to death by hanging.

William's mental condition further deteriorated, and in another appearance before The Honourable W.M. Jervis he was quite incoherent, referring to the magistrate as 'Pontius Pilate'. The Home Secretary, William Harcourt, ordered Benn's removal to Broadmoor and declared that 'the case against him has been abandoned.' On 6 April 1883, William Benn was removed to the infamous criminal asylum, where doctors concluded that he would never recover his sanity.

Meanwhile, a memorial fund was set up to support the widow and dependent children. A large committee of local ministers and dignitaries, including Thomas John Barnardo, founder of the children's homes, convened to enlist the help of the Reverend's parishioners and local residents, who also contributed to the fund.

On 26 July 1890, following a period of seven years in Broadmoor, William was discharged to the care of Florence. His devoted wife, who had acquired a lease on a house in Balham, south London, had never given up hope of being re-united with her husband and had written to him regularly. Although they had been married for nearly eight years, the couple had spent only a few brief unhappy weeks together, and clearly must have rekindled their relationship with some trepidation. Because of the family's status and the public knowledge of the murder, William had now changed his name by deed poll to William Rutherford, adopting his middle name as his surname.

There is no question that this time the marriage was consummated; their daughter, Margaret Taylor Rutherford, was born on 11 May 1892 at 15 Dornton Road, situated on the edge of Tooting Bec common and then in the Borough of Wandsworth. The 'occupation of father' on baby Margaret's birth certificate signposts the family's next move: William Rutherford is now described as an 'East India Merchant'. Within a few months of Margaret's birth, the three Rutherfords left London to make a new life in India. For them, it was Balham – gateway to the East.

Little is known of their life in the Raj but it has been suggested that William was greatly affected by the poverty and disease that he observed, and dedicated himself to working in the slums of Madras. According to Tony Benn, William was a shipping clerk by trade but supplemented his income with journalistic commissions. He also found time to compose topical songs for his brother John.

Margaret Rutherford was extremely young during this period in India, and in later life her only memory of this time was that her parents bought her a very small white pony for her birthday, although this recollection may well have been a fantasy resulting from a desire to produce at least one happy experience from her childhood. In any case, the family did appear to be settled and William's mental health was stable.

Within a year of their arrival in India, however, all was to change. Florence became pregnant again, and, to all intent and purposes, the Rutherford family were to be complete. Sadly this event brought her no happiness. Instead, as the months passed, Florence became increasingly miserable and disturbed. William was obviously no stranger to the torment of mental illness and recognised that his own dear wife, who had never before exhibited such behaviour, was suffering some kind of breakdown. He immediately made plans to return to England, but her depressive illness had already taken hold, and the strategy to save her proved to be belated and tragically unsuccessful. One morning at dawn, a servant found Florence hanging from a tree in their garden. Like her sister before her, Florence had killed herself.

Three months later, in the spring of 1895, William returned to England and immediately made his way to Florence's sister Bessie's house in Wimbledon. He banged on the door, in a frenzied state with the three-year-old Margaret in hand, and implored Bessie to look after her niece, to which she immediately agreed. Margaret never referred to this incident, and may well have involuntarily erased it from her memory.

In reality, William never recovered from his wife's death and suffered a number of breakdowns. According to the official hospital records held at Broadmoor, after bringing Margaret home William returned to India and then lived in Paris, working as a journalist. David Benn is of the opinion that William returned to India with the thoughts of re-marrying, but that, 'When his brother John heard of this, he felt obliged to stop the marriage.' Following his return to England in 1903, William Rutherford was admitted to the Northumberland House Asylum in Finsbury Park on 22 January. It is not known if a specific incident precipitated his re-incarceration, but two days later, when he could no longer be contained, he was transferred to Broadmoor.

On Margaret's arrival at the cosy but modest home of Berkeley Place there followed a family discussion about what she should be told. It was felt that she should be shielded from her father's incarceration at Broadmoor, and she was thus told that he had died. What she knew of the circumstances of her mother's death is unclear. Whatever her plight, it was agreed that in light of William Rutherford's wishes and Aunt Bessie being an eminently suitable guardian, Margaret – or 'Peggy', as she was known to family – should remain in Wimbledon. Thus for the next five years she lived with Aunt Bessie and maintained contact with both paternal and maternal sides of the family. Bessie did not live alone, so there was initially some company for Margaret: in addition to Bessie, who was aged 44, also in residence were her brother, Guy, his daughter, Muriel, aged five, and two servants, Amy and Elizabeth. According to Dawn Langley Simmons' biography, 'The Benns retained a lively interest in the child – they never forgot her birthdays, Easter and Christmas.'

Margaret described herself as 'a grave child, my face was oval like a bantam egg and I had green eyes as round as pennies. My hair was auburn tinged and fine as floss and I wrinkled my nose like a rabbit. I was also a lonely child.' Margaret had no school friends, her aunt deciding to educate her charge herself at home. An interview with the *Ladies Journal* in 1950 provided a glimpse into her somewhat bohemian upbringing: 'I had a wonderful aunt, who I called my adoptive mother, one of the saints of the world – and a gay saint too, who cheered the days of someone who would otherwise have been quite a sad little girl. The knowledge of French that she gave me by reading aloud each day as I lay on the floor by doctor's orders (having an inclination to curvature) has been a stand-by all my life.'

Bessie also introduced Margaret to the notion of the afterlife. She imparted her belief that although people died in a physical sense, their spirit lived on. 'Aunt Bessie believed herself to be gifted with psychic powers. She was quite sure that if one asked a dead relative to intercede personally with God for something sensible like a new pair of Sunday shoes – of course in a nice, ladylike way – there was a good chance that the prayer would be granted.'

Bessie Nicholson was interested in the theatre and encouraged 'Peggy' to participate in family productions. 'I was eight years old when I made my mind up I was going to be an actress. I was playing the bad fairy in a play to entertain some people in their home in Kensington. It was difficult enough to be playing a fairy dressed in black net, threaded with gold and a tall hat studded with gold stars. Then a cousin, Graham Nicholson, fell ill and I literally stepped into his shoes and doubled as the part of the prince.' Margaret later recounted her first entrance: 'It was spectacular. As an adult beat the tin tray, I tripped in. That night I went to bed filled with dreams of being an actress. This was to be my life – there could be nothing else.'

An example of Margaret's early life and possible career choice is also referred to. 'Like most girls of five I wanted to be a nurse. I even made a patient of my tennis racquet. I often pretended that the racquet had ear ache and gave it ear lotion which promptly ran through the gap in the handle and soaked the pillow.'

Fortunately for Margaret, Aunt Bessie decided that she required some formal education and, in September 1900, at the age of eight, she was enrolled at the nearby Wimbledon High School. The all girls' school opened in 1880 and was then situated in Wimbledon Hill. The first headmistress was a Miss Hastings, whose initial address seems to have incubated Margaret Rutherford's life philosophy: 'Be fair, be open and truthful in your work, in your games, in your homes. Every girl must do the best she can for herself but you can all think of others too. The characteristic I beg you all individually to cultivate still more, is loyalty.'

Peggy was recorded as number 1288 on the Register and in her full name of Margaret Taylor Rutherford. There were no details of her parents and her guardian was named as her aunt, Miss Nicholson of 4 Berkeley Place, Wimbledon. The Register confirms that she did not attend any schools prior to Wimbledon High.

Although socially Margaret had been isolated, Aunt Bessie's educational methods must have been effective, because soon after enrolment Margaret was moved up a year. The school archive possesses the earliest surviving photograph of Margaret Rutherford, aged about eight and pictured with her class, accompanied by a sample of her writing – already neat and elegant. There is also a hand-painted cast list and colour drawing, sketched in 1901, to mark the twenty-first anniversary of the school. It was in this year that Peggy gave her first public dramatic performance on a proper stage – when she undertook the role of Jack in a selection of Nursery Rhyme Quadrilles. In the hand-painted cast list, that records her debut, Margaret receives equal billing with Bridget Young, who played opposite her as Jill.

Her friends at this time included Clarissa Graves, sister of poet and writer Robert Graves. In his account of his early life, *Goodbye to All That*, Graves describes his fear of having to meet his sister after school and being terrorised by her classmates – one of whom we must suppose was the frightening Peggy Rutherford. Peggy and her classmates produced a newspaper entitled the *Pinc*, named after its contributors, editors and printers, namely Peggy, Irene, Nancy and Clarissa.

The more official organ of the institution, the Wimbledon High School Magazine, reported that the annual distribution of certificates took place respectively on 30 November and 1 December 1900. The following account appeared in the *Wimbledon News*: 'The concerts were witnessed by a large assembly of parents and friends of the pupils. Songs were excellently rendered, carefully played piano solos were given, and five little girls from the Lower Preparatory recited "The cat's tea party" very prettily . . . Before presenting the certificates at the close of the concert, Miss Hastings, the school's head mistress, read a report of the year's work which showed that the school was full, the work had been satisfactory and good progress had been made during the year.' The junior concert on 30 November contained a pianoforte solo, 'In the Garden' (OPUS 82) by Cornelius Gurlitt, which was performed by 'P. Rutherford, of Form 1'. The young Margaret Rutherford was already exhibiting the musical prowess which was to be extremely useful to her in years to come.

According to other school records, Margaret was absent for the whole spring term in 1902 and most of the spring term and the first half of the summer term in 1904. The first long absence is unexplained but, for the 1904 spell, there is a likely and somewhat disturbing explanation.

About this time, Margaret recalled opening the front door of the Wimbledon house to be confronted by a dishevelled old man with the appearance of a tramp. He told her that he had brought her a message from her father. She was naturally astonished and told the man that this could not be, for her father had died in India. The 'tramp' told her that her father was very much alive, but locked away in Broadmoor, adding, 'He sends you his love.' With those words, he departed. The distraught Margaret confronted Aunt Bessie, who then decided to tell the twelve-year-old girl the truth about her father. She explained that William Benn was indeed in a hospital for the criminally insane, and also spelled out the tragic story of her family background.

Damaris Hayman, Rutherford's great friend for twenty years, is convinced that Margaret, following this visit, was panic-stricken that her father – who, she had just learnt, had murdered her grandfather – might escape from Broadmoor and cause her harm. There is absolutely no evidence that William was anything other than a doting father to her, but there is equally no doubt that Margaret was shocked and terrified by this revelation, and by the visit of this fellow patient of her father's, who in later life she likened to King Lear.

Margaret was inconsolable and reacted by sinking into long periods of non-communication, deep gloom and much crying. This was the first in a series of depressive breakdowns. The news did not just cause her immediate shock and misery – it was to have profound and lifelong consequences. From the age of twelve she would be afflicted by the fear that she was herself as unstable as her psychotic father and her suicidal mother.

In November 1904 the Broadmoor Medical Superintendent recorded that a relative* of William Rutherford requested that all William's correspondence should be forwarded to him first. On 21 March 1905 William Rutherford sent a lengthy letter to the Medical Superintendent which included a brief mention of Margaret. 'If I wanted news of my daughter,' he wrote, 'I had to trouble you to stir them [his relatives] up for a letter,' and also that 'owing to the thoughtfulness of a rich old lady, my little girl is placed beyond the reach of discomfort and is being well educated and cared for'.

Throughout her life, Margaret publicly maintained a completely different story. In her 1971 autobiography she described her father as a 'complicated romantic who changed his name to Rutherford as it was more aesthetic for a writer. My father died in tragic circumstances soon after my mother and so I became an orphan.' We can assume that Margaret's version of events was concocted to protect herself and her extended family from this desperate story of madness, murder and suicide. It was a fabrication that she took to her grave.

* Whose identity is not known.

Peggy was deeply affected and remained an 'unhappy child' in the year following this dramatic disclosure. She left Wimbledon High School in July 1905, at the age of thirteen. The School Register noted that there was 'no reason stated' for her departure. The explanation she later gave was that 'Aunt Bessie felt I should mix more with girls of my age and that a spinster's house might be too lonely for such an introspective girl'. Aunt Bessie might well have felt that the overwhelming responsibility of caring for her niece was too much for her and that a new environment might be beneficial for both of them. She decided to send Margaret to Raven's Croft, a private boarding school in the country, run by two redoubtable sisters, the Misses Mullins. The school was originally established, in 1895 by Miss Isabel Mullins and her sister, Miss Margaret Mullins, in Surrey but relocated in 1909 to newly built premises near to the English Channel at Seaford, Sussex.

Margaret reacted surprisingly well to being away from Aunt Bessie and the genteel environs of Wimbledon, although her attendance was not without some difficulties. She admitted that she found most of the subjects arduous simply through lack of interest, but that she was proficient at English and French. 'I was never really good at games. It wasn't that I didn't try – I used to put my chin down and charge down the hill clutching my hockey stick. At the school cricket match I made four runs and thought I was sensational.'

A calamitous timekeeper throughout her life, Margaret's problems with punctuality seem to have begun here. 'I was often late for lessons,' she wrote. 'I have never been too occupied with time, unless it affected my work as an actress.' It was also at Raven's Croft that she met a girl who was to remain one of her closest friends for the rest of her life. Dorothy Whatmore, later Vaisey, was instrumental in helping Margaret's career, and Margaret referred to her on occasions as her 'Fairy Godmother'.

Mark Cardale, Dorothy's grandson, learnt through the family that both Peggy and his grandmother had won some form of scholarship which gave them a reduction in the school fees. In return, the two of them were expected to become governesses with 'well-to-do' families following their education. Dorothy's father was a teacher and later a county education officer who became involved in amateur dramatics; Dorothy's mother was also a teacher and ran her own nursery school, her own parents having been 'travelling players'. The eldest Whatmore son, Arthur Reginald, was born in 1889 and known to the family as 'Reg', although in his professional theatrical career he remained A.R. Whatmore.

Mark Cardale also reported that, 'Dorothy herself was a gifted pianist, who also much enjoyed all things theatrical.' The girls had much in common, and, even then, 'Peggy was resolutely determined to be an actress, and I believe that she and my grandmother used to put on little shows at the school together'. Apart from these playlets, Margaret gained useful experience in a Raven's Croft production of *The Tempest*, in which she was cast as Prospero.

In addition to their shared theatrical interests and the fact that they were both 'scholarship' girls, Dorothy was also extremely protective towards Peggy. 'Peggy's physical appearance, which helped so much in later years to make her such a beloved character, was very much against her at school, where she was occasionally teased as a result,' explained Mark Cardale. 'I remember a story about Dorothy rescuing Peggy from trouble with the headmistress after a dormitory pillow fight.' One hopes that this loyalty was reciprocated, although Dorothy Vaisey did indeed comment on the fact that Peggy Rutherford was a great favourite of the younger girls, in whom she took a special motherly interest. Rutherford made a habit of looking after and mothering her friends and acquaintances throughout her professional and personal life.

When the question of future employment was raised by Isabel Mullins, Margaret replied that she wished nothing more than to be a professional actress. Miss Mullins was suitably shocked and the following day both Miss Mullinses confronted Margaret and firmly proclaimed that young ladies at Raven's Croft just did not become professional actresses. Instead, in Rutherford's own words, 'They decided that I showed promise in piano playing and I was to be prepared for the Associateship of the Royal Academy of Music.' In an appearance in the BBC radio show *Desert Island Discs* many years later, Margaret declared that her music teacher offered to train her for her ARCM at a greatly reduced fee.

In addition to music tuition, Margaret was the recipient of elocution lessons while still at school. Mark Cardale is convinced that both she and his grandmother benefited from such teaching, 'I think it is said that Peggy's speaking voice was much developed by the elocution classes she took after leaving school. This may be so, but I think the process will have been started at school. I say this because my grandmother also had a most powerful voice with the clearest possible diction. I am sure they must have had something like Speech and Drama classes at Raven's Croft, and someone who was probably rather good at teaching the subject.'

Neither Dorothy nor Peggy became governesses, although Margaret did stay on an extra year to teach some of the younger children. The school closed in 1965, but right up until then the name of P. Rutherford remained visible on one of the prefect boards that hung in the school's assembly hall.

There is no doubt that Margaret's school days were extremely influential. She remained in contact with both Wimbledon High School and Raven's Croft and visited whenever she could. An article by Wimbledon old girl Lesley Anderson in the school magazine in December 1918 recalled one such event: 'When I was in Upper IV there was an old girls' conference and for some reason we were invited to take part in a performance of Gilbert and Sullivan's *Trial by Jury*, which was to entertain the conference. I was fortunate enough to be included and for the first time heard the name Margaret Rutherford. I never spoke to her but in the front row of the jury box I had an uninterrupted view of the wonderful performance she gave us as the judge. Often since then I have watched her with the same keen admiration and enjoyment.'

Margaret was also approached by the school some years later, when appearing on the West End stage in *Blithe Spirit*. There were plans to make a film of the history of the school, so the headmistress had written to one of her most celebrated old girls. The actress replied and enclosed a number of photographs from various theatrical appearances.

THE PICADILLY THEATRE
DECEMBER 12TH 1941

Dear Miss Wedgwood,

Herewith are photographs of the parts I have played in the West End. They are rather large but perhaps your photographer will be able to make negatives to his satisfaction.

The idea of a film is very good and enterprising one. Very good luck to it.

Yours sincerely
Margaret Rutherford

Her devotion was also acknowledged by the wonderfully named Elfrida Down Kettleborough in Simmons' biography: 'In 1952 I was asked to help nurse Miss Margaret Mullins, former headmistress at Raven's Croft, who suffered a stroke. Peggy never failed to ring and ask after her – even when she was in great demand as an actress.'

'I spent many happy years at Seaford and I still claim that Sussex air is the loveliest in England,' said Margaret in the *Ladies Journal* interview. 'It gave me a tremendous appetite as a child, our headmistress believed in feeding us well and I can still remember my feeling of greed on seeing my plate piled high with bread and butter at tea time and how speedily I used to reduce the mountain to plate level.'

TWO

Articulation and Arpeggios

'A Tudor who tooted a flute
Tried to tutor two tooters to toot.
Said the two to their tutor,
"Is it harder to toot
Or to tutor two tooters to toot?"'

MARGARET RUTHERFORD LEFT Raven's Croft in 1911 to return to live full time with her Aunt Bessie in Wimbledon. At the age of nineteen she still held a deep desire to be an actress but, armed with her music qualification (ARCM in piano), embarked reluctantly on a teaching career. Money was short and she could at least earn some kind of living giving piano lessons. Already too much of a free spirit to teach in the school system, Rutherford decided private tuition was more suited to her character and was successful in finding work locally. She also utilised a cheap form of transport: 'During the years that I taught music I used to hang my leather music bag on the handle bars and cycle around Wimbledon in all weathers visiting my pupils.'

This image of a determined woman, pedalling furiously away, hair flowing and cape flying, was replicated in her most famous role as

Madame Arcati in *Blithe Spirit* at the Piccadilly Theatre, and later in the film version. Her time commuting around the leafy Wimbledon streets proved efficacious. 'Cycling became second nature to me so that when I played Madame Arcati in the stage production of many years later, it was no problem for me to come cycling on to the stage and pull up before I hit the footlights.'

The freewheeling Miss Rutherford admitted, however, that she was not a good music teacher. 'My thoughts were always far away with an unseen audience. To me, unfortunately, being a music teacher was only a way to make a living and help my adoptive mother, now noticeably older and slower of step. I was not patient enough. It was merely a means of making money and meant no more to me than if I had taken a milk or paper round . . . besides I was often far too honest in telling the parents, when their unfortunate offspring hated music, that no power in the world could ever make it like playing the piano.'

It is quite evident that teaching music was not her raison d'être. Margaret had been stage-struck since a little girl and remained desperate to tread the boards professionally. She considered all the options and discovered that there was another avenue in which she could learn more about her intended craft, and at the same time gain another teaching qualification: she would study for a diploma in elocution.

Before such phrases as 'A noisy noise annoys an oyster' and 'The rain in Spain stays mainly on the plain' became synonymous with the art of elocution, the discipline had long been formalised. The leading exponent during the eighteenth century was the Irish actor Thomas Sheridan, author of the influential *Lectures on Elocution*, which he presented on a tour around Britain in 1762. He was also the father of playwright Richard Brinsley Sheridan, who was to provide two of Margaret Rutherford's more important roles in future years.

Elocution was not just a tool for actors in regard to clear diction and projection, it was also used for gesture and posture. Performers could study voice in detail while perfecting pronunciation, grammar, tone and the rhythm of the English language. Non-thespians soon realised that speaking clearly and being able to hold oneself with confidence could enhance their social position. Thus, a half-century after Sheridan's tour, elocution became popular with the middle classes, who began taking private lessons. School teachers realised the importance of speaking with confidence and saw what difference it could make to their pupils' careers. The subject of elocution was added to the school curriculum in certain schools.

While continuing to teach piano, Margaret duly studied for her LRAM (voice). She subsequently passed her exam – one imagines, with distinction – and was now a 'Licentiate of the Royal Academy of Music'. Armed with twin diplomas, Margaret visited homes all over south London, imparting her knowledge of music and elocution and in the words of Eric Keown, 'leaving behind her a thickening trail of pure "Es" and rounded "Os"'.

Margaret recalled these formative days as a would-be actress with due respect: 'I am a great believer in repertory as the best training for an actress but I would strongly advise any stage applicant to include in their training a study of speech and all that goes with it in the way of breath control and so on, in order to have the most necessary thing for an actress – a good mechanism, or shall we say instrument, upon which to play.'

She continued to work throughout the First World War, and maintained a love of poetry, which she would recite to wounded soldiers in military hospitals. In order to gain acting experience, she joined the local Wimbledon Amateur Dramatic Society and paid for lessons from an old Shakespearean actor, Acton Bond, who was recommended by a confident family member: 'Acton has impeccable manners and will not make unseemly advances towards Margaret.'

Although only in her sixties, Aunt Bessie suffered a series of strokes and became more dependent on her devoted niece. Bessie's brother Guy had moved away and she was now Margaret's charge: their roles had reversed. It seems the servants had long departed, and it was left to Margaret to care for her aunt, which she did with kindness and devotion – although other family members would have ensured that the couple were not left to their own devices. According to Dawn Langley Simmons, 'On Sunday afternoons, if the weather was fine, Margaret Rutherford pushed Bessie throughout the familiar streets in her wicker bathchair, which the latter steered with the aid of a sticklike device. Margaret Rutherford and the large bath chair dwarfed the regal little lady wearing the big hat overly decorated with whatever flowers were in season – and always holly at Christmas.'

Margaret's relationship with her father during this period is less coherent, although behind the scenes, and probably unknown to Margaret, the family, most likely in the guise of William's brother John Benn, continued to be involved in William's welfare. In early 1909 the Home Office refused a family request to conditionally discharge William Rutherford. A telling comment on file states that, 'Whether he is allowed to visit his daughter, or is prevented doing so, the result will probably be the same so far as his mental condition is concerned. His daughter's sanity would be endangered if she were allowed to associate with him.'

Later in the year, another family member[*] wrote to the Broadmoor Superintendent that 'William's recent correspondence makes us all anxious on account of his daughter . . . he has written direct to her contrary to the promise made it should go through my hands.' The hospital authorities decided to encourage correspondence between father and daughter, but only if William remained discreet about his situation. A memo on the medical records indicates that Broadmoor staff complied with the family's request to filter William's letters to his daughter, although they 'saw nothing objectionable in his correspondence'.

Between February and March 1911 there is further correspondence between Broadmoor staff and a third family member. The hospital's Medical Superintendent, Dr Baker, stated that, 'I am under the impression that William Rutherford's immediate object is to get into more direct touch with his daughter.' As the years of institutionalisation

[*] Again, the identity is unknown.

passed, Rutherford grew more desperate to see Margaret, but the family's response was to become increasingly protective of his daughter. On 25 May 1919 a family member wrote that 'William's actions, in regard to his daughter, render it necessary, from my point of view, that all his outgoing letters . . . should be sent to me for censorship . . . this is the more important to us just now for he seems to be making desperate efforts to get his daughter to see him, doubtless to use her to further his release. Further efforts in this direction will, I fear, result in the poor girl's collapse. She is already having sleepless nights.'

In August of the same year, there is a note on the file that William had told a visiting relative that 'the time has come when he should be allowed to see his daughter'. The relative replied that 'he could not possibly do this . . . for his daughter's sake.' The thought of poor William Rutherford being deprived any contact with his 'Peggy' is heart-rending but there is no doubt that the Benn family was acting in her best interests. The various relatives clearly believed she should be protected from the unpredictable behaviour of her father, which might have a harmful effect on her already frail mental state.

By 1921, William's physical health had begun to fail and, in a letter dated 3 July, the family requested that the hospital authorities consider transferring him to a more suitable institution where he could spend his last days. The correspondence also stated that Margaret agreed to this arrangement. William Rutherford was duly moved to the City of London Asylum at Stone, near Dartford, Kent. After suffering two strokes, he contracted pneumonia and died on 4 August 1921, aged 66.

It is difficult to know how Margaret was affected at this time. There is no evidence from the hospital records of her ever visiting her father. She may have written to him, but any correspondence would have been sent via her relatives, and might not have been archived at Broadmoor. She had publicly denied his recent existence and history. There must have been a palpable sense of relief: finally *her* truth had become reality. And yet, kind and sensitive as she was, she must also have felt extraordinarily guilty – she had after all, in her own mind, 'killed' her father. Now, at the age of 33, she really was an orphan.

Within four years, another death, which may have had a less profound psychological effect on Margaret, actually provided a physical release from her prevalent existence. Bessie Nicholson, following yet another stroke, passed away in 1923. Margaret inherited a small legacy, which she was determined to invest in some formal theatrical training. She had no connections in the world of professional theatre, so was grateful when her old school friend Dorothy Whatmore, now Dorothy Vaisey, initiated a series of introductions which led to a meeting with Andrew Leigh, head of the Old Vic School. One morning a letter arrived, advising Margaret of an audition with the legendary Lilian Baylis. 'All heaven had opened for me,' she later reflected. 'I rushed out to buy some shoes and chose my most stylish green silk dress from my modest little wardrobe. I never had any money to spend on clothes in those days. All the way down to Waterloo I wondered if this would be my chance. Lilian Baylis was the Queen of the Old Vic.'

Lilian Baylis had originally become involved in theatrical production by assisting her Aunt Emma Cons in running the Royal Victoria Hall and Coffee Tavern near Waterloo station. Following the death of Emma Cons in 1912, Miss Baylis took over complete control. Bryan Forbes, in his biography of Edith Evans, described Lilian Baylis as, one of the most improbable figures ever to achieve theatrical immortality, 'Even coming from Shaw's pen the idea of a 39-year-old spinster running a theatre would have seemed outlandish, yet here was Lilian Baylis, an under-educated woman, a one-time child violinist to whom Art was "a kind of medicine dispensed to the poor and needy" daring to attempt it single handed. . . Aunt Emma had bequeathed the passion but not the cash and the continued existence of her beloved Royal Victoria – the Old Vic as it became known would have been dismissed as hopeless by anybody who relied on orthodox methods.' Taking on the puritanical governors, consisting of 'evangelical peers and do-gooding ladies', Baylis insisted that the programmes, which included lantern slide shows, lectures on electro-magnetism and weekly temperance meetings, were dull. She introduced a variety performance including an act entitled 'A Man with a Goat', which caused great consternation among the trustees. However, her aims were not just to provide novelty acts for the audience; she gradually transformed the theatre into a cultural haven, producing operas and Shakespeare plays. In the process, Lilian Baylis was responsible for furthering the careers of, among others, Peggy Ashcroft, Sybil Thorndike and John Gielgud.

It was thus with some trepidation that our own Miss Rutherford arrived for her audition. The dumpy and short-sighted Lilian Baylis spoke with a distinctive cockney accent and out of the side of her mouth – the result of a slight stroke. She kept two spoiled and bad tempered terriers in her office. Margaret recalled that, 'Out in the stark auditioning room she crisply asked me to do my piece. I drew a deep breath and walked onstage, it was then that my shoes let me down. They let out a squeak every time I moved. Somehow I stumbled through my piece, squeaks and all, only to hear Miss Baylis remark gloomily, "I think production might be a safer line than acting." I minced out in my awful shoes and my heart was heavy.' She needn't have worried. Several days later Margaret received another letter from the Old Vic, informing her that she was to be taken on as a trainee actress for the 1925/26 season.

In September 1925, at the age of thirty-three, Margaret Rutherford made her theatrical debut at the Old Vic, appearing as Portia's attendant in *The Merchant of Venice*. The following month she was a bridesmaid in *The Taming of the Shrew*, and in November she was cast in non-speaking parts in *Measure for Measure* (Citizen) and *Antony and Cleopatra* (Slave). She had to wait until 21 December for her first speaking part, as the Fairy with the Long Nose, a role especially written for her, in a pantomime called *Harlequin Jack Horner and the Enchanted Pie*. Immediately following the panto on the same bill was Cicely Hamilton's nativity play, *The Child in Flanders*. Margaret found herself in a bit of a dash: 'I always remember the experience of leaving the stage, wearing my long nose, squeezing behind the backcloth to rush to my dressing room to get tidy and in my right face, whence I flew to the wings to speak the lines of the Angel Gabriel, while Edith Evans played the part on stage. Needles to say I regarded this as a tremendous honour and one of the highlights of my career.' Edith Evans was celebrated for her diction, and to recite her lines was quite a compliment for Rutherford.

Rutherford described the Old Vic as 'A hard school, but a just one. There was no question as to whether you thought that a part was right for you – the actors had to play any part that was given to them.' Edith Evans also stressed the uniqueness of the theatre, 'A season at the Vic can do more than anything I know to break down the shyness and inhibitions that are such "a holding back" to an actor's development. You launch one big part one night and the next morning you start work on another. What can you do but plunge again? We must always have a living theatre, where actors can go to learn their job.' Evans was a firm favourite at the Old Vic and always brought in full houses. Although the theatre could hold up to 1,200 and, apart from the fortnight of the General Strike in 1926, was sold out every night, the Old Vic operated within very tight financial restraints. Costumes were used again and again and every way of making and indeed saving money was utilised.

By May 1926 Margaret Rutherford had been seen in half a dozen further productions, and, as the result of winning a students' competition, she made an appearance as Lady Capulet in *Romeo and Juliet*. Edith Evans played the Nurse for the first time and other cast members included Frank Vosper, Baliol Holloway and Esmond Knight. Margaret told Eric Keown that she returned home on the bus after those little triumphs, 'Clutching my ticket, hands trembling with excitement'. Sadly these triumphs were not to be repeated in the following months.

*

The deeply religious Lilian Baylis often asked her colleagues to pray with her. It's not known whether Margaret Rutherford was ever asked to join her in this genuflection – perhaps if she had she might have received more mercy at the hands of Miss Baylis. Unfortunately, at the end of the nine months, Margaret had been neither 'discovered' by a talent-spotting impresario nor offered the chance to return the following year. She was devastated. 'I have a philosophy of life which leads me to believe that everything that happens is meant to be . . . but I found it terribly hard to bear when Miss Baylis told me that there was no room for me in next year's production. There was nothing to say. I supposed that I just did not fit in. My world had crashed.'

Her theatrical dreams shattered and without any other source of income, Margaret was forced to remount her bicycle and return to her former profession. 'For two years I continued to pedal around Wimbledon teaching music but not a day passed without my planning my return to the stage. There was no question of giving up hope – I had faith that one day I would be an actress.'

Margaret continued to seek acting work but 'couldn't get arrested'. In her mid-thirties, it seemed all was stacked against her: she was plain looking and wasn't going to get romantic leads – yet she was too young and inexperienced for character parts. A few members of the Nicholson family offered advice and the steadfast Dorothy Vaisey continued to see Margaret regularly during this period, providing her with moral support and encouragement when she grew depressed. Dorothy also provided the occasional meal and somewhere to stay for a change of scenery.

In desperation, Margaret returned to the amateur stage. In 1928, at the invitation of Margaret's cousin Guy, the actress Ethel Royale attended a production of *Hay Fever* by the Wimbledon Amateur Theatrical Society. According to Margaret, her uncle wanted to know whether she should be encouraged further to pursue a career on the boards – or was just not going to make it. At the end of the performance Ethel Royale told Guy, 'I don't know whether Peggy is a good actress or not. But she is lovable and will make people laugh, and that is very important.' Margaret always maintained that these encouraging words inspired her and gave her the motivation to continue in her chosen path. With a newfound optimism and a grand naivety, Margaret now decided to leave Wimbledon and try to seek professional stage work. She moved to a hostel in Bloomsbury so that she could be nearer to the West End theatres. While she was residing at 24 Coram Street, an acquaintance gave her an introduction to Sir Nigel Playfair, who was producing plays at the Lyric, Hammersmith.

In her day-to-day life, Margaret wore no make-up and was not a follower of fashion. If her looks disappointed, then so be it. Other than a pair of decorative earrings or a little costume jewellery, she resisted any attempts at accentuation or primping. But now, invited for an interview at the Lyric, for some reason she decided that she must change her image for a more sophisticated incarnation. She thus purloined an entirely unsuitable dress, slapped on copious amounts of rouge and powder and entered Playfair's office with the exaggerated confidence of a woman who knew what she wanted and 'how to get it'. The actor manager's face fell, and Margaret was immediately discommoded by his apparent embarrassment. She exited swiftly and returned home in deep sorrow. She had completely misjudged the situation and, worse still, was concerned that the producer might consider her 'a loose woman'. The following day, she penned a letter of apology, explaining that she had acted totally out of character. The understanding – and probably terribly relieved – Playfair rewarded her with an audition, subsequently engaging her to understudy Mabel Terry-Lewis, as Dona Filomena in the play *A Hundred Years Old*.

Margaret Rutherford only played one night but she was well prepared. 'It was in November 1928 and was lucky that I knew of it a whole weekend before. Mabel Terry-Lewis was ill over the weekend and her doctor said she needed three days off and so not to appear on the Monday night. I rehearsed with the company and then I played for that one night. Some of my family were there to see my first professional night as an actress. I was abysmally nervous, but when the curtain rose I seemed to gain confidence and a magical calm came over me.'

Unfortunately no further work was incubated from this performance and she was yet again out of work until the following spring when she discovered that the Grand Theatre in Fulham was looking for someone to play Madame Vinard in *Trilby*. Following another audition, in which she presumably committed no cosmetic or couture crimes, Margaret was gainfully employed. She opened on 29 April and remained for an eight month season with the English Repertory Players, playing every conceivable role. 'The Grand must have been rather fun,' wrote Eric Keown. 'A box for four cost ten and sixpence, the gallery sixpence, and productions were advertised as "A Human Vivid Play of Life and Laughter", and "The Great Farcical Comedy, Positively 100% Laughter". Margaret threw herself into the gruelling but useful turmoil of weekly repertory.'

Among her many parts, Rutherford appeared as Eustasia, a spy in *The Three Musketeers*. The programme of 23 September listed her as appearing in the unlikely role of Chi Li in *The Green Beetle*, 'a drama of love and revenge, set in the Curio Shop of Chang Hong, San Francisco and the bedroom in a hotel near Chinatown'. This was one of the roles that Margaret Rutherford enjoyed the most at the Grand: 'It was a fairly dramatic part with some magic in it, which I always enjoy. I was dressed in a Chinese kimono and found it very difficult to get the right make-up with my shape of face and fair colouring – however it did teach me the rudiments of stage make-up.'

She loved 'the whole ambiance of this theatre' and played twenty-seven roles in all during the season. 'All my free time was spent in learning my parts. I used to get up at first light to study, hugging a hot water bottle to keep me warm.' The company also included Leslie Harcourt, who went on to appear in a couple of Will Hay films. One of the season's productions, a play called *Tarnish* publicised with the line "We only invite adults for it depicts the realities of life", suggested an avant-garde edge to the theatre's programming, but in reality it was

the kind of throbbing family theatre for which no canned entertainment can ever be a satisfactory substitute. And it left Margaret
Rutherford with a lasting respect for the training value of repertory,
'provided always that the hard driven apprentice can somehow find
time to study speech and breath control'.

The Grand experience was followed in the ensuing year by a role in
Dear Brutus in repertory at Epsom Little Theatre, and in 1930
Margaret received a telegram from the Oxford Repertory Company.
The troupe was desperate for an actress to play 'a Mary Brough part'
in a Ben Travers Aldwych farce, *Thark*. The role required her to appear
'rotund', but in those days Margaret was extremely thin, so she
crammed an old trunk with a selection of 'wadding' to make her fatter,
and referred to this as 'my Salomes', because of the likeness to Salome's
voluptuous shape. She hurried to the station and took the train to
Oxford, making her way by taxi to the Playhouse. It was at the stage
door that a rather significant but brief encounter took place.

Margaret recalled the moment in her autobiography. 'Just as I was
arriving, I saw a handsome man leaving. I noted his clear blue eyes,
debonair dress and courtly style. I could not take my eyes off him. It
was obvious that he was an actor. He had that special something. He
was in a hurry to attend the five minute Armistice service on the corner
of the Woodstock Road. His name was Stringer Davis.' Having
deposited her belongings in her digs, Margaret returned to the theatre
that evening to get the feel of the place. The production was *Thunder
in the Air*. 'I was not only taken by Stringer's performance but taken by
him altogether . . . we did not speak at all at the theatre but I went back
to my boarding house with a strange feeling of disquiet.'

The following day the newest member of the repertory company
turned up to rehearsal wearing her 'Salomes'. She managed to have a
snatched, nervous chat with Stringer, being somewhat encumbered by
her costume. 'I tried so hard in these early days to hide my private
feelings about this man in my life. I apparently failed, as everyone later
told me that they were aware that I was in love with him. At the end

of the season we did *Outward Bound*, in which I played a young charwoman who turned out to be the mother of the young man played by Stringer. I think he must have known by then that I was beginning to get very fond of him.' Not, one would imagine, the ideal way of initiating a blossoming romance, this also highlighted the fact that Stringer was seven years younger than Rutherford.

Margaret appeared on the cover of the programme for her role as Madam Denoux in *French Leave*, a light comedy in three parts by Reginald Berkeley. The production was enriched by the presence of a full orchestra – not to mention the possibility of 'afternoon teas at matinées served by the Sheilan Tea Rooms, Woodstock Road, one shilling per person. Please apply to the attendant not later than the first interval.' She also appeared in the following week's play, *The First Year* by Frank Craven.

Margaret returned to Epsom for a special Christmas engagement in *The Sport of Kings*. She did this with some reluctance, as she had to part from Stringer. Before leaving, she gave him a gift of a small travelling mirror bound in a leather case. He apparently returned the favour by presenting her with an 'outsize Jerusalem cherry bush in a red flowerpot'.

In the spring of 1931, she returned to the Oxford Players to appear in two more productions – one of which was a more substantial role as Lady Bracknell in *The Importance of Being Earnest*, a play in which she was to feature in several productions over the years. Another landmark of her time in Oxford was her meeting of actress, and subsequent lifelong friend, Joan Hickson. She was also able to renew her relationship with Stringer Davis and discover more about the man with whom she had professed to have fallen in love.

Stringer Davis, born in Birkenhead on 4 June 1899, attended Uppingham public school, where he served in the cadets. As soon as he was eighteen, and while still at school, he applied for a Temporary Commission in the 3rd Battalion South Lancashire Regiment. Second

Lieutenant Davis was subsequently posted to France in August 1918, where he saw active service and was demobbed in September 1919. Stringer had worked as a jobbing actor and director since then. His father, George, was a bank clerk and had separated from his wife, Ethel, Stringer's mother, some years previously. Ethel owned a rambling house near Reading and Stringer lived nearby above a boat house on the Thames.

Margaret recalled time spent with her beau during this period with great fondness: 'We went walking in the country lanes and boating together. They were idyllic days and when the weather was warm we used to bathe from the sides of Stringer's canoe . . . we had a splendid time. It was then that Stringer discovered I was rather a good sprinter and it was all he could do to keep up with me at times . . . I called him "Tuft" because of a tuft of hair that stood up on the top of his head.' Stringer, on the other hand, wasn't quite so forthcoming, and it was only much later that he confided in Margaret that, 'She had made a very deep impression on him.' He was more open with advice about her career, however, concerned about how often she was cast in eccentric roles and how this prevented her from obtaining more serious parts: 'He felt he must stop me wearing funny clothes. He wanted to see me as I really was . . . in a sensitive part.'

Although Margaret then left for a stint at the Croydon Greyhound Theatre, the couple were still able to spend time together, as Stringer was also recruited to the company. The admiring Miss Rutherford had been instrumental in persuading the producer, Esme Church, to take him on, singing his praises as an actor but with a clear ulterior motive. Other members of the company included Donald Wolfit, May Whitty and Margaret Webster. 'To her rapidly growing collection she now added a formidable list of plays,' commented Eric Keown, 'some of them froth – Arnold Ridley's *The Ghost Train*, in which she excelled as the hilarious Miss Bourne – but some with a sharper edge – Ibsen, Maugham, Pinero.'

Esme Church was yet another significant figure in Rutherford's fledgling career. Margaret described Church as 'A brilliant woman, a wonderful producer – firm and strong minded. We all took her decisions without questions. I suppose I was a strange choice for rep as I was already beginning to be type cast much against my will. The parts I had been given had begun to show signs of the eccentricity that I later developed into my own special technique.' Esme Church later recalled her protégé stating that her burning ambition was to be in *Romeo and Juliet* and mistakenly assuming that it was the Nurse that she wanted to play. Margaret, in fact, wanted to be cast as Juliet, but at the age of 39 was already considered too old.

It was during this season at Croydon that C.B. Cochran came to the theatre and saw Rutherford act. Charles B. Cochran, known as 'Cockie', was one of the last great showmen. Although he never referred to himself as an impresario, Cochran produced shows which featured the most talented performers of the day – be they actors, composers or writers. He also promoted Wild West shows, circuses, rodeos and wrestling and boxing bouts, and counted among his clients Harry Houdini. He also supposedly introduced roller-skating to France and Germany. Quite what he was doing in the leafy suburbs of Croydon is anybody's guess – unless he had been invited by Esme Church. The company was presenting Ibsen's *The Master Builder*, in which Margaret played the builder's tragic wife, Aline Solness. Esme Church described the scene, 'I was sitting behind Cockie and the play had been going for some time. It had come to the scene when poor Mrs Solness tenderly cherishes her plants as if they were her children. Suddenly Cochran turned round to me and in a loud stage whisper said, "Who is that woman? She's brilliant. Where did you find her? I wonder why I have never heard of her before."' Cochran's opinion of Margaret Rutherford was shared by Sir Donald Wolfit, who stated that she was the best Mrs Solness he ever played with and that he greatly admired her qualities as a great tragic actress.

In October 1931 Margaret returned to Oxford for another six plays and remained there until December. She had worked hard for a year, gaining inestimable experience, but yet again she was unable to capitalise on the previous twelve months. She just could not find regular work and so entered a particularly unhappy time. Her unlikely romance with Stringer did not sustain her. This was not a simmering, tempestuous affair. Stringer was still very attached to his mother – a somewhat overbearing woman who dominated her son's life. To sustain demanding relationships with two resolute women was a little too much for Davis.

Margaret was given an introduction to Tyrone Guthrie, then a young and promising producer who was making his mark in the theatre world. She wrote to him and arranged a meeting. Margaret reported that he appeared to be interested but could not provide her with any promises to use her. He somewhat patronisingly told her to keep reminding him of her existence: 'Bombard me!' She did just this, and whenever she managed to procure a night's employment she wrote and informed him. 'Many times he did not even answer my letters but I just kept on – letter after letter. Even then I was already being classed as a character actress, rather than a romantic lead, so roles were far fewer.'

Throughout this period Margaret's spirits were buoyed by friends and family. David Benn recalls that she was a permanent figure at Christmases and other family gatherings. Tony Benn wrote in his memoir, *Dare to Be a Daniel*, 'We had a another sweet great-aunt called Auntie Tweenie, who lived in Oxted in a tiny house, where we had tea on Boxing Day with cakes that she had baked; Margaret Rutherford watched her carefully and affectionately and I have an idea that some of her stage characters were based on her observations.' This was confirmed by his brother David, who later saw her in her first West End performances and noted that some of her mannerisms were similar to those of their Aunt Tweenie.

Margaret also used to visit Blunt House, the home of her cousin, publisher Ernest Benn, eldest son of John. Tony Benn recalled, 'She seemed to me to be quite old, though she was only in her early forties and was doing repertory theatre, hoping to make it big on the stage. Many young girls want to go onstage, but it is unusual for that desire to be so strong later in life, and we used to treat this as an eccentricity. Margaret was always very kind to me, and I have many happy memories of sitting with her on the beach at Bexhill as a child.' In one of these memories, then ten years old, Benn, in short trousers and ankle socks, is happily settled in a deck chair, inevitably sipping tea. Next to him, wrapped up against the cold and clutching a Thermos flask, is his redoubtable 'Cousin Peggy'.

For such a prominent family, Julius Benn's murder those fifty years ago still had to be kept secret, and it was forbidden for anyone to talk about it. It was many years before Tony Benn discovered the truth. 'I had often wondered how Margaret Rutherford was related to us and, if she was, why her surname was not Benn. When I asked about her father I was always brushed aside. If I tried to press my mother about William Benn, all she would say was, "Darling, he never did anything to be ashamed of."'

Years later, when he was a Member of Parliament, Tony Benn conducted some research about the incident and came across reports about the murder in the *Times* archive. His parents were apparently somewhat annoyed that he had discovered the truth. The tragedy had inevitably caused much distress within the family and its implications were far reaching, 'When my dad was about to marry my mother in 1920, my grandfather John actually wrote to my mother's father to report this history, though it never occurred to him to write direct to my mother, who was, after all, the bride about to marry into a family with this tragic background. This absolutely incensed Mother's mother, who came out against the wedding and stood outside the church while the marriage took place, announcing to all and sundry that she was not in favour of it.'

Margaret was in her early forties and no nearer to her goal of supporting herself as a full time professional actress. She would try to cheer herself up by 'replenishing my small wardrobe, as in those days it was essential for an actress to keep up her performance . . . we still had to dress with special distinction.' Writing in the 1970s, she stated somewhat enigmatically, 'There was no question of turning up to rehearsal in skimpy jeans and shapeless poncho as today.'

Yet again Rutherford was on the brink of giving up. And yet again she was rescued. This time deliverance came in the shape of Olive Walter, who in 1932 had taken over the running of yet another repertory group – the Greater London Players, who toured the suburbs. Wherever possible, Olive gave Margaret a part with the ensemble, a well respected and talented company that featured such actors as Roger Livesey and Rex Harrison. Margaret thought Harrison was 'suave and well groomed and even then showed the authority and accurate timing that we were to see later in his acting.' Among a number of parts, Margaret featured as Mrs Nelly Fell in *The Torchbearers,* a comedy by George Kelly; Mrs Tabret in *The Sacred Flame* by W. Somerset Maugham; and, in a part she was to reprise some thirty tears later, Mrs Candour in *The School for Scandal,* in which Charles Vane and Leslie Harcourt also appeared. She was paid the princely sum of £4 a week and took part in one-night performances in Ilford, Greenwich and Watford.

The year ended and Margaret's hopes of further employment at the beginning of 1933 proved fruitless. Then she received a telephone call that marked an important milestone in her professional life. Dorothy Vaisey, who had continued to support and encourage her friend, cajoled a family member to help Margaret. Her eldest brother, A.R. Whatmore, was a respected writer, actor and producer. Dorothy had never ceased to remind him about her talented friend who was trying hard to become an established actress and seemed always to be in need of work. Finally having a project that was eminently suitable, Whatmore contacted Margaret to say and that he was directing a play entitled *Wild Justice* at the Lyric, Hammersmith, and just wondered whether if she might be interested in a very small part.

THREE

A Member of the Strolling Tribe

'Drama – what literature does at night.'

GEORGE JEAN NATHAN

T HE LYRIC THEATRE, Hammersmith, which was once known locally as the 'Blood Tub' because of its 'uninhibited melodramas', recaptured some of its earlier reputation with James Dale's *Wild Justice*, which opened on 21 April 1933. 'There was genuine excitement in the play,' according to Eric Keown: 'it gave rich parts to Barbara Couper and Henry Oscar, and a slim one as Mrs Read, the murderer's charwoman, to Margaret Rutherford, who went unnoticed by the critics.'

Unnoticed she may have been but when the production transferred to the Vaudeville the following month, coinciding with her forty-first birthday, Margaret Rutherford had finally reached the West End. Unfortunately the play only enjoyed a short run and she spent the rest of the year in a variety of jobs, including understudying Jean Cadell and Muriel Aked in *Birthday* at the Cambridge Theatre. Not exactly the stuff that dreams are made of – but she maintained a connection with the West End theatre world and there was, at least, a little remu-neration. Other avenues had to be explored.

Margaret had been in touch with the BBC about radio work earlier in the decade, but her first West End appearance prompted her to try again. On 2 January 1934, from an address in Gunter Grove, Chelsea, she wrote to the Drama Director at the BBC.

> Dear Mr Rose,
>
> You may perhaps remember seeing me play 'Miss Reade' (sic) in Wild Justice. I write now to ask if you would be good enough to consider me for work at the BBC. You gave me a 2nd class pass on my last audition but if you would give me another chance I feel I could do better next time . . .
>
> Yours truly
> Margaret Rutherford

The reply was swift and helpful:

> Dear Madam,
>
> Thank you for your letter of the 2nd January.
>
> Mr Rose will be in Edinburgh for the next three months and I am looking after the dramatic auditions in his absence. I shall be pleased to send you an appointment when I have fixed a date for my next auditions.
>
> Yours faithfully
> THE BRITISH BROADCASTING CORPORATION
> (for Drama Director)

Unfortunately Margaret did not give herself the opportunity to deliver a '1st class audition'; a BBC memo confirmed that, although an audi-tion appointment had been arranged for 25 January at 3.30pm, Miss Rutherford failed to arrive.

Eventually some further stage work did materialise. Donald Wolfit invited Margaret to appear in a special Sunday night performance of *The Master Builder* for the Scandinavian Society at the Westminster Theatre. The production transferred to the Embassy Theatre, Swiss Cottage, and opened on 30 April 1934 for a short run. Margaret repeated her role of Aline, opposite Donald Wolfit's Solness. Beatrix Lehmann and John Clements were also members of the cast. The Embassy was situated several miles from the West End and the programme reflected a more suburban attitude to theatre-going, in the form of two gentle reminders to the house: 'Ladies are respectfully asked to add to the comfort of the audience by removing their hats. No alcohol will be served after 10pm.'

This time the critics did take notice of her work: the much respected Ivor Brown declared that he was 'especially struck by Miss Margaret Rutherford's livid portrait of Aline Solness, warped slave of duty, a dreamer whose dreams are dead'. The *Evening News* reported that, 'There is a quite terrifying performance by Miss Margaret Rutherford as his wife, the poor woman who has been spiritually dead for 12 years.' The *Morning Post* wrote of the 'Excellent Miss Rutherford' and *The Times* subscribed that, 'Miss Rutherford brought the shades of the madhouse close to the elusive, frustrated spirit of Aline.'

This description must have conveyed a sinister resonance, although Margaret admitted that she particularly enjoyed the part, 'because of its tragic perception'. Eric Keown remarked on the importance of this production in terms of Miss Rutherford's career, 'To be acting at The Embassy in 1934 was much more than filling in time, for under Ronald Adam's adventurous leadership this theatre had earned a glowing reputation: in that year no less than five of its productions were running at once in the West End. Now, at last, a small bonfire was lit, by Ivor Brown. Not just yet the big critical conflagrations, but she had made her mark.'

Since leaving Berkeley Place Margaret had occupied various lodgings and hostels and had enjoyed the hospitality of friends. She was now much more settled and had rented rooms at 57 Parkhurst Road, close to Holloway Prison in North London. Finally having somewhere of her own, she was determined to make it as homely and comfortable as possible, but in creating such a haven, she would need some help.

It would be fair to say that Miss Rutherford was something of a stranger to the day-to-day tasks of life. In terms of housekeeping she was more Mrs Doubtfire than Mrs Thursday. She had never learned to cook and was less than obsessive when it came to tidiness, and a propensity for anything practical was sadly lacking: 'I was very bad with a needle,' she admitted. Margaret's former classmate, Dorothy Vaisey, did by all accounts attempt to inculcate Margaret with some basic skills, but to no avail, and later spoke of her friend's impracticality with a sort of resigned amusement.

The answer to Miss Rutherford's domestic failings, which might also supply some companionship, was to acquire a live-in help. An advertisement was placed in the local newspaper for a resident house-keeper and was answered by a West Country woman in her sixties. Elizabeth Orphin was a gentle but practical woman who took charge of the house immaculately. She also professed to possess 'second sight', which would have appealed to Margaret's interest in spiritualism. Elizabeth Orphin, who referred to her employer for the next few years as 'Missy', was skilled in stretching the household budget and, accord-ing to Margaret, 'saw that nothing was wasted and we had plenty of nourishing soups and stews'.

Now that her home life was settled, Margaret was to feel the warm embrace of good fortune again. She was still 'bombarding' Tyrone Guthrie with requests for work and he finally caved in. This was not because he was knee-deep in missives from the determined actress but because he was facing a production crisis. The excellent Athene Seyler had been cast for the role of Lady Nancy in a new play in the Haymarket, when on the eve of rehearsal she was denied release by her existing management. Tyrone Guthrie could now hardly ignore Margaret Rutherford's persistent pleas for work. In any case, which actress could he possibly find at this late notice who was more equipped to play the part of a troublesome aunt?

In an interview with the *Ladies Journal*, Margaret recalled, 'One Saturday evening, Tyrone Guthrie rang, asking if I would like to come down to His Majesty's Theatre the next day to read a part in the play *Hervey House*. It was Palm Sunday, the clocks had just been put on, the sun was shining, the clouds were flying and I went up the Haymarket in a glory.'

There are a couple of accounts of this audition. In her autobiography, Margaret wrote, 'I went, I read. After 24 hours of suspense, I received the favourable verdict. I was told, "Well, there's not much to say because we want you."' Dawn Langley Simmons' version is inevitably more fanciful. 'She had forgotten to put her own clock forward, arriving an hour late for the audition. Sensing her embarrassment, Guthrie was quick to forgive her. He took her hand and led her onstage. There, standing in the raw glare of the spotlight, she read her part for the first time, pausing only at the end, only to blurt out her inadequacy, "I wish I were more innately this woman." There was a long pause, the Guthrie shouted out, "Read it again. I think you can do it." Again Margaret read the part and then, after what seemed to her an eternity, a young man who had been sitting next to Guthrie, Hugh Beaumont, better known as 'Binkie', announced, "There is nothing else to say except that we want you."

The Welsh born Binkie Beaumont was mentored by the legendary Henry Moncrieff Tennent, theatrical producer, impresario and songwriter, whose offices occupied the top floor of the Globe Theatre (renamed the Gielgud Theatre in 1995). Binkie was later to take over Tennent's, known in the business as 'The Firm', and would exert extraordinary control over productions in the West End. Indeed in Michael Billington's seminal book about post war theatre, *State of the Nation*, he described Beaumont as a 'silky Welsh authoritarian who enlisted many of the star actors, writers and director. He dominated theatrical fashion for many years. Although the common allegation that Beaumont ran a gay mafia from which heterosexual talent was excluded is hard to substantiate, there is little doubt that he did operate a velvet tyranny in which those who crossed or displeased him were cast into outer darkness.'

Tyrone Guthrie, who was asked by Beaumont to direct *Hervey House,* was, however, fulsome in his praise of the producer, and defended Binkie's theatrical conservatism. 'He is methodical, good tempered, reasonable. His mind moves like lightning, he is observant and uncannily intuitive – he has been content to farm with splendid efficiency soil which has proved its fertility and to leave the pioneering to others.'

Hervey House, set in a fictitious mansion in London during the Edwardian era, was written by American actress Jane Cowl under the pen name of C.R. Avery in collaboration with Reg Lawrence. It was a complicated drama, a sentimental and affectionate view of feudalism with a large cast and stock characters that included the Duke, the Duchess, the Duke's mistress, character aunts and uncles, devoted servants and a number of footmen, grooms, gamekeepers and pantry boys. The scene changed at least fifteen times and the story bore little resemblance to historical fact but, according to Tyrone Guthrie, 'The play was written with great verve and conveyed a rather charming admiration for the good old days. We thought it would be an appropriate offering for King George V's Jubilee, done on the grand scale and with a whopping star cast and lavish production.'

The day after the audition, Margaret Rutherford attended a wardrobe fitting and found herself a member of an all-star cast. Nicholas Hannen played the Duke, Fay Compton was his Duchess and Gertrude Lawrence, who was deep in debt at the time due to unpaid taxes on both sides of the Atlantic, was engaged in the comparatively small role of the mistress.

Margaret was extremely anxious at the start of rehearsals, which she joined belatedly because of her late casting. She was filled with self-doubt and wondered whether she could fulfil the expectations that had been placed upon her – especially in such distinguished company. She wrote, 'I am always so uncertain until that first night is over. It is not even the critics I worry about – it is whether I have done my best for all those people who have paid to see me and whether I have satisfied myself.' Happily, the other actors set her at ease, especially Gertrude Lawrence, who on the first day offered kind words of encouragement and support. Lawrence later commented, 'Margaret was so sweet . . . so eager to please; in addition to which she was quite unaffected and blissfully innocent of life.'

Margaret, who described her character of Lady Nancy, the Duke's Aunt, as 'a somewhat tragic spinster', was attired totally in black, sporting a luxurious hat adorned with a swirling osprey feather. She was also to puff contentedly on an expensive Cuban cigar and added a character trait by giving Lady Nancy a nervous but explosive laugh.

After some performances in the provinces, *Hervey House* opened in May 1935 at His Majesty's Theatre, Haymarket. Margaret Rutherford needn't have worried about her performance, for she received marvellous reviews: 'all the play's ingredients are popular. There is a man torn apart between two women and a Duke to boot . . . there are at least a dozen extremely good sketches of character, there are lovely clothes and plenty of opportunity for wearing them. There is lively dialogue on the safe side of wit . . . I shall select Miss Rutherford's as being the best of the sideshows.' And there was another excellent review from Ivor Brown: 'Miss Margaret Rutherford offers a most lively sketch of a troublesome aunt, an incubus which not even the Duke is spared.' He added that Fay Compton as the Duchess showed some 'clever touches' and that Gertrude Lawrence 'acted with dignity and a restraint of which she has not always been a mistress'.

Unfortunately the play suffered from some problems of staging. Jane Cowl had always been concerned about Guthrie's ideas and was worried that, because of the size of the theatre, the play would lose its intimacy. Guthrie reluctantly concurred. 'In the end the play was a failure, and for just the very reason which Jane had foretold. The actors did well; the sets by Molly MacArthur were handsome, but so compli-cated that, on the opening night of the tryout in Manchester, one of the actors got lost and flew about in frenzy through room after room, pre-set on a turntable. The actors on stage, making up the lines and pretending to look for their lost colleague in the garden, were startled to see him crawl through the fireplace.'

The costly play closed after a few weeks and lost Tennent a great deal of money. Margaret was, of course, extremely upset but, as usual, magnanimously unselfish: 'We all thought the play was set for a long run but it was not a success. Some critics thought the plot was too slight, others that it was almost an impossible task for any American to try and crystallise our English peculiarities in such a feudal setting and give them authenticity. The play came off after a few weeks and we were all dispirited and sad – I felt especially for Gertrude Lawrence, who was not used to failures.'

According to Dawn Langley Simmons, Stringer Davis sent a message of consolation tied to a rather wilted bunch of mistletoe and signed simply 'Tuft'. Margaret's other principal source of support, Elizabeth Orphin, summoned up all her psychic powers and prophesised, 'You will soon hear of another part.' Whether Miss Rutherford's maid possessed second sight or had the ear of an indiscreet impresario, she was proved to be correct in her prediction. In the autumn of the same year, Margaret was offered the memorable role of Miss Flower in a yet another Guthrie production, Robert Morley's *Short Story*. A strong cast including Marie Tempest, Sybil Thorndike and A.E. Matthews was assembled.

Robert Morley wasn't altogether confident about his drawing room comedy. He recalled that during the six months of writing, 'I used to despair a good deal . . . I had a few good jokes that I hoped would pass for wit. It also had a rather vague plot, but a splendid part for the leading lady. So I sent it to the most brilliant comedy actress of her day – Miss Marie Tempest via her manager.' Somewhat disappointingly, Tempest's manager Alban Limpus returned the manuscript, informing Morley that he couldn't possibly pass it on to his client because it was, in his opinion, 'one of the worst plays he had ever read'.

Undaunted, Morley sent it directly to Miss Tempest, who agreed to do it if the author made changes to the play and Tyrone Guthrie directed it. This was readily agreed to – Morley was no doubt persuaded by a 'sweetener', a cheque for £100 given to him by Marie Tempest's husband, Willie Graham Browne. It was possibly the hardest £100 that Mr Morley ever earned as he was then required to rewrite the play, removing nearly all the comic devices and situations. The plot centred on the fact that the leading lady, now retired, had never been a good actress. In his autobiography, Robert Morley recorded that Marie Tempest's principal objection was that 'her public would never swallow such a ludicrous idea and consequently Kitty Danvers, her role in the play, must have been a star. Thus under her instructions I removed every comic situation I had painstakingly striven to achieve.'

Tyrone Guthrie felt Marie Tempest to be 'the greatest light comedienne of a generation, but by now was aged seventy and a tremendous tartar. She was a fascinating, brilliantly clever and talented little woman, but she had a considerable sense of her own importance and expected others to have the same.'

Rehearsals with Miss Tempest were never dull. Morley explained that, 'Miss Tempest started off worshipping Tony Guthrie until she found that she wasn't going to have her own way with him.' Director and actor then started to argue the arrangement of the furniture – he laid it out one way and she positioned it differently, so that there wasn't anything between her and the audience. 'Once, picking up a pouf, she flung it over the footlights into the stalls.' Miss Tempest insisted that the Adelphi Theatre was hired for a month so that the cast, which included Rex Harrison, A.E. Matthews, and Ursula Jeans, could rehearse there in the evenings. 'Miss Tempest would arrive in an evening dress, and most of the rest of us in dinner jackets, and work would start about six-thirty and go on till nine, when Miss Tempest would go across to Rule's for dinner, returning about eleven for another hour or two.'

Short Story enjoyed a successful opening in Edinburgh, followed by even better reviews in Manchester. There was only one dissenter – a member of the public who sent a telegram to the startled author:

YOUR PLAY THE ROTTONEST I EVER HEARD STOP SO MUCH THAT I AM BACK HOME AT 9.30PM STOP THE STORY IS CHRONIC THE TECHNIQUE IS TERRIBLE STOP THE ARTISTS GARRULOUS STOP WHY MAKE THE UPPER MIDDLE CLASSES APPEAR SUCH UTTER FOOLS STOP.

James Agate's account in the *Sunday Times* on 3 November 1935 denotes the blossoming of Rutherford's characteristic performance. 'The play rather resolves itself into a contention for a bone which isn't there. There is no play to run off with. But if there were, it would now be in the reticule of Miss Margaret Rutherford, who as a ruthless village spinster convulses the house every moment she is on stage. The scene in which this tigerish mouse wrestles with another caller for the telephone, and finally secures it with a kick on the ankle, is the best thing in the play.' The play's protagonist was played by Rex Harrison, and it was Rutherford who introduced the idea of kicking her co-star on the ankle. She was delighted with her little bit of business, which 'brought a round of laughs'.

Marie Tempest wasn't, however, so terribly thrilled, and Margaret bore the brunt of the diva's fury, in what was to be her first taste of theatrical jealousy. Rutherford had always respected Marie Tempest's work and enjoyed the style and formality that she brought to rehearsals, and was surprised when summoned to her co-star's dressing room. 'Miss Tempest sent for me and in no uncertain manner told me that she was not accustomed to have a play stolen from under her nose . . . it was not the thing to do to stand up to Miss Tempest. But I was quite firm and told her very quietly that I intended to play my part as well as I could and that was that.'

Miss Tempest would have been further annoyed by the *Telegraph* review: 'Margaret Rutherford gives an extremely funny study of a spinster in charge of the village fete.' *The Times* concurred: 'Miss Margaret Rutherford is at the same time astonishing the audience by the amount of fun she is getting out of the intense spinster whose soul is in the nice conduct of a village fête.' Robert Morley concluded that Rutherford stole *Short Story* and bested Marie Tempest both on and off the stage: whereas Marie Tempest 'dictated laughs', Margaret Rutherford 'commanded' them. He also paid tribute by remarking that Miss Rutherford could 'root out a laugh like a truffle hound'.

The play itself received mixed reviews and its run ended prematurely. But it was her performance in *Short Story* that convinced Margaret Rutherford she was destined to play comedy for most of her professional life. She described an event which supposedly illustrated this notion: 'I had gone to the wardrobe department and chosen for myself a fantastic outfit which I thought was suitable for the part. I wanted something comical and yet would suit the parochial soul of Miss Flower. I made my entrance to an amazed look on the producer's face. Then I was quickly taken aside and told to re-dress in my own clothes. They were just right for the part. I felt hurt until it was explained to me that it was just my acting that conveyed the real clue to Miss Flower's character, not the clothes.'

Margaret didn't need to bedeck herself in ridiculous stage clothes to produce a reaction from the audience. It was her acting ability that they had come to see and not her outlandish costumes. She now realised that her own individual style was being appreciated by theatre-goers. Eric Keown described it as 'the Universal Aunt emerging from her chrysalis, a rare and most lovable specimen'. Rutherford herself referred to one night in Edinburgh when, making her entrance, she felt, for the first time, the instant warmth of an audience so genuine that it was almost palpable.

Yet despite her growing confidence and an increasing number of admirers, theatre work remained elusive. *Short Story* was followed the next year by the prophetically named *Farewell Performance*, which opened at the Lyric, Hammersmith, in September 1936 and closed nine days later. Margaret returned to the Embassy Theatre for two productions in 1937. In February, she appeared as Aunt Bella in *Tavern in the Town,* a comedy by Arthur Macrae, whose cast included Max Adrian and Esma Cannon. The play, set in a Mayfair pub, provided Margaret with a meatier role as a crotchety aunt. Her notices were universally praiseworthy. Ivor Brown in the *Observer* continued to be impressed: 'Mr Macrae's brisk comedy should go well, because he can write good lines and he has in Miss Rutherford an actress who is amusing before a word is spoken, and is doubly so when she has words of wit and character to speak. She is admirable in a kind of spinsterish petulance, her special talent lying in the ability to keep this petulance from being mean, ugly and pathetic . . . nothing could be more useful to a play than the ability to get all the fun out of a nasty woman's part and yet to remain, by some personal magic, likeable and nice'. The *Daily Mail* described the play as a 'crazy comedy of Mayfair drug peddling . . . Miss Margaret Rutherford romped away in last night's performance with her overwhelmingly funny study of a touchy maiden aunt.'

Up the Garden Path, based on a story by Richmal Crompton, was produced in July. Margaret, instead of being an understudy to Muriel Aked (those days were long gone and never to be repeated), now played opposite the Yorkshire-born actress in the role of Emily Deveral, 'a foolish old woman'. Although the plot was a little lightweight, the two principals received much praise: 'Margaret Rutherford and Muriel Aked were as usual great fun in characters of which audiences never tire.' In fact Ivor Novello was so taken with the leads that, immediately after one of the performances, he went backstage and offered to buy the play for the West End. Unfortunately this did not come to fruition because some of the other cast members had other engagements, but it brought Margaret Rutherford to the attention of the popular writer and director for the first time.

In January 1938, the Phoenix Theatre staged *The Melody that Got Lost.* Margaret Rutherford was 'Mother' in a musical comedy which co-starred Esmond Knight. The notices were decidedly mixed, although yet again Margaret came out of it well. 'Whimsicality can be a good servant to the dramatist, but a bad master,' wrote the *Observer*'s critic, '. . . over-stylised . . . reiterative . . . dull . . . but let us admire, in passing, the prowess of Miss Margaret Rutherford, whose suburban matron was far more amusing than an army with banners.' Another critic called the play, 'Demonstrable tosh . . . possessing a highbrow assumption that people who live in small houses jammed together in a row know nothing but misery . . . the best acting comes from Miss Margaret Rutherford.'

Miss Margaret Rutherford had continued to work for the BBC during this period – in both radio and the relatively new medium of television. In February 1938 she received a contract for eighteen guineas for two performances of a television programme entitled *Have you brought your music?*, to be recorded at Alexandra Palace Studios on 7 and 11 March. If she had become concerned about her professional duties, her mind would, no doubt, have been put at rest by the note that accompanied the script: 'Please don't be alarmed at the prospect of having to sing and dance – it is only Burlesque.' The show was delayed for three weeks due to the indisposition of deviser Quentin Tod, but was eventually broadcast on 29 March and 2 April. It may have been 'only Burlesque', but Margaret obviously liked it, as she agreed to appear in further episodes of the show.

She was, by now, in a production of *Spring Meeting* at the Ambassadors Theatre, and there were some concerns about a clash of times. A somewhat officious letter from Elsie Beyer, General Manager at H.M. Tennent, clarified the situation: 'It will be quite alright for you to approach her but I would call your attention to the rehearsal on October 7th (10.30 – 1.30 p.m.). It is our matinée day and I think it will be driving it very close if she does not finish her rehearsal until 1.30. Wouldn't it be possible to arrange for her to finish about one o'clock, as she is on very shortly after the rise of the curtain at the Ambassadors? Perhaps you will kindly let me know.' The time was duly changed so that Margaret Rutherford could end her rehearsal at 1 p.m.

A letter from the BBC's Bruce Belfrage to Binkie Beaumont at the Globe, dated 25 July 1938, referred to a radio production. 'We are approaching Miss Margaret Rutherford to take part in *She Stoops to Conquer*, which we are broadcasting to the Empire in two parts on 19th and 20th August and would entail the following rehearsals. We would be very grateful if you could see your way to grant permission for her to undertake this engagement.' The contract was for twenty-one guineas and Binkie agreed.

Further radio broadcasts in 1938 included playing the part of Mrs Pemberton in the series *Detectives in Fiction* (programme number four, 'Mr Fortune'), and appearances in radio plays *The Missing Kitten* and *The Snow Man*. She agreed to guest on a radio show, *Newsreel and Empire Variety Theatre*, on 17 December, despite the fact that the show was to be broadcast live between 2.20 a.m. and 3 a.m. and rehearsal started at midnight. Her fee was twelve and a half guineas, although she was a little tardy with her correspondence. The familiar spidery handwriting, penned in her favourite green ink was, as ever, suitably mannerly:

> My dear Mr Belfrage,
> My humble apology for the delay in returning my contract.
> Rather a wealth of affairs is responsible.
> Yours sincerely
> Miss M Rutherford.

The contrite Miss Rutherford was not, sadly, referring to affairs of the heart. Although she and Stringer remained friends, the romance was decidedly lukewarm. Neither is there any evidence that she was involved with anyone else. Her preoccupation related to the fact that she was now much in demand for the silver screen. Her film debut was in *Dusty Ermine* (also known as *Rendezvous in the Alps* and *Hideout in the Alps*), adapted by Arthur Macrae from a long-running stage play, the plot revolving around a counterfeiter attempting to go straight.

Directed by American Bernard Vorhaus and using some Alpine location shooting, the film is visually quite interesting. Rutherford was cast as Miss Butterby, a gangster's moll and would-be jewel thief. She made her mark by walloping a detective with a lead-filled umbrella, and even indulged in some 'stunt work', scrabbling around a fast moving car.

Margaret was delighted to be approached for the part. Endearingly, she refers in her autobiography to the character as 'Miss Butterfly', but is correct in her account that she had to fly down from Edinburgh while appearing in *Short Story* to participate in a screen test. 'Of course I was apprehensive and played my first takes of Miss Butterfly with that extra sensitivity that comes at such times. It was the kind of role that was to pursue me all my career. When I came to make the film, as so often happened throughout my career, the part was written up each day to make it more important.'

She played a housekeeper in her next film, *Talk of the Devil*, which was co-written and directed by Carol Reed, whom she referred to at the time as 'a charming young man'. Rutherford was very taken by the young director, and particularly impressed by his technical skill and understanding of actors. Reed went on to become one of Britain's greatest film directors and is probably best known for his 1949 masterpiece, *The Third Man*.

Talk of the Devil was the first film to be made entirely at Pinewood Studios in Buckinghamshire. Margaret followed it with a role as an irritable grandmother, Lady Parke, in the comedy *Missing Believed Married*, also filmed at Pinewood. *Catch as Catch Can*, a tale of smuggling – more jewel thieves, but this time on board an ocean liner – came out in July 1937 and starred James Mason and Finlay Currie. Margaret Rutherford played Maggie Carberry and the film was also released under the titles of *Atlantic Episode* and *Crooked Passage*.

In 1933, the Triumph Film Company bought a former factory warehouse in Crisp Road, Hammersmith, and transformed the engineering works into two large film studios, marking the start of a long tradition of film and television production at Riverside Studios. The first major success for the studios came in 1937 with *Beauty and the Barge*, starring the young Jack Hawkins as a handsome lieutenant. The film features a rarity: as Gordon Harker's housekeeper, Mrs Baldwin, Margaret Rutherford actually gets a love scene. In the same year, she also played an uncredited cameo role as 'Nanny' in *Big Fella*, a light-hearted musical vehicle especially written for the actor-singer Paul Robeson and also starring Elizabeth Welch and James Hayter. The plot revolves around the mysterious disappearance of a young English boy in Marseilles. Robeson is Joe, a vagabond who helps search for the child.

These were by no means starring or even substantial roles for Margaret, but they did provide her with another outlet for her talent. More importantly, she was learning the craft of film acting. The fact that the merest change of expression and facial movement could be seen by the whole audience, and not just those at the front of the stalls, appealed to her, as it showed the benefit of her methodical preparation and the precise nature of her acting. She always maintained that the stage was her true career, and that the theatre was 'the mother of it all'. She did, however enjoy some aspects of working in films: 'There is something exhilarating about film making because although the technique differs so much from the stage it has an intimate magic of its own. Unlike a play, in which you can grow into a part during rehearsals, in a film your reactions and emotions must be instantaneous.'

Margaret said that she enjoyed film work because it put her on her mettle. Once the scene was over, her thoughts could turn to the following day's filming. 'There are of course a few rehearsals and several takes of each scene but at the end of the day you realise that the three minutes in the can was only a fragment to fit into the final mosaic. Sometimes an actor can give it a unique quality through brilliant directing or some other outside influence. Other times the lustre is elusive but the effect is there, captured for all time on the screen.' She was also grateful that she had received training in elocution so that she was able 'to use my voice even in a mere whisper'. At times feeling isolated on the set, she did miss the instant reaction and warmth of an audience. To compensate, she befriended the crew and extras. Naturally inquisitive, she would engage them in conversations about their part in the film, be it in front of or behind the camera, and also liked to quiz them about their families and personal lives.

Another positive aspect of her work in film, and one which she failed to mention in her autobiography, was that of her fees. She had been struggling financially for some years, dependent on her teaching when times were hard. Now she was working full-time as an actress and was able to afford more clothes and to equip her humble accommodation with some furniture – although not of the most tasteful nature. 'She treated herself to the first of a long line of green woollen capes and a rather large antique gilt Regency mirror with tiny whitish glass lilies popping out of every corner,' reported Dawn Langley Simmons.

In May 1938 Margaret returned to the theatre in spectacularly successful fashion. At the request of Tyrone Guthrie, she was sent a script of a new play by its writers. M.J. Farrell (a pseudonym for novelist Molly Keane) and actor John Perry had seen Rutherford in *The Melody that Got Lost*, and had been extremely impressed with her sensitive performance. They wanted her to play Aunt Bijou in the play *Spring Meeting*. Margaret loved the script and accepted the role immediately. She described Aunt Bijou as 'a gem of a part' as it gave her the opportunity to stretch her skills.

Directed by John Gielgud, *Spring Meeting* opened at The Ambassadors on 31 May, with Roger Livesey and Joyce Carey alongside Rutherford. The comedy, set in a crumbling mansion in Tipperary, featured a group of endearing, impoverished gentry. The family, supposedly based on John Perry's kith and kin, are financially embarrassed because of the patriarch's twin obsessions, horses and brandy. His two daughters are thus forced to survive on a paltry £25 per year. Rutherford's character, Aunt Bijou, is an old lady driven to dottiness by a lifetime of tedium in the Irish countryside. Her only enjoyment is having a flutter on the Punchestown races, although her bets have to remain surreptitious and are, more often than not, disastrous. It is only her confidant, the butler, James, who is aware of her predilection: 'They must never, never know I have a bet, James. Such an example for the girls.'

Rutherford's opening line – a request to her long suffering butler: 'Skin on the milk and no biscuits' – always elicited a laugh from the audience, and from then on the house was convulsed with laughter at her every action. The actress was always surprised by this as she never really considered Aunt Bijou humorous: 'I have never thought of Aunt Bijou as being comical . . . to me a woman like Bijou had a deep streak of disturbing pathos that one finds often in the so-called comic characters of life.' Consequently, Rutherford didn't just play the part for laughs. Eric Keown commented: 'All her absurdity lay in a haunting consciousness of futility, of a life wasted and withered in barren gentility. She meant much more in the play than just a comic aunt, because she stood as a symbol of everything her two nieces were desperate to avoid; and it was Margaret Rutherford's triumph that while making her a devastating figure of fun she gave her at the same time an extraordinary sympathy.'

Sydney Carroll in the *Daily Telegraph* wrote: 'If I had to award a prize for the perfect representation of the company it would go unhesitatingly to Miss Rutherford . . . her Miss Bijou is a study which is both hilarious and almost painful in its pathological exactitude.' The *Tatler* proclaimed that, 'This performance is the best which I have ever seen Miss Rutherford give, it threatens at times to disturb a play of which the texture is too bright and slight to contain pathological drama.' Ivor Brown continued to show his admiration for Rutherford's abilities: 'Miss Rutherford's performance is indeed remarkable . . . she presents a fussy, irritable, absurd old maid with a great contempt for marriage and a wide, if secret knowledge of the turf, where she punts secretly. If sometimes one feels that the kind of fevered gamester's eagerness and the flash of spinsterish temper which Miss Rutherford so forcibly puts into the play are too large and too vivid for the compass of comedy, it is also true that her performance is in many ways vastly amusing, as one discovers when she is packed off to bed during far too much of the Second Act. The play does tend to wilt when she is away.'

Margaret Rutherford had triumphed and had, at last, 'conquered the gallery'. She was finally receiving the recognition for which she had long strived. As one of the country's most acclaimed character actresses, her services were now to be in constant demand. Not only did the critics enjoy her performance, theatregoers also took her to their hearts, beginning to demonstrate the affection she was to enjoy for the rest of her career. Her autograph was in demand and bouquets were left for her at the stage door. *Spring Meeting* was a hit and enjoyed a long run at the Ambassadors before touring. But Margaret left the cast of her first major success after six months. She was exhausted. The strain had taken its toll: Miss Rutherford needed a rest.

FOUR

The Smell of the Ectoplasm, the Roar of the Crowd

CHARLES CONDOMINE: Would you like a cocktail?
MADAME ARCATI: If it's a dry martini – if it's a concoction, no. Experience has taught me to be very wary of concoctions.

BY THE END OF 1938, the domestic responsibilities of her employer had proved too much for the ageing Elizabeth Orphin and she had retired to a tiny cottage in the Devonshire town of Dawlish. This was not, however, the end of their relationship as the two spinsters maintained contact. Indeed, so exhausted was the 46-year-old actress by her first long run that Margaret Rutherford took a rest cure in the West Country. Staying in Elizabeth's small cottage wasn't an option and so she took a room at the nearby Queen's hotel. Rutherford had always been a fresh air fiend and her spirits were revived by coastal walks and the stiff sea breeze. Around this time, she also moved into a new abode. Buoyed by her West End success, she took out a lease on a flat at 160 Ebury Street in the upmarket Belgravia district of London, within a few minutes of theatre-land and, it appears, without any live-in help.

John Gielgud, who had been terribly impressed with her performances in *Short Story* and *Spring Meeting*, sought her out for his next
production. She was suitably thrilled and 'accepted with joy' when in
January 1939 she was offered the part of Miss Prism in *The Importance
of Being Earnest*. The first performance was on 31 January 1939 – a
charity event in aid of the Hospital for Women, Soho Square – and
there followed eight matinées in February.

The lavish production, which attempted to capture the authenticity
of the 1890s, even using dresses from that era, was well received. The
Observer recounted that, 'It is a magnificent comedy . . . Margaret
Rutherford flowing over with that show of elderly farce which this
actress so vividly commands.' The *Daily Telegraph*'s critic agreed: 'The
acting of this brilliant company make this likely to be as distinguished
a revival as the year is likely to see. Margaret Rutherford's Miss Prism
lends a large lunacy not in the character Wilde drew but her period
sense was admirable.' A critic in *The Times* wrote: 'The play and the
cast glitter, Miss Rutherford's bridling over the restored handbag, as if
it were a favourite cat, long lost and now astonishingly mewing in her
lap, being as restrained and effective a piece of drollery as one could
wish for.' An extract of the play was recorded by the BBC for radio
broadcast on 21 February and a letter, sent to her Ebury Street address,
informed Margaret that 'the fee which will be paid to J. Gielgud for
distribution amongst the cast will be our usual one of £50'.

The production did not transfer to The Globe Theatre, Shaftesbury
Avenue until 16 August, when a glittering cast including Gielgud
himself, Peggy Ashcroft, Jack Hawkins and Edith Evans, as Lady
Bracknell, assembled for what they hoped would be a long and successful run. Rutherford considered Miss Prism her most testing and
significant part yet. She was delighted to discover she had been granted
a full-page photograph in the programme, and proclaimed that she felt
she had really arrived as an actress.

Eric Keown was of the opinion that the part challenged Rutherford
in new ways. He asserted that the play's 'traditional outlines left little

room for fresh creation'. He also questioned whether there was 'just a touch of *Spring Meeting's* Bijou in her portrayal, whose aberrations seemed at times to stray into a slightly larger field of lunacy. If so, no-one minded. It was a farce and it was madly funny; and in spite of being farce, the character appeared complete, so that Prism became a real and familiar person, and not just a symbol of dithering spinsterhood.' Rutherford denied that she had intentionally linked the two roles but admitted that she observed a deep strain of loneliness in both characters, 'a withdrawal from the world', and to this added poignantly, 'This I have always personally understood.'

During a brief revival of the play at the Golders Green Hippodrome in the same year, an unscripted incident in the play caused her great amusement. Authentic antique chairs had been procured for the production and one of them, riddled with dry rot, collapsed under her. The whole audience saw what had happened and it was impossible for the floundering Miss Prism to carry on nonchalantly. She grasped George Howe, the actor playing Dr Chasuble, and both burst into a helpless giggling fit – with which the audience joined in, equally enjoying the moment and then applauding the two delirious actors. Margaret had always held the belief that when such an incident occurred it was better to go with the moment than attempt to ignore it, and this proved her theory right. Strangely, history repeated itself some years later when exactly the same thing happened while Rutherford was playing Lady Bracknell in *Earnest* in Boston. She described herself as being the only actress to have been 'grounded by woodworm on both sides of the Atlantic!'

There was, however, more to worry about in September 1939 than a little furniture beetle. At the outbreak of war, every theatre was compulsorily closed down, many of them not re-opening for at least a year. Margaret considered what she could do to help the war effort. 'I was not trained for canteen cooking, I had no practical nursing experience. I was also worried about my own family, for all those mothers and children in London who nightly crowded down in the

shelter of the Underground stations.' There was also Stringer to
consider. Although the couple had maintained a close relationship in
recent years, there was still no sense of total commitment, and wartime
could only mean further disruption. Margaret was, however, somewhat
shocked when Stringer, at the age of forty, showing the same sense of
duty and patriotism that he had exhibited during the First World War,
applied for an appointment to an emergency commission in His
Majesty's Land Forces. On 15 October 1939 he was appointed Second
Lieutenant in the East Yorkshire Regiment. His address then was 5
Queen Alexandra Mansions, Grape Street, London WC2, and in his
application, he described himself as 'Actor and Theatrical Producer'.

He was sent for training straightaway and wrote to Margaret on 18
October 1940: 'Time is more precious to me than in any Repertory
Company. We're doing a fortnight's intense course so I'm sorry I can't
write letters or I'll never catch up . . . I really am beginning to get the
hang of the Bren gun and can take it to bits and nearly put it together
again. My drill is terrible and my lungs will never be the same again .
. . please send me an arty photograph of yourself.' We can only assume
she did as requested, as well as posting regular parcels of the Turkish
cigarettes for which he had a fondness. Stringer also had a propensity
to catch chills and colds and Margaret kept him stocked with a supply
of handkerchiefs.

His subsequent correspondence proudly advised her that, 'I am now
a first class shot – nobody is more surprised than myself. I passed by the
comfortable margin of three Bulls! We dug trenches for three hours in a
blizzard; however, I did not distinguish myself – I gave in completely
when we were suddenly told to put gas masks on. I had a rather nasty
cold, but the extreme exertion seemed to make it better.' In another
missive, he adopted a slightly snobbish tone: 'I have invested in a Battle
Dress and have also bought a forage cap. I don't think you would like me
in them very much. I look rather common and am inclined to swagger.'

Second Lieutenant Davis was given a week's leave at the end of
December. Margaret met him off the train in London, and they were

able to spend a little time together. She was in a fret, not just because of the likelihood that he would be posted to France in the near future, but because he chose to spend most of his leave with his mother, who had now been evacuated to Bournemouth.

Margaret and Ethel Davis just did not get on. Stringer's mother was generally dismissive of her son's relationship with Margaret and had always referred to her as 'that older actress woman you have been seeing over the years'. Stringer just wasn't able to stand up to his overbearing mother, and, while she was still alive, the likelihood of committing himself to, never mind marrying, Margaret was extremely small.

Margaret was also unsettled, in early 1940, by a letter she had received from an old friend of her father's from the family's days in India. G.H. Gilpin had nursed William during a bout of ill health in Madras and had remained in contact with him, apparently even visiting Broadmoor during Rutherford's second admission to the asylum. 'I only learned recently,' wrote Gilpin, 'that you were the "Peggy" who was so constantly in his thoughts and of whom he used to talk with much love. How thrilled he would be at the success which your talent has so justly brought you.'

Although touched by the tone of the letter, Margaret was flustered by this unexpected reminder of her past. She was concerned that the tragedy might be revealed and that her contemporaries and growing number of fans might discover the unhappy truth about her background. Might she be singled out as the daughter of a murderer? Her career was finally taking off, but if the newspapers were to get hold of this things might be very different. Margaret sought advice from her Aunt Tweenie, who replied by letter, dated 20 February 1940, 'Gilpin was one of your father's choicest friends and a sweet soul . . . I hope you see him sometime.' She added, somewhat mercurially, 'He comes from Quaker stock I think.'

The sinister Mrs Danvers, Manderlay's gloomy housekeeper, was not the type of character Margaret Rutherford would ideally have chosen to portray. Daphne du Maurier's book, *Rebecca*, had proved phenomenally successful, and now a theatrical version was planned. The director George Devine sent Margaret the play to read, which she did with great care, while noting that, 'In my heart I knew that Maurier's Mrs Danvers did appear evil but I tried to see her differently. Pathologically faithful to the first Mrs de Winter, she dedicated herself, rightly or wrongly, to protect the memory of the first wife. She chose a cruel and sadistic way of persecuting the new wife.'

Rutherford knew at once this was a part which would challenge her both professionally and emotionally. She had never played such a harridan. 'I had to make Mrs Danvers a terrifying dragon, but I wanted my audience to understand why she was so deeply motivated by hate.' There was also a financial motivation for accepting the part: the play was assured of success – the book had been a bestseller and was a perfect subject and setting for adaptation for the stage. It was a thrilling melodrama and was fortunate in having a top-notch cast. The actress admitted that from the very start she found the role exhausting, and gave a clue as to her acting method at the time: 'Whenever I act I give my all, and this part had a kind of eeriness about it. A play always fills my thoughts entirely in the early days of rehearsing and becomes my life – a bit of their soul creeps into mine. I like to be still and quite alone before I go on stage every night. I concentrate and transform myself into the character I am playing. I get into my broody mood well beforehand.'

The broody mood was exacerbated by the departure of John Gielgud, who was originally to have played the part of Maxim de Winter. He left after several rehearsals and, according to Rutherford, this was 'a decision made in the devotion to more serious theatre and wanting to play some of the great Shakespearean roles'. Despite some teething troubles, *Rebecca* was staged in Manchester in March 1940 before transferring to London.

The H.M. Tennent production opened at the Queen's Theatre on 5 April 1940. The beautifully produced programme listed the featured performers as Owen Nares, Celia Johnson, Raymond Huntley and Jack Watling. It also gave a warning about procedure during an air raid, while an advertisement extolled the virtue of Craven A cigarettes: 'They never affect the throat.' Despite the backdrop of the war and intensified bombing, the theatre was packed every night. In July Barbara Mullen replaced Celia Johnson as the second Mrs de Winter.

The *Daily Mail*'s critic was not particularly impressed by the play but was, at least, relieved 'to see on stage, in these days, a stately home of England which is neither a war hospital nor a hive of evacuated children'. *The Times* pronounced that, 'Miss Rutherford's madly jealous housekeeper is another accomplished thing in an evening of accomplished acting', and the *Telegraph* noted that, 'Daphne du Maurier has taken the bare bones of her successful novel, *Rebecca*, and made from them the very effective drama . . . much depends on the sinister housekeeper and Margaret Rutherford acted so well that one almost shuddered at the thought of her next appearance on the stage.'

'Margaret Rutherford conquered the role,' was Eric Keown's conclusion. 'Mrs Danvers' aim, knowing that her master had killed his first wife and hating him for it, was to scare the daylights out of his second . . . wherever poor little Mrs de Winter crept for a momentary breather, she was sure to find the evil face of the obsessed housekeeper lowering behind her.' Although the character was of a deeply saturnine nature, Rutherford disclosed that she did have some fun in experimenting with her make-up. 'I wanted her to look dignified and frightening and yet not absurd. I concentrated mainly on the way I held myself and my eyes.' Her eye shadow matched the deepest black of her clothes, creating a sinister menace. Keown noted that, 'It was an astonishing jump from Prism, and a triumph in that although the author had pushed the character to the very brink of the ludicrous, so certain was the performance that it remained proof against even the involuntary titter. The play was melodrama, prepared to be purple in places . . . and it told its odd story with a force that kept it running all through the desperate summer of Dunkirk.'

Stringer Davis had actually been a member of the British Expeditionary Force that had sailed for France on 25 April 1940. He wrote to Margaret: 'We had a good crossing . . . and already getting that happy satisfied feeling of an inevitably tough job done as well as we can . . . I can tell you nothing of what part of France I am in – but it's beautiful in its spring foliage and we've had some lovely sun – also thunder and a bitter east wind – quite like England!' In fact, Stringer and his comrades were overseas for less than six weeks and the British Expeditionary Force had to flee for their lives and from capture. The retreating Second Lieutenant recorded: 'We marched backwards and forwards – always zig-zagging away from the front line as we thought, until it closed in on us. We repeatedly did rear guard action, and were incessantly under fire. Absence of information and the extreme scarcity of Orders of any sort gave us a sneaking-unofficial kind of feeling.'

'Tuft' was among the hundreds of thousands of British and French troops who were rescued by 4 June. 'I came through without a scratch but was, I'm afraid, completely exhausted by lack of food and sleep.' Following his return to Blighty and having been granted leave, Stringer planned to visit his mother in Bournemouth. He had wired Margaret ahead, hoping to meet her somewhere on the way, but she didn't receive his telegram so knew nothing of his plans. Stringer took this lack of response on Margaret's behalf as a sign of indifference and went straight to Bournemouth, where he was immediately laid low by an attack of bronchitis.

Stringer remained with his mother, Ethel, who was delighted to have his sole attention. He did not visit Margaret during his post-Dunkirk leave, nor did he even see her in *Rebecca*. Margaret was naturally distressed and for a while refused to have any contact with him, the consequence of which was an accusatory letter from Stringer: 'As you're in an emotional mood, I'm afraid it's more than I can stand to see you . . . I'm going out and I want some cheerful society.' Quite where he found it while under his mater's thumb we can only fantasise. He did write later, however, with further news of the town's social status. 'Mother likes Bournemouth in spite of the air-raid alarms. She derives great comfort from being amongst real gentlefolk and feels content. The great point is that in Bournemouth her class and type predominate, and will be sympathetically handled by the authorities.'

Meanwhile, in less genteel Piccadilly, the highly successful production of *Rebecca* came to a premature end after five months. On 24 September a German bomb was dropped on the theatre, thankfully not during a performance, but destroying the whole front of house area along with part of the rear stalls. The production was revived briefly on tour in 1941, with Peggy Ashcroft as Mrs de Winter. Rutherford recalled sitting in a Hull hotel with Raymond Huntley and experiencing a heavy air raid. 'We sat and nibbled cheese biscuits to take our mind off matters.'

Although no student of Stanislavsky, there was something of the method style in Rutherford's preparation for some parts. 'It is simpler to fashion a character that convinces an audience than to convey a valid expression or feeling of the world in which the character has its existence. In my opinion a character is not revealed until you have transmuted yourself into it. First there is the study of the part, when your instincts begin to get to work. Then comes the building up and the gathering of the elements you hope to fuse into a whole. To me the great moment of acting is when I am transmogrified into the part I am playing and I lose my own identity. Until it is achieved, nothing of vital importance happens. But it is not possible to hope for it with every kind of part, and success is in proportion to the possibility.'

If Rutherford did indeed throw herself into such a demanding and unappealing character with total abandon, it is not surprising that at the end of *Rebecca* she was left feeling unhappy and depressed. In addition, with the war going badly, the strain of blackouts and bombing raids were taking their toll on Margaret. Her relationship with Stringer was also extremely confusing.

About this time Margaret became friends with Stephen Tennant and was a regular visitor to his home at Wilsford Manor in Wiltshire, where she met the writers E.M. Forster and L.P. Hartley. The Honourable Stephen James Napier Tennant, cousin of film director Anthony Asquith, was an aristocrat best known for his decadent lifestyle. He was a member of the 'Bright Young Things' and his friends included Rex Whistler, Cecil Beaton, the Sitwells and the Mitford girls. The flamboyantly camp Tennant had an affair with the poet Siegfried Sassoon but his need for attention and desire to be outrageous led him to proposing marriage to novelists Elizabeth Bowen and Rosamond Lehmann. Unfortunately, he also professed to have romantic designs on our Miss Rutherford and, whereas the sophisticated writers were probably not fooled by his behaviour, poor unworldly Margaret was totally taken in.

Tennant, once described by an acquaintance as 'the meanest and bitchiest of men', fawned all over the actress, demanding more and more of her regard, time and company. Eventually, according to the dilettante's biographer, Philip Hoare, 'Stephen Tennant proposed to Rutherford but then refused her admittance when she arrived for the weekend at his home, Wilsford Manor.' Subsequently, it appears, the butler felt sorry for the humiliated actress and let her into the house: 'She was later found by the butler, in the coal cellar, eating coal.'

If true, this is a desperately sad scene. The likelihood is that she had suffered a breakdown. John Gielgud confirmed that an incident had occurred, but wasn't entirely surprised: 'Margaret was not only a wonderful actress but a naïve and sweet woman . . . [Tennant] treated her very badly though I never ventured to ask her about the episode.' Certainly she later admitted to feeling depressed and under stress during this period, but it is possible that Margaret's infatuation with such a character, who made Stringer Davis look like Errol Flynn, resulted from her ongoing psychological condition.

More evidence of Margaret's condition is provided by a letter from her agent, Dorothy Mather, to the BBC in regard to an unnamed radio programme: 'As you probably know, she had no break after finishing the tour of Rebecca . . . and just at present her free mornings are really of more use to her as rest than to use tackling something quite new. Had you been able to pay £30 for each transmission she would have been persuaded in spite of her need for free time to do it, but I think from everyone's point of view it really is much better that just at present she should have all the rest she can.'

Rutherford was thus not in the best frame of mind when Noël Coward approached her to undertake a part in his new play. It was a part with which she was to be associated for the rest of her life. The play was *Blithe Spirit* and the role was that of eccentric medium, Madame Arcati. Ironically Noël Coward's play was originally born out of pecuniary needs rather than artistic aspiration. 'By 1941 Coward's finances were under pressure,' explained Philip Hoare in *A Talent to Amuse*, his biography of Noël Coward. 'At the beginning of the war, the government had closed down all non-essential media; BBC radio was reduced to non-stop news and organ music, and its television transmissions had been suspended for the duration. Theatres and places of entertainment were closed, putting the entire profession out of work. (Two weeks later, the authorities gave in to the entertainment industry and the ban was lifted, but only for performances during daylight.)'

In his entry for 22 April 1941 Coward wrote, 'Spent morning discussing financial troubles which are considerable. Discussed play as a possible solution. Title, *Blithe Spirit*. Very gay, superficial comedy about a ghost. Feel it may be good.' In the company of actress Joyce Carey, Coward travelled to the resort of Portmeirion, Wales. For a week he wrote constantly and created a beautifully constructed piece and was on such top form in the Italianate resort that only two lines were ever cut from the final draft. Initially, Madame Arcati had only been a minor character, which Coward had intended to be played by his great friend, the writer Clemence Dane. However, as the story developed, Arcati became more and more of a centre-piece to the comedy and eventually quite crucial in driving the plot. On his return to London, Coward negotiated a production with H.M. Tennent on the understanding that the play, which he would direct, would be staged at the bomb damaged 'but still serviceable' Piccadilly Theatre.

Cecil Parker was cast as author Charles Condomine, harassed by both living and dead wives. Kay Hammond was Elvira (named after Binkie Beaumont's housekeeper) and Ruth, Condomine's second wife, was played by Fay Compton. Now that the part of the dotty Madame Arcati was a more substantial part, Coward was convinced that Margaret Rutherford would be ideal. There are several versions of what happened next. In one, Coward and Binkie Beaumont went to see Rutherford backstage while she was on tour in *Rebecca* and read her the script. She was tired and uninterested and rejected the part. In another rendering, Coward sent her the script of the play, which was returned accompanied by a letter in which she stated with due reverence and politeness that she was refusing the role.

However, actor Keith Baxter was actually told the definitive story by Binkie Beaumont himself. Margaret Rutherford was invited to Coward's house, where he read the play in front of some friends, who laughed all the way though. At the conclusion, the author turned to Rutherford expecting equal praise and an immediate acceptance of the part – instead she refused to have anything to do with the play. In any event, Coward, infuriated at this rejection of the best part that Rutherford would ever be offered, and one that he had developed especially for her, telephoned Binkie Beaumont. His exact words to Beaumont were: 'The cunt's turned me down.'

Rutherford's tragic family background had remained a secret but, according to Philip Hoare, both Coward and Beaumont would have been aware of her fragile mental health at the time, and were wary of pushing her. However, the success of the play was at stake and neither of them was prepared to accept the actress's response. Binkie duly invited her out to lunch, to discover what had prompted her decision. Rutherford was distressed and torn between her professional career and a personal conviction. She knew Madame Arcati was a wonderful role, but was loath to ridicule mediums. In her view, Madame Arcati wasn't funny: 'I know women like that.' Her main objection was that she felt it made a mockery of the hereafter. Rutherford was a deeply religious woman who held firm views about spiritualism – a phenomenon which she took very seriously. Hoare described their conversation, in which Beaumont pointed out that the play poked fun at fake mediums, not genuine ones, and that, as she was a fraud, mockery of Arcati was justified. Rutherford retorted, 'Will you explain how she raises two ghosts if she is a fake?,' to which Beaumont countered, 'By chance, Margaret, dear. Even fake mediums can have a stroke of luck.' The next day Beaumont received a telephone call from Rutherford, agreeing to take the part, on the understanding that she must play it straight. 'I regard this as a very serious play, almost a tragedy. I don't see it as a comedy at all.' Beaumont assured her that she should play it her way and was equally adamant with Coward, requesting him not to give Rutherford 'a single note' in rehearsal so as to keep her happy. Of course, once on stage, when the audience immediately responded to her performance, Rutherford played it for every laugh imaginable. Beaumont later declared, 'Of course she always wanted to do it. She's far too sensible not to realise what a terribly good part it is. But she needs a face saving way of saying "Yes" and that's exactly what I gave her.'

Eric Keown was a little more understanding about Rutherford's reluctance to accept the part of Madame Arcati. 'She hates hurting, and that her immediate thought should be for the feelings of the professional mediums, a small percentage of whom she believed to be genuine, and not for the chance of a fat part, was dead in character. She is not a satirist . . . she is whoever she happens to be playing. Madame Arcati, that dazzling comic performance was not a caricature. She played her seriously; or rather it is probably truer to say that her immersion in the character was so complete that she believed she was playing it seriously.'

Rutherford did take the role seriously enough to arrange an audience with a celebrated medium, and some years later, 'when she attended a psychic luncheon, she was vastly relieved to find the profession friendly, indeed full of praise for the skill with which she had avoided guying it'. Rutherford embarked on the rehearsal process with some trepidation and her concerns were justified, although not in the way she envisaged. Coward apparently demanded that the cast be word perfect from the very start of them coming together. 'Sadly I was not word perfect and felt the strain,' Margaret wrote. 'After a few days of mental unhappiness I felt I could not go on. I rushed out of the theatre, phoned my agent, Dorothy Mather, and told her it was no use. She listened attentively, arranged to meet me and gave me a nice strong stimulant while I wept.' The stimulant was brandy, and with much sympathetic listening and support, Mather persuaded the shaky actress to return to the production. Rutherford was further undermined during rehearsals when, having been delayed by a wardrobe mistress, she returned late to find that 'The Master' was standing in for her. Coward delivered the lines with such skill and panache that, although admiring of his technical ability she was left feeling even less confident about her own interpretation.

After two try-out weeks in Manchester and Leeds, *Blithe Spirit* opened at the Piccadilly Theatre on 3 July 1941. Rutherford described the first night as, 'A splendid occasion. Noël Coward, looking very bronzed and handsome, sat in a box chain-smoking. In the audience was Captain Lord Louis Mountbatten, who accompanied Mrs Randolph Churchill.'

Although 'a splendid occasion', the first night did not augur well: the audience had to walk across planks laid over the rubble caused by a recent air raid 'to see a light comedy about death'. There was some concern from the clergy about the nature of the play. A Reverend James Colville wrote a piece entitled 'Should We Laugh at the Dead?' He was of the opinion that death and the hereafter were not suitable subjects for farcical treatment. Graham Greene, then Literary Editor of *The Spectator*, described the play as 'a weary exhibition of bad taste'. One audience member on the first night shouted out, 'Rubbish!'

Coward referred to the intrusion as coming from 'our old friend in the gallery', so it's possible that the dissenter had followed the play around the country in a one-person protest movement. The *Daily Express* critic wrote, 'Mr Coward made a graceful speech afterwards and the ill-mannered gallerite was very rightly howled down . . . it was a very typical Noël first night . . . and everyone, including the Minister of Information, was there.' The only other negative reaction was from John Gielgud, who didn't think much of the play: 'I thought it was terribly over-written . . . a good joke, but he spun it out too much.' Everyone else, however, felt that the play was going to be a huge success, and one critic decided that Coward had written, 'An ideally escapist entertainment, flippant and careless about death yet funny and sturdy enough to be a constant source of joy and hilarity to wartime theatre-goers.'

Rutherford needn't have worried about her own performance. She received rave reviews. The *Tatler* declared: 'Miss Rutherford is not one of your pale anaemic dabblers in the psychic but a thoroughly hearty, bicycling *bon viveuse*, breathing deeply and skipping about with a triumph when she brings off a coup. To see her Madame Arcati get up from an armchair is a lesson in eccentric observation.' Ivor Brown noted: 'This part, superbly played by Margaret Rutherford, is the saving of this farce about the dead, a new play, a gay play, and one irresistibly propelled into our welcoming hearts by Miss Rutherford's Lady of the Trances, as rapt servant of the séance as ever had spirits on tap.' *The Times*' James Agate was yet again complimentary: 'Nothing could be more wildly funny than this grotesque embodiment, now pursuing the humdrum of her craft as soberly as a monthly nurse . . . a wonderful synthesis of Ariel and Miss Mowcher.'

The author wasn't quite so fulsome in his praise of Rutherford's portrayal. A note, written on 18 July 1941 and included in *The Letters of Noël Coward*, stated: 'The great disappointment is Margaret Rutherford, whom the audience love, because the part is so good, but who is actually very, very bad indeed. She is indistinct, fussy and, beyond all her personality, has no technical knowledge or resources at all. She merely fumbles and gasps and drops things and throws many of my best lines down the drain. She is despair to Fay, Cecil and Kay and mortification to me because I thought she would be marvellous. I need hardly say she got magnificent notices.' This sits somewhat at odds with Margaret's own account: 'Noël Coward told me recently that there had never been, never would be another Madame Arcati like mine and that I was dazzlingly funny, the greatest comic performance of my career' she wrote in her autobiography.

According to Keith Baxter, 'Rutherford and Noël Coward were poles apart. As an actress and a woman she had no instinctive sense of humour, while Noël saw the ridiculous side of everything. His slant on life was puzzlement to her, and she was equally beyond his comprehension.' Rutherford obviously admired Coward's work, but admitted to David Benn that the playwright could be 'cruel and catty'.

On the whole, the notices were marvellous and, despite a heatwave engulfing London, Coward described business as terrific. He was also delighted with his own directorial skills. 'Fay (Compton) is better than she has ever been and was lovely and easy to direct. I've cured her of all her bad mannerisms . . . Cecil is really first rate – the best performance is Kay Hammond, who is absolutely bewitching . . . with a wonderful sense of timing.'

Margaret declared herself to be very happy in *Blithe Spirit* and got on famously with all her fellow cast members. She was, despite her misgivings, delighted with the role of Madame Arcati and the crowd's warm response. 'It is a rewarding feeling when you hear an audience laughing and sighing with happiness. It comes over the footlights like a great wave. For me it used to begin when I entered on my bicycle and Coward had me say, "It was wonderful cycling through the woods this evening. I was deafened with bird song."'

Rutherford was on stage for a significant part of the play but managed to eke out some rest periods whenever she could. She would often enjoy a quick nap backstage, something she needed increasingly to sustain her energy throughout her career. At other times she professed to catch up on her correspondence or fan mail during breaks – although she treated her work with such intensity that it is hard to imagine her dropping a line to an admirer in Tunbridge Wells before unleashing herself on stage in a whirling dervish of a performance. During the run she took part in a couple of charity events: a concert in aid of the Fire Service Benevolent Fund, in a sketch with Rex Harrison and Lili Palmer, and a special matinée in aid of the Red Cross and St John Fund, in which the programme stated: 'Noël Coward will probably appear during the afternoon and will speak on the work of the Red Cross.'

Blithe Spirit ran for 1,997 West End performances, although Margaret Rutherford only remained in the cast for a year. She blamed an unspecified illness for coming out of the show, but it was true that a year was the longest time she had ever remained in one production. She may not have been a blithe spirit but she was certainly a restless spirit, both in her professional work, where she longed for change, and in her search for a suitable place to call home. Between 1942 and 1943 Margaret moved several times. The lease on her flat in Ebury Street had expired and she found it difficult to get settled. She finally found a small flat at 143 Richmond Bridge Mansions, Twickenham. Situated next to Richmond Bridge, it was perfect for Margaret, as the flat accommodated several large and airy rooms overlooking the river. Margaret enjoyed walking along the tow path and observing the activities on the Thames: 'I have always enjoyed water – it gives me such a sense of freedom.'

The waters of the Devon coast were also a draw for Margaret, who continued to visit Elizabeth Orphin in Dawlish. Miss Orphin encouraged her former employer to pursue the complicated relationship with Stringer, being convinced he was the right man for her 'Missy Rutherford'. Elizabeth even maintained a separate relationship with Stringer, sending him pots of his favourite clotted cream. Margaret and Stringer had now got over their tiff, forgiven each other and resumed contact. In fact Tuft wrote to her regularly from overseas.

While undertaking some radio work herself, Margaret tried to procure some work for Stringer, who had served in North Africa and was attached to the Concert Party in the Actors Battalion. She wrote to the BBC with an idea of Stringer's about the Army Concert Party. The reply of 16 December 1943 from Mary Allen, a drama radio producer, was sympathetic: 'I have been trying to find the right channel to get Lieutenant Davis's case launched. Talks Dept are very sympathetic and interested and are going to write to you asking whether Mr Davis would come and see them.' Allen later suggested a show, *As the World Goes By*, presented by Freddie Grisewood, as a possible outlet. 'It seemed to me on the face of it an awfully good place for Mr Davis to give a description of his concert party . . . thanking you so much for the lovely performance you gave in *Lady Precious Stream* and for doing it at such short notice.'

It later transpired that the topic had already been covered by Eric Maschwitz and Macdonald Hastings on Boxing Day 1943, so Stringer's show never came to fruition. The communication with Mary Allen did, on the other hand, lead to further work for Margaret. In February 1944, she was approached by the producer to take part in a recording of *Miss Elizabeth Bennet*, originally a stage play by A.A. Milne, based on *Pride and Prejudice*, at the Oxford Street Radio theatre. Unfortunately Margaret got the wrong end of the stick and thought that she had been cast in the title role and wrote enthusiastically to Mary Allen, 'I am both pleased and flattered that you have cast me for Elizabeth Bennet – a young part!'

Mary Allen replied swiftly and flatteringly, ignoring Rutherford's error: 'Delighted that you will be able to play Mrs Bennet . . . I think she is a very amusing character and it will be lovely to hear your interpretation . . . a lovelier Mrs Bennet, I cannot imagine.' A few months later, on 16 May, she wrote again to Margaret with another suggestion.

Dear Miss R,

Walter de la Mare has written the most exquisite story of a slightly cracked old lady called 'Miss Duveen' who talks to a small boy across a stream which divided their gardens. I think this is one of the most profound and moving as well as one of the most amusing characters Walter de la Mare has ever created. I have admired this story for years . . . and I feel convinced that if you would play her it would make the most beautiful radio script. Mr De la Mare and I feel that no other actress could possibly understand, let alone put across Miss Duveen's flights of spirit. Unless you are able to fit in rehearsals and recording I will shelve the whole programme.

As soon as Miss Duveen is typed I will send you a script.

Margaret, who was a devotee of the poet, replied on 2 June 1944, having received and read the script: 'It is, of course, a very delicate, poignant, little thing – a work of art. My first reaction was that of hesitation in giving voice to anything so movingly sad – but we must face the truth – it will be a most intriguing piece of work. I have spoken to Mr De la Mare, giving him my impression – he has reassured me so I hope much to be able to give an interpretation worthy of this creation of his mind. July will suit me well on the dates you mention.' There followed a letter from a grateful Mary Allen: 'Mr De la Mare seems to think he may be able to look in at the last rehearsal.' Margaret received twenty-five guineas for her work and the play was broadcast on General Forces Radio on 23 July 1944.

The themes of *Miss Duveen* appealed on many different levels to Margaret, and the poignancy of the old lady's predicament must have been deeply affecting. Novelist Russell Hoban described *Miss Duveen* as 'a story about a deep affection that grows between a boy and an elderly woman who is, in a fond and magical way, somewhat wandering in her wits. It is about the death of the heart and the river that appears in the first line is always mystically present.' The boy,

Arthur, lives in his grandmother's house across the river from Miss Duveen, who introduces herself to him by tapping her forehead and saying, 'I am Miss Duveen, that's not, they say, quite the thing here.' She also tells him, 'One thing, dear child, you may be astonished to hear, I learned only yesterday, and that is how exceedingly sad life is.' Later Arthur poignantly recalls the nature of their relationship, 'I begin to see we were ridiculous friends, especially as she came in now in ever dingier and absurder clothes.' When the first ice appears in the garden his grandmother tells him that Miss Duveen's friends 'have been compelled to put her away'.

Apart from her stage work and occasional forays into radio, it was mainly film work that occupied Margaret Rutherford during this period. She was very much in demand for 'the pictures' during wartime, commencing with the celluloid version of *Spring Meeting*, which was filmed in 1940 and released on 31 May 1941 (two years to the day after the West End opening night). It was re-titled *Three Wise Brides* for the American market and featured Michael Wilding, Basil Sydney and Winston Churchill's daughter, Sarah. Bijou Furze was one of Rutherford's favourite stage characters, so, unsurprisingly, Rutherford stole the film.

Next came *Quiet Wedding*, released in 1941 and directed by Anthony 'Puffin' Asquith, who was the son of former Prime Minister Herbert Asquith and had been given the unflattering nickname by his mother because of his 'beaklike' nose. The screenplay was written by Anatole de Grunwald and Terence Rattigan, and the film starred Margaret Lockwood as a bride-to-be who, under pressure from intruding friends and family, escapes with her fiancé for a few hours' peace. The couple are arrested for dangerous driving by a simple country policeman (Bernard Miles) and end up in front of the bench, where Rutherford makes a brief appearance as the 'Second Magistrate'. Eventually they are bailed by their family and the quiet wedding takes place. A strong cast featured Athene Seyler, David Tomlinson, Peggy

Ashcroft and Muriel Pavlow. Terry-Thomas made an uncredited appearance as an extra. A review in the *New York Times* observed: 'Few pictures have possessed the richly human qualities of this beguiling little English comedy drama. A foreword to the film states that its production was interrupted five times when Nazi bombs fell on the studio, but all their destructive fury has left no visible mark on the quiet humor and the atmosphere of hearthside warmth that permeate this wisp of a tale . . . all the characters have been expertly drawn and Anthony Asquith has directed with tender appreciation of his material this completely unpretentious and charming film.'

Two years later Rutherford appeared in *The Demi Paradise*, the first British film to make use of the Anglo-Russian alliance. Again directed by Asquith, it starred Laurence Olivier, in splendid form, as Ivan Kouznetsoff, a Russian inventor. *The Demi Paradise* combined propaganda with a gentle satirical look at British national values. Among others, the cast featured Leslie Henson, Joyce Grenfell and Wilfred Hyde-White. Margaret took the role of Rowena Ventnor, the village Lady Bountiful, full of good works and community spirit. Rutherford enjoyed working on this film – not just because she liked Anthony Asquith and Olivier but also because she recognised 'the glimmer of the genius that was yet to be seen in its fullest from Laurence Olivier. His uncanny mastery of a foreign accent made him tower over everybody else in the film'. She also took succour from Olivier's final words of the film in which he proclaims, 'They [the English] have developed a religion of making the best of things and their sense of humour is the guiding spirit of their lives.' Rutherford wrote, 'They were lines that I was often to remember during the darker periods of my life.'

Yellow Canary, also distributed in 1943, provided a small but satisfying part for Margaret, who described it as 'a very saucy spy film about the U-Boat days and a British convoy' and 'a great commercial success'. She was originally only contracted for one day's work, but the director Herbert Wilcox kept adding to the part and she ended up on the set for three weeks. The plot revolved around the character of Sally Maitland (Anna Neagle, Wilcox's wife), who is accused of being a Nazi sympathiser and embarks on the SS *Carina* bound for Canada. She is inevitably romanced by Polish aristocrat and gauche British Naval officer Jim Garrick (Richard Greene). It transpires that Neagle is in fact a double agent, working for British Intelligence. Rutherford played Mrs Towcester, a busybody passenger on the ocean liner, and her cameo included one memorable line: 'Wouldn't it be nice to do something violent?' In fact, she created a bit of spontaneous business to this effect by kicking a Nazi on the ankle. Stringer Davis later told the story of how one night when in North Africa he had overheard a couple of soldiers talking of how much they had enjoyed this incident in the film.

After filming, Herbert Wilcox wrote to Margaret: 'I have never known anybody quite so unique, with 100 percent projection. You were a joy to direct. You brought light and shade into an ordinary situation and gave a very dramatic story the touch of lightness that it needed . . . I have never met anyone in my long experience so completely camera and audience unconscious, and this is why you are such a rare personality.'

The 1944 film *English Without Tears* (US title: *Her Man Gilbey*), written by Terence Rattigan and Anatole de Grunwald and produced by Sydney Box, starred Michael Wilding, Lili Palmer and Peggy Cummins. The wonderful Irene Handl had a small role as a Romanian delegate and violin virtuoso Stéphane Grappelli appeared as himself. Harold French's comedy has Rutherford as bird fancier Lady Christabel Beauclark, demanding territorial rights for migrating British birds, which are forgotten when war breaks out.

By 1944 Rutherford had moved out of London and was living in Beaconsfield (11 Highway Court, High Street, Beaconsfield New Town) with her friend and professional stand-in Grace Bridges. They managed to rub along nicely, although Grace was sometimes discommoded by her flat mate's precipitous need for fresh air and exercise. Geoffrey Green, a retired solicitor, still living in Buckinghamshire, remembers Margaret regularly attending St Michael and All Angels church: 'She always sat in the front pew and wore her cloak. Of course she was instantly recognisable, but was never actressy or overbearing. She was the most dear lady!' The flat was situated close to the studios at Denham, where by now Margaret was filming *Blithe Spirit*, so commuting was relatively easy. Margaret and Grace had a number of visits from London friends taking refuge from the 'doodlebugs' – the V1 rockets aimed at the capital. Rex Harrison and Lili Palmer lived nearby and Margaret recalled that, when Miss Palmer had a baby, 'She was rushed up to London during an air raid in an ambulance and the traffic was so confused and slow she barely got to the hospital on time.'

The film of *Blithe Spirit* was made in 1944 and released the following year. Rutherford enjoyed the work, though the filming was tiring and took six months instead of twelve weeks – 'something to do with the colour film, which, then fairly new, had to be sent to America to be processed and then returned each time to match up'. One of the film's stars, Constance Cummings, noticed the effect of the punishing filming process on Margaret: 'In the middle of shooting she would suddenly disappear – nowhere to be seen. And then we would find her in a corner or in her dressing room tucking into a pile of sandwiches.' Margaret admitted that she 'must have caught the habit from Madame Arcati with whom I, by then, completely identified myself. In the film she was always nibbling a tiny cucumber sandwich when she got a chance. I used to look forward to that last scene when I was trying so hard to get rid of the two wives who were causing Rex so much trouble. It went on for quite a long time and poor Madame Arcati used to get exhausted and have to nibble cucumber sandwiches to keep her ectoplastic strength up.'

Cummings said of the cast: 'we were a happy company and we knew we were on to a winner judging by the success of the play and the fact that the film was in colour.' She recalled that a large set containing a living room, dining room, and bedroom was constructed at Denham. The film was directed by David Lean, who, according to Miss Cummings, 'wanted much more of the film to be shot outside or on location but Noël insisted it be filmed as presented on stage, i.e. two thirds in the living room. David disagreed with him but Noël was adamant and very powerful. Noël didn't come near the studio. He was away being an Ambassador for Britain somewhere and that made proceedings more relaxed. I don't think David would have coped with his presence on the lot.'

Lean did, however, have to cope with Rex Harrison, who had been granted special leave by the RAF to appear in the film. 'Dear Rexie was edgy about other male actors – he didn't like to think he was being challenged in looks or talent stakes,' remarked Cummings. 'He was rather immature, very intense and wrapped up in himself – several of my theatre friends said he was difficult – he was never aware of anyone else's problems.' The cast also included Coward himself as an uncredited narrator, his Portmeirion holiday companion Joyce Carey as Mrs Bradman, a neighbour of the Condomines, and the seductive Kay Hammond, reprising her stage role as the deceased Elvira. Her make-up was incredibly effective for the time, a fluorescent thick green liquid applied to her face and body, topped off with a wig of greeny-grey hair. The chiffon costume was dyed and the glow was produced by special lighting. Tom Howard won the Academy Award for visual effects in 1947 (due to a delayed release in the USA).

It was, however, Rutherford's performance that should have been rewarded with an Oscar. From the moment she appears, cycling furiously through the Kent countryside, cape flying, jowls quivering, she is an absolute joy. Cummings concurred: 'Margaret Rutherford was such a funny lady. A unique person rather like Madame Arcati herself, exuberant and active – I think she did not know quite how funny she was and how amazing she made that part. She stole the film, however, as she always does.' Rutherford's line about the downside of uphill bicycling – 'Just knack again. Down with your head, up with your heart, and you're over the top like a flash and skimming down the other side like a dragon fly' – is beautifully dismissive and, when she realises that she has actually managed to summon up a spirit, her unbridled rapture is absolutely truthful. 'Coward had given her some wonderful lines,' wrote Eric Keown, 'and she crackled them out with the hearty gaiety of an optimistic games mistress. When Elvira warns Charles Condomine, "If you are not careful, the old thing will materialise a whole hockey team," one saw exactly what she meant.'

Although beautifully played by the rest of the cast, and inevitably containing some extremely witty dialogue, the film is much enlivened when Rutherford is on the screen. She attacks the role with huge exuberance and her unique physicality is allowed free reign: arms akimbo and twirling around, she bursts into verse to attract her spirit – the little girl with the cold. But, as *Time and Tide* reported, 'it's not the arty-craftiness that Margaret Rutherford gets so right, it's the faith behind them. In the mad world in which all the characters find themselves after Elvira has materialised, Madame Arcati is the sanest and most purposeful character. She is also extremely resourceful. Observe her mounting the steps and declaiming rather insulting medieval rhymes while she shakes herbs over the phantom Ruth and Elvira. If any acting could be too good, hers would be too good . . . I suppose she is one of Coward's cruellest creations, and yet there are moments in which she eludes our mockery and mocks us.' Madame Arcati was a defining role for Margaret Rutherford and brought her to the attention of cinema-goers on both sides of the Atlantic. Yet despite the commercial and popular success of *Blithe Spirit*, Coward himself was disappointed with the final cut and, after seeing it for the first time, said to David Lean, 'You've really fucked that up.'

While Margaret was still working on *Blithe Spirit*, in June 1944, Stringer came to stay with her and Grace Bridges in Beaconsfield. The two actresses were very close, to the extent that Stringer was sometimes jealous of their friendship, as he was of a number of Margaret's friends.

Tuft did, however, manage to grab a little time with Margaret before he rejoined his battalion. Rutherford remembered Stringer taking her out on to the flat's balcony and pointing out 'the bold, magical moon suspended in the sky'. He put his arm around her shoulder and said, 'That is a very special moon but just now I cannot tell you the reason.' She later wrote: 'I did not realise then of course that this beautiful moon, so bright and hopeful, was in fact to be remembered as the D-Day Moon.'

Stringer was duly posted abroad and while he was away, on 19 August 1944, Margaret Rutherford joined an ENSA tour. The Entertainments National Service Association (not Every Night Something Awful, as coined by a number of personnel who had to endure some of the less successful shows) was set up in 1939 to provide some distraction for the armed forces during the Second World War. This particular show, Ivor Novello's *Love from a Stranger*, featured Jessie Matthews, Gertrude Lawrence and Diana Wynyard.

Ivor Novello had only just been released from Wormwood Scrubs prison, having served a month of an eight week sentence for illegally obtaining petrol coupons for his Rolls-Royce – a serious offence in wartime Britain. He had also allegedly tried to bribe the officer delivering the summons, and his 'not guilty' plea was based on the fact that he needed his car to drive to and from the theatre and Redroofs, his country house near Maidenhead. In his defence, he also maintained that his stage appearances were 'very important work for morale'.

Despite this jail sentence, Novello remained as popular as ever on his release and, no doubt wishing to make amends, immediately made plans to travel to France. Margaret described the background to the trip: 'We were to visit British airfields in Normandy and Belgium and were to leave from Southampton, but at the time it was very hush-hush. When we got to the gangway, poor Jessie was terrified. She was such a young elfin, endearing creature and had just had a terrible week of high temperatures and injections. Her doctor had ordered that she should not make the trip but good trouper that she was Jessie was determined to do so. On the ship Jessie's fever became worse and none of us thought she could land.'

In fact, Matthews made a remarkable recovery, and the following day the company set up their portable stage in a Normandy orchard, close to the front line, with some of the dialogue having to be shouted above the background roar of an endless steam of warplanes. In addition to the play, Margaret Rutherford read poems, mainly from her favourite Edward Lear book, and the rest of the touring troupe, which included the marvellous Sandy Powell, George Formby (inevitably accompanied by his wife) and Flanagan and Allen, performed their own material. After the show Ivor Novello banged out some songs on a battered piano, always starting with 'Keep the Home Fires Burning', but also including a new number, 'We'll Gather Lilacs'.

Soon after she returned from France, rehearsals started for her next stage venture. In December 1944, Clemence Dane's adaptation of *Alice in Wonderland* opened at the Palace Theatre. Peggy Cummins was Alice and the show was directed by Esme Church. Music was provided by Richard Adinsell, who later became well known as the composer of Joyce Grenfell's songs. Margaret undertook the role of the White Queen in the afternoons while Sybil Thorndike performed the role every morning at 10.45 a.m. According to Margaret, Sybil was already 'a proficient aeronaut and could fly in and out of the wings on the wires with ease, but I had to learn from the ground upwards.' Once she had learned the skill of a smooth landing and not bouncing in the wings, she apparently looked forward to her 'daily flight'.

'The White Queen is a figment of the imagination and not an ordinary character,' she said in a magazine interview, describing a different approach from that of her other roles. 'I find it particularly fascinating to try and represent a creature of spirit and fantasy, although it is an extremely difficult job! I think it is better not to analyse too much . . . it is possible to be too concerned about ways and means, and to be over-anxious about the wonderful thing – call it what you like – inspiration. If inspiration does not flow, no matter how carefully you have worked out the details of your performance, very little of significance can happen. Analysing and worrying tend to tighten you up and make you look into yourself too much. It is more helpful to look outside yourself when things are more likely to become clear and open up to you.'

Actor and director Frith Banbury appeared in *Alice* as the White Knight. He was a legendary figure of British theatre, having met Mrs Patrick Campbell at the age of six and starred in Gielgud's 1931 *Hamlet*. When I interviewed him in 2008, just a few weeks before his death at the age of 95, he was still as sharp as a Noël Coward barb, and had fond memories of the wartime production of *Alice*, recalling having to perform above the din of the sirens: 'It was no different from acting in peacetime other than the fact that you might have a bomb drop on you.' Although he and Margaret Rutherford didn't have a scene together, they became very friendly, and discussed the possibility of working together on a play in which she might enjoy a principal part. 'Unfortunately we couldn't find anything that we considered suitable, Margaret being a very idiosyncratic performer who needed leading parts because of her star status, yet was very difficult to cast.'

The director had met Margaret prior to *Alice* through Stringer Davis and was always somewhat astonished at their romance. They did, he remarked, 'produce some strange bromides together'. Banbury was wonderfully waspish about the sexual side of their relationship: 'I can't imagine there was much action in bed – neither of them would have known what to do!' In fact, he was convinced that Stringer was bisexual, something hinted at by several contemporaries. He did concede, however, that Stringer and Margaret were extremely happy in each other's company, and that he was devoted to her. Banbury was also pretty disparaging about Davis's acting abilities: 'He didn't strike me as an actor at all! But if a director needed a solicitor, lawyer or Army officer, he was okay.'

In contrast, Banbury was effusive in his praise of Davis's inamorata. 'She was always perfectly on the ball when she got the part. She used her eccentricity unconsciously – this was her true character and she really didn't know how funny she was until the audience laughed. She loved imaginatively romantic productions and used to say, "I want to produce a theatre of fantasy." Margaret Rutherford was such an individual and so different from anyone else. She was so very sweet-natured and very kind. Because of her work in film, her performances will be remembered forever.'

Frith Banbury died in May 2008. His obituaries in the national press informed readers that his power as a director was at its zenith during the 1950s, when H.M. Tennent, under Binkie Beaumont, ruled over Shaftesbury Avenue. 'With Beaumont's backing he assembled glossy casts and worked with names that made the box office happy.' His father was a distinguished rear admiral, and Binkie Beaumont referred to him rather mischievously as 'the admiral's gifted daughter'. Banbury was 'well informed, precise and withering', 'successful in revue where his slightly camp manner was an asset, but always a safe pair of hands with a script'.

At the same time that Margaret Rutherford was regally flying across the stage in *Alice in Wonderland*, Stringer had been posted to North West Europe. But in March 1945, as the war in Europe entered its final few months, he was granted leave. Stringer was initially posted to a camp at Tilbury and then, after a quick stay at the Battalion's headquarters in York, he was free to travel. This time there was no reason to go to Bournemouth. His mother had died. Finally, there was only one woman in his life. He headed straight to Buckinghamshire.

FIVE

Taking the Plunge

'It's never too late to be happy.'

MARGARET RUTHERFORD

SECOND LIEUTENANT DAVIS was a man with a mission. Catching a train from Paddington, he arranged for Margaret to meet him at Beaconsfield railway station before returning to her Highway Court flat. This time there would be no romantic balcony scene. In the hallway, Stringer finally proposed to Margaret, using the words from the actual marriage service: 'Wilt thou have this man to be thy wedded husband . . . for better or worse, for richer for poorer, in sickness and in health?' He was word perfect. He had, after all, had plenty of time to rehearse. For once, Stringer was convincing in his part as the would-be husband, and his prop – a solitaire diamond engagement ring – completed his performance. Margaret accepted immediately. 'I had always wanted to get married and had loved Stringer Davis since I first saw him, so it was with joy and relief that I accepted his proposal of marriage. I felt very happy indeed.'

Rutherford described their romance as 'one that took a long time to bloom'. True: about fifteen years. She cited her career and Stringer's devotion to his mother as the principal reasons for the dilatory blossoming, but maintained that, 'It was the war separation that changed everything. "Tuft" suddenly realised that there is nothing worse in life than loneliness and that perhaps after all he might be husband material. It took him all that time to find himself in that respect, if you see.'

There may have been another, more fundamental reason for delaying the nuptials. Margaret was fifty-three at the time of her wedding, and by then it was far too late for her to conceive. She had been in her late thirties when she first met Stringer and, even if a whirlwind romance with him was unlikely, a precipitous marriage, despite Frith Banbury's misgivings, might have resulted in pregnancy. Margaret did have a maternal nature, but she was always convinced that her parents' mental illness was hereditary. Not only did she suffer from breakdowns, caused by depression and occasional manic episodes, but she also feared – and this was confirmed by her doctors – that any child of hers would also be at risk of suffering from the same fate in future years. In this respect, it was thus now safe to enter the institution of marriage.

Margaret had just been offered and was already rehearsing a part in Ivor Novello's new musical, *Perchance to Dream*. The first person she informed of her news was Blanche Wright, wife of Ivor Novello's dresser, of whom Margaret was very fond and intriguingly described as 'a gay French cockney'. Novello himself was then told, and when word got out, a delighted crowd congregated in Margaret's dressing room. Soon after, in the middle of a full rehearsal, Margaret lost the ring. Novello, realising that she was upset, immediately signalled for the musicians to cease playing and asked everyone in the theatre to get down on their hands and knees and hunt for it. Margaret later found the diamond ring when Blanche suggested she look in one of her gloves.

The actress had other reasons to be grateful to her dresser, Blanche Wright, who protected Margaret throughout many productions. 'Blanche was all that embodies the loyalty and devotion of real theatre people. She cherished but never fussed me. Never in all those long years we were together did I ever find my clothes anything but spotless.

No matter who came around to see us after curtain, Blanche always stayed to tidy up and put every last thing away. She watched over me with the ferocity and tenderness of a lioness over its cub. Everyone at my door was inspected before Blanche would bother me.' On matinée days Blanche would satisfy Margaret's newfound predilection for cucumber sandwiches by preparing a traditional afternoon tea (with cakes) between performances. 'When I came off the stage there she would be, with the table all laid with a pretty cloth and some of my own china just as if I was at home . . . rehearsals were chaos. The director Jack Minster would be frustrated by Ivor and I giggling – it was such fun. There were last minute cuts and alterations to the script. The cast gave Ivor everything that we could because we all felt that this was the kind of enchanting escapism that the public needed after the war, and Ivor was the undoubted master of it.'

Every summer Novello held an annual garden party for everyone connected with his productions. 'There was always a most lavish tea with strawberries and cream and gooey cakes – in the afternoons there would be a cricket match for the men and running races for the women.' Novello also had a swimming pool in the grounds, in which Rutherford would often be found. She had always been keen on swimming and would, whenever the opportunity arose, immerse herself. 'Cold water has never bothered me and though I prefer the sea I will swim wherever I can. There is something so cleansing mentally and emotionally in feeling yourself weightless in water.'

Stringer was now very much part of Rutherford's theatrical world. Novello was happy for him to spend as much time as he wanted backstage so that the betrothed couple could be together. In fact, from then on, Stringer barely left Margaret's side. In almost every theatre production and film that she made, he was present, earning himself the peppery soubriquet of 'Stringalong' from Margaret's fellow artistes.

Plans were quickly formulated for the couple's wedding, which was to take place at St Michael's church in old Beaconsfield but performed by The Reverend Donald Nicholson, Margaret's vicar from her church of St Michael and All Angels. The date was set for 26 March 1945. Margaret and Stringer wanted a quiet wedding with a few family members and close friends in attendance. Her cousin, John Nicholson, was best man, and another cousin, Professor Graham Nicholson, whose illness all those years ago had presented Margaret with her first acting part as the 'Bad Fairy', gave her away.

Elizabeth Orphin made the trip all the way from Devon and arrived in a London cab which she had taken all the way from Paddington, at the insistence of and paid for by Margaret. According to Dawn Langley Simmons, Miss Orphin had brought two pots of Stringer's favourite clotted cream as a gift. Margaret described her wedding outfit as, 'A biscuit coloured coat and skirt and a jaunty snood of veiling scattered with golden stars.' She later, inexplicably, left the wedding ensemble in a telephone box which, judging by the description of the outfit, doesn't sound such a terrible thing. By comparison, Stringer was dashingly attired in his Army uniform.

Rutherford wrote that when the service began she was so nervous that she pushed Grace Bridges in front, alongside Stringer. 'When the vicar said, "Do you take this man, for better or for worse, to be your lawful husband?" Grace said, "I am not taking anybody. Margaret, you ought to be here, not me."' Margaret also maintained that, having signed the register, she and Tuft mixed up their exits, only to emerge in the graveyard at the rear of the church: 'I was so dazed with happiness as I took his arm that neither of us realised that we were alone as we walked down the yew-lined back garden path. In the front of the church there was the usual excitement. Grace Bridges stepped out of the front door and was showered with rose petals and confetti as they mistook her for me again.' Although these anecdotes are very possibly apocryphal, the accounts of Margaret's stand-in nearly overdoing her role might explain a little of Stringer's jealousy towards Grace Bridges. The reception was held at the Bull Hotel in Gerrards Cross, where the vicar surreptitiously presented the bridegroom with a little booklet which explained the carnal nature of marriage. The text was augmented by a diagram, just in case Stringer and Margaret needed a little extra help.

Ten days later Stringer returned to Army headquarters in York, and Margaret continued rehearsing in *Perchance to Dream*. It was not until three months into the run that Margaret was allowed a fortnight off so that she and Stringer could enjoy a proper honeymoon in Cornwall. Margaret was extremely grateful to 'the kind-hearted' Ivor Novello and felt this to be a generous gesture: 'Few producers would have allowed a name in the cast such a break so early in the run.'

Perchance to Dream opened at the Golders Green Hippodrome on 21 April 1945. The musical romance, devised, written and composed by Ivor Novello, is set in Huntersmoon, a magnificent old English house, in three time periods (Regency, Victorian and Modern) and tells the story of two families who are linked by unhappy love affairs. Novello's biographer James Harding describes it as 'a mixture of usual Novello romanticism tempered by a gentleness and nostalgia that were entirely English and were perfectly suited for the time in which he wrote and performed it'.

Novello thus had three roles, and Rutherford played opposite one of them, as his wife, Lady Charlotte Fayre. She had never appeared in a musical and didn't sing in the production. She did, however, have one ballroom scene in which she began to dance. She recalled the moment: 'How I loved that sweeping velvet dress, the vivid green of an Irish spring, my elegant bonnet with its swirling green feathers, and the lorgnette I wore on a golden chain. I have always loved to dance and at that moment each night it seemed that I floated round the stage. The whole scene had seized my imagination.'

Despite the fact that audiences loved the show and it ran for over a thousand performances, the reviews were not positive. James Agate described the show as 'pretentious and wordy', and went on to state: 'I hasten to say that the curtain, when it went up, took with it the entire audience, which remained in seventh heaven, until after three hours and a half, the curtain descended and automatically brought the audience down with it. Mr Novello's nonsense had obviously suited their performance . . . the production has been shortened and improved since opening night but Mr Novello can do better than this. I am certain that someday he will.' John Trewin was equally disparaging: 'We have left Margaret Rutherford to the last. What in the world is she doing at Huntersmoon with that unquenchable sense of comedy and the voice that – like Byron's cocking of the pistol – is a 'strange quick jar upon the air'? Her part hardly exists; but ingeniously she makes a personage of a phantom and at the end – in Mr Novello's odd little ghost scene behind the gauzes – a phantom of a personage.'

There were a number of reasons why Margaret Rutherford agreed to appear in such an unlikely vehicle. Delighted to accept a role which she felt escaped the stereotypical comedy characters with which she was already associated, she had also been flattered by Ivor Novello when he had gone backstage to meet her during the production of *The Master Builder* in 1934. 'There was a knock at my door and a shy young man stood there. "My name is Novello." As if I didn't know. "I just wanted to tell you how much I enjoyed your performance. You were quite marvellous."' She was enormously impressed by Novello's charm, grace and classic good looks. (Noël Coward once remarked: 'There are two perfect things in this world – my mind and Ivor's profile.')

In France the previous year Rutherford had been terribly moved by Novello's dedication and inspired by the troops' affection for the musical star and his songs. He remained modest and approachable, she felt, despite the adulation of his fans. Eric Keown wrote: 'She has something approaching a missionary feeling about the duty of the artist to bring entertainment to as many as people as possible – her sense of duty would only allow one answer. The bleak house of highbrowism is not for her. She was therefore delighted when he asked her to accept a peerage in *Perchance to Dream*.' This may be a little fanciful, but Rutherford had a strong sense of loyalty and in some way wanted to repay Novello for his belief in her.

Novello not only admired Margaret Rutherford's work as an actress, he was also extremely fond of her for her eccentric ways and generous nature. Unashamedly homosexual, Novello lived in a flat above the Strand Theatre in the Aldwych. Margaret was invited to one of his dazzling parties and, as he opened the front door to her, revealing ornate furnishings, twinkling lights and, in the background, Noël Coward, Siegfried Sassoon and a host of matinée idols among an array of impossibly beautiful young men, Margaret gasped with excitement. 'Oh, Ivor! Enchanting! It's like fairyland . . .' Novello resided in the flat until his death in 1951 and, in 2005, following extensive refurbishment, the Strand Theatre was renamed the Novello in his honour.

The best known song from the production is 'We'll Gather Lilacs', which was first performed in France during the ENSA tour. The wartime song captures the themes of returning home and the allure of the English countryside. The lyrics referring to 'gathering the flowers, walking around country lanes . . . happy in each other's company' had special meaning to Margaret and her new husband. Stringer would pick delicate bouquets of wild flowers for her while on their country walks: 'We knew all the roads around Beaconsfield and each had its special magic. Perhaps our favourite was Hedgerly Lane which in those days was quite unspoilt. I used to stride out with my cloak flying behind me.' Tuft considered himself something of an ornithologist and would identify for Margaret the various birdsong that he recognised. Stringer's Army career was drawing to a close. He was granted release leave on 4 July 1945 and was finally demobbed on 8 October 1945.

In May 1946, Rutherford appeared in a television recording of *The Importance of Being Earnest* at the BBC's Alexandra Park studios. For the two performances she was paid sixty guineas. She and Stringer were now living at 22 York Avenue, East Sheen, London. The 1947 edition of *Who's Who in the Theatre* listed her recreations as music and walking, and noted that she belonged to the London Arts Club. In the same year Margaret made two more films. *Meet Me at Dawn* was a romantic comedy set in 1900 Paris, about a man who makes a living from duelling. Margaret Rutherford played Madame Vermorel and the cast was strengthened by Stanley Holloway and Wilfred Hyde-White. The film was panned – summed up by a review in the *New York Times* which described the movie as 'just plain boring'. *While the Sun Shines*, a romantic farce, was Anthony Asquith's first post war effort and based on a play by Terence Rattigan. Set in London, the story involves an aristocratic pair whose lives are complicated by a French expatriate and an American lieutenant. Rutherford was cast for the first time as a doctor (Dr Winifred Frye) and the film also featured Miles Malleson, Joyce Grenfell and Wilfred Hyde-White as a collection of British caricatures.

Nineteen forty-seven took the actress to New York to play in another of Gielgud's productions of *The Importance of Being Earnest*. Jean Cadell was to be Miss Prism, with Pamela Brown and Jane Baxter also in the cast. John Gielgud had originally wanted Dame Edith Evans to play the role of Lady Bracknell – a part with which she was synony-mous – but she declined. This was in part due to the fact that she was tired of the role, but she was also much in demand for film work, and had recently lost her father.

Gielgud turned to Rutherford as a safe pair of hands and she readily agreed – on the understanding that she was provided with costumes 'identical to those Dame Edith wore, down to the last detail'. Margaret was concerned she wouldn't be able to play the role as effectively as Edith Evans, but wanted to mould her performance on those of Evans, using the costumes as a kind of professional safeguard. Even more security would be provided by the presence of Stringer, who was cast as the butler, Merriman, and thus able to accompany his wife on her first major theatrical tour abroad.

The play initially toured in Canada, and Margaret prepared herself for the inclement weather: 'Everyone had warned me it would be cold. I looked at my tired wardrobe – I'd used up all those odd dresses from lengths bought at Liberty's. Then I had the idea to have a yellow blanket with green stripes made into a trouser suit by my dressmaker. It looked rather dashing when it was finished. I wore it to a late night party in Montreal with scarf and green earmuffs.' Only Rutherford could have got away with this sartorial disaster – she was already a popular character with the Canadian public, who knew of her work and particularly her portrayal as the freewheeling Madame Arcati. While walking to the summit of Mount Royal in Montreal, she was rather surprised by one of the guides calling out, 'Where's your bicycle?'

The first Saturday night in Toronto was not an auspicious start for our Lady Bracknell. There was a full house, Rutherford was extremely nervous and was playing a scene with Gielgud. 'John had got to his knees and Lady Bracknell has to enter and say, "Mr Worthing, rise from this semi-recumbent posture," which always got a big laugh. He turned around and there was no Lady Bracknell. I was offstage thinking that the Act was over and I had begun to change for the last Act. The stage manager called me and I rushed out just as I was. No feather boa, no jabot, no handbag or umbrella. But worse still I had taken off my hat and was in a half-wig. I was so upset and that I was trembling in every limb. The audience was sympathetic as I heard my voice saying, "Good Morning Mr Worthing," and then exited through a blind door.'

The play was then taken to the Royale Theatre, New York, where the influential *New York Times* critic, Brooks Atkinson wrote, 'As the overbearing Lady Bracknell, Miss Margaret Rutherford is tremendously skilful; the speaking, the walking and the wearing of costumes all gathered up into one impression of insufferability.' It was not just the critics who enjoyed her performances: Alfred Lunt and Lynn Fontanne were among a number of distinguished fellow actors that came to see Rutherford on Broadway, and, as in Canada, her American fan base was growing. One night she was crossing a Manhattan street when a young motorist, whose car was filled with flowers for some celebratory event, screeched to a halt. He decamped from the car, approached the startled actress and enquired, 'Excuse me, but are you

Margaret Rutherford?' On her forthright confirmation, he handed her an enormous long-stemmed tulip with the words, 'Then, enjoy this!'

Margaret did indeed enjoy the gift, and the rest of the adventure, and was particularly pleased with her treatment by the American press. She found their directness 'refreshing', and questions such as 'Are you an eccentric?' she found to be more 'candid than impertinent'. Still, she wasn't terribly pleased with the description of her in *Time* Magazine: 'her bulbous eyes swivel in deep pouches. The nose is impertinent, and her great jaw is pillowed in an accordion of jowls.' She was relieved when the article added, 'She is so British that by comparison with her even John Bull himself seems the son of a miscegenetic marriage.'

Rutherford was reported as saying that she divided the press into two camps: 'The people whom we like and would do anything for and the others whom we deplore and can be quite beastly to. I am not an intolerant woman but I abominate stupidity.' Although extraordinarily polite and well mannered, Margaret would speak her mind if the occasion demanded – but there is no evidence of her being 'beastly' to anyone who knew her.

On returning to England, she was approached by director Ken Annakin for a part in the fantasy film, *Miranda*. Annakin's diverse body of work includes the Disney production, *Swiss Family Robinson* the star-studded account of the D-Day landings, *The Longest Day*, and grand scale comedy, such as *Those Magnificent Men in Their Flying Machines*. Born in 1914, he began his career as an assistant cameraman for the Ministry of Information, which led to work with Carol Reed. Annakin worked on a 1942 government documentary, *We Serve* (not to be confused with Noël Coward's *In Which We Serve*), which focused on the contribution of women to the overall war effort. Margaret Rutherford had been recruited for the documentary, along with other British actresses including Edith Evans, at a nominal £5 per day.

Miranda, based on Peter Blackmore's popular play about a flirtatious mermaid, starred Glynis Johns, David Tomlinson and Googie Withers. Rutherford played Nurse Carey, a part she was to reprise in the 1954 sequel, *Mad About Men*. It was at the request of Mrs Davis that husband Stringer made his screen debut in the film as a museum attendant. He was to appear in over twenty of Margaret Rutherford's films throughout his career; in fact, in later years, a clause was written into each of her contracts that a part should be provided for him.

The plot of this quirky film pivots around Harley Street specialist Dr Paul Martin, who is on a Cornish fishing holiday. He is rescued from drowning by a mermaid who threatens to keep him in her cave unless he takes her to London. He reluctantly agrees and takes her home in the guise of a wheelchair bound patient. Once in the city, the sexy Miranda captivates every male she meets. Glynis Johns is gloriously alluring as Miranda, her feline features and purring voice reducing the hapless David Tomlinson to a ball of wool. Yet there is surprisingly little visual comedy – just two short sequences: one where Miranda devours a street-vendor's entire stock of cockles, and the other at London zoo, where she catches a fish in her mouth during feeding time. Eventually Rutherford's eccentric nurse and the doctor's jealous wife (Googie Withers) become suspicious of Miranda's disconcerting addiction to seafood.

Annakin was delighted with Margaret Rutherford's performance: 'Margaret did a great job for me as Miranda's nurse. She had the gift of making a character real, but also full of imagination. Her reaction to the string of pearls which Glynis Johns gives her as a reward for pushing her around in the wheelchair was indeed magical. Maggie took the pearls, looked at them as if they were the most priceless treasure from a fantastic ocean bed and, despite her weight and age, did a spontaneous pirouette, delicate as thistledown. I think we made five takes and the last one gave me goose pimples, so I printed it!'

The director described Rutherford as a natural scene stealer, even when she was not delivering dialogue: 'She used to do something quite unique with her mouth and lower jaw. Sometimes I would be explaining a scene to her, and I would say with a smile, "At this point, you should do one of those things you do with your mouth." And I would try, weakly, to imitate her. With wide-open, serious eyes she would stare back at me and say, "I don't know what you mean, young man. I never do anything like that with my mouth."' To keep Rutherford's spontaneity and instinctive acting, Annakin chose to rehearse as little as possible. He thought her charm quite individual and not at all contrived: 'You had to set the mood of the scene, and nine times out of ten she would give you something wonderful. I would say that Margaret was one of our great British character actresses. She had hard features, but the inner workings and emotions almost make her beautiful.'

The professional performances from Glynis Johns and Margaret Rutherford were tempered by the difficulties Annakin encountered with Griffith Jones, who played Dr Martin. Inevitably, having a mermaid as the film's principal character presented a few technological challenges for the director, who positioned one of the crew up on the gantry with a piece of piano wire attached to the mermaid's tail. Whenever Glynis Johns came out of the water, the grip gave a tug on the tail to make it flap. Although Miss Johns was very petite and the rubber tail wasn't heavy, every time Griffith Jones had to lift her he caused a terrible commotion, 'insisting, with great public show, on putting on a truss and elastic knee pads'.

Although Annakin thought he had a coaxed a reasonable perform-ance from the actor, the actor's attempts to hog the scene had not made it easy. Annakin recalled one scene with Margaret Rutherford, in which Griffith Jones sat on the edge of a desk interviewing Nurse Carey about her employment: 'He knew very well I was going to shoot a front-on close-up for his key lines and this particular set up was to favour Margaret . . . the camera operator kept asking him to keep his position in the foreground, but he continued to find reasons to play with his face turned away from her. At last I ordered him to hold his look to Maggie, to which he replied, "It's like this, Ken, old boy, something inside of me keeps saying, 'Griff, it's up to you to keep the old fizz in the picture,' and that's what I intend to do!" For once I lost my cool and told him I was the director! I would look after the fizz, and he should be ashamed of himself for trying to steal the scene from an old pro like Maggie! Griff obeyed sulkily and we made the shots.'

When *Miranda* was due for release in the USA, the censors reached a most bizarre conclusion about mermaids. In order to protect the sensibilities of the American public, they adopted the amphibian equivalent of the bedroom scene where actors had to keep one foot firmly on terra firma: it was decided that only married mermaids were allowed to have tails. So the tail of poor spinster Miranda was never seen in America. So much for the piano wire.

Rutherford's next film was another 'piece of whimsy', albeit a little starker. Bombardier Billy Wells bangs the Rank gong to herald a very busy opening in *Passport to Pimlico*, in which a multitude of principal and minor characters are introduced. Post-war ravaged London is grimly depicted: bomb sites, clothing coupons, food rationing and the inimitable spirit of the community making the best of it. The cast list is truly a who's who of British films: Michael Hordern, Hermione Baddeley, Stanley Holloway and the delightful double act of Basil Radford and Naunton Wayne (immortalised in *The Lady Vanishes*) playing bewildered but decent Whitehall Civil Servants; plus Richard Hearne (later Mr Pastry) as a drunken bicyclist, Sydney Tafler as wide-boy bookie and even Charles Hawtrey as a piano-playing 'potman' accompanying the pub vocalist's rendition of 'I Don't Want to Set the World on Fire'.

An unexploded bomb (nicknamed Pamela) is accidentally deto-nated in Pimlico, revealing a treasure trove and paperwork alluding to the fact that the area is in fact part of Burgundy. History academic Professor Hatton-Jones (Rutherford) is called in to give her expert opinion on the matter, and the residents duly declare themselves Burgundians and therefore not governed by British law. Local bobby, PC Spiller, comes to a sudden realisation with the words, 'Blimey, I'm a foreigner,' and the general state of disorder is beautifully summed up by the grocer's wife (Betty Warren) who, when it is suggested that the people of Pimlico are now a bunch of foreigners, declares: 'We were always English, and we will always be English, and it's just because we're English we're sticking out for our right to be Burgundians.' The British Government, in the form of Foreign Office bureaucrat Naunton Wayne, closes 'the border' and Pimlico comes under siege. However, the great British public join the fight against government bureaucracy, supporting the Pimlico community by throwing provisions over the barbed wire – even a pig is parachuted in. Eventually Pimlico is returned to the UK, the heatwave that has gripped this little piece of Burgundy disappears and, inevitably, rain immediately starts to fall.

Written by Ealing regular T.E.B. Clarke and directed by Henry Cornelius of *Genevieve* fame, the film was nominated by BAFTA in the Best British Film category. The idea of the film much appealed to Rutherford, who is slightly manic in the blustering role of Professor Hatton-Jones: 'It was a romp from start to finish and Cornelius handled the film with light-hearted sophistication.' She also approved of the way the British were portrayed, accentuating their individuality and decency, while acknowledging some parochial idiosyncrasies.

After completing her work on *Passport to Pimlico*, Rutherford took another of her 'rest periods'. When combining theatre and film parts, she would leave her home by 9.30 a.m., only to return by midnight: 'But of course this takes its toll of one's physical strength and nerves, and so in between productions my doctor always ordered me to rest. The weeks just flew as I went for long walks, caught up with my private life and spent hours reading poetry. In the beginning it was always a relief to have some time to oneself, but then I noticed that gradually I became a little bored, even irritable.'

The theatre production which occupied her at the time – along with Stringer, who enjoyed a small role – was *The Happiest Days of Your Life*, which was first seen at the Theatre Royal, Brighton, in January 1948, before transferring to the Apollo Theatre in March. Author John

Dighton's plot involved the British Ministry of Evacuation mistakenly billeting the all girls' school of St Swithins with the boys of Hilary Hall. Aware of the potential damage to their institutions' reputations, the two combative head teachers conspire together to prevent the parents and inspectors from discovering the terrible truth. Rutherford played Miss Evelyn Whitchurch, headmistress of St Swithins, and George Howe was the embattled boys' headmaster, Mr Pond.

The production opened to excellent reviews. The *Tatler and Bystander* reported that, 'Margaret Rutherford, fighting with might for both schools against the parents, always the common enemy of pedagogues and pupils, rejects no subterfuge however obvious and gets herself and everybody else into bigger and better trouble.' Rutherford herself loved the character and, although she often described parts as among her favourite roles, there is no doubt that that the personality of Miss Whitchurch appealed greatly: 'She has a heart of gold but is no marshmallow. I have never found any challenge in playing a weak woman.'

'Mr Pond is a pompous bumbler on the verge of tears but in Miss Whitchurch he is up against a woman accustomed to command,' wrote Eric Keown wrote. 'She was Margaret Rutherford, who has never lent herself to a more disgraceful exhibition of ruthless femininity. She passed over poor Mr Pond like a trumpeting steam roller; no demand was too outrageous, no cunning too low. It was an unflaggingly funny performance, in her wildest vein; and yet as always with her, disbelief was suspended, so that for a couple of hours one would have been prepared to swear that here was a typical member of that notoriously hilarious body, the Headmistresses' Conference.'

It was during this production that Rutherford became friendly with *It's That Man Again* actress Molly Weir, who played the head girl. Rutherford was intrigued by the Scottish actress's varied background: Miss Weir had worked in a munitions factory during the war and was once shorthand champion of Great Britain, with a speed of 33 words per minute. 'Molly was a darling girl and many a laugh we had together. She had digs in Clapham and once went down with a very bad flu. Rationing was at its worst and so was her temperature when I stood outside her bedroom on the third floor in my green coat and four little brown eggs. I wonder where I got those eggs from?'

Rutherford left the show after 400 performances, although Stringer remained in the cast. The couple also moved again – this time to an elegant Nash residence in Regent's Park (9 St Andrew's Place) – and the Davises celebrated their fourth wedding anniversary in March 1949 in their new house with a musical party for friends from the production. Rutherford had by now stopped playing the piano, and told a journalist, selflessly and disingenuously, that in any case she was much less gifted than her husband, who was known to tickle the ivories occasionally.

Two years after the stage version, *The Happiest Days of Your Life* was adapted for the screen. Rutherford reprised her stage role, but her old friend George Howe was replaced by Alistair Sim. The director Frank Launder had seen the play and 'was convinced that it offered the opportunity for Launder and Gilliat to develop a comedy form to rival that of Ealing', according to Sim's biographer Mark Simpson. 'The opening cartoon graphics to *The Happiest Days* had been drawn by Ronald Searle, whose series of cartoons describing the grisly antics of a group of unruly and anarchic schoolgirls had become very popular with the readers of *Lilliput* magazine.' The rights were purchased and filming began in 1949.

Margaret was less comfortable in the film role than she had been in the stage version two years earlier: 'I found doing the film a bit tiresome. Film actors are, by nature, more complicated than stage actors. Mr Sim is a brilliant actor but most competitive.' Although Rutherford found Sim slightly difficult, he was quite superb in the renamed part of Wetherby Pond and the two played off each other brilliantly. They were two scene-stealers trying to outdo each other in a film which is very funny, well plotted and beautifully paced.

Joyce Grenfell, of whom Rutherford was very fond, played hockey mistress Miss Gossage ('Call me sausage'). Gossage is extraordinarily gauche and skips along like a toddler – Grenfell deliberately gave her a bouncy walk to underline her immaturity. Richard 'I love monotony' Wattis is superb as ever as the drily cynical maths teacher Arnold Billings; Guy Middleton is a Terry-Thomas type in the sports master role of Victor Hyde-Brown; and the uncredited George Cole, junior assistant caretaker at the Ministry of Education, has one line. Stringer also made an appearance, as Reverend Rich, a school governor.

It is Rutherford, however, who catches the eye every time she is on screen. As the headmistress of St Swithins, one of her finest film roles, she is indomitable. On seeing their new abode for the first time, she barks to her assistant Miss Jezzard (old friend Muriel Aked): 'The infant animal needs space to breathe and blow – see our girls get a south-facing dormitory.' On entering the grand interior, and surprised that no member of staff has come to greet them, Grenfell bangs the gong to gain attention, far too energetically and loudly. Rutherford shouts down the stairs: 'A tap, Gossage, a tap. You're not introducing a film.' Observing a plaque on which the Nutbourne College boys school motto – 'Guard Thine Honour' – is boldly emblazoned, Rutherford's beautifully understated reaction is a mere purse of the lips.

The headmistress's name was changed from Evelyn to Muriel Whitchurch, but otherwise the character remained identical. A feminist before her time, Whitchurch is a determined woman, who we can imagine must surely have been a leading light in the suffragette movement. Her approach is very much at odds with Pond's need for order and convention, and she has absolutely no qualms in occupying his school. Although the needs of her girls are paramount, her own requirements are not unimportant, and Pond's personal living quarters are duly purloined for Whitchurch's own benefit.

Frank Launder was full of praise for Rutherford's performance and felt that she embodied the part of Miss Whitchurch: 'We could never put marks down for her, we just had to keep the camera rolling wherever she was likely to be. She can always make any line sound funnier than it really is. She would never do one take the same, but I like an artist like that. Margaret is an artist who has great moments, many great moments.'

Happiest Days was filmed at the Byculla School in Hampshire and featured some of the Byculla pupils, supported by students from the Corona Theatrical School. After filming, Margaret and Joyce Grenfell would spend genteel evenings with the school's real headmistress, who had a cottage in the grounds. Occasionally Grenfell helped the teaching staff with the huge amount of sewing that such a large institution generated. Rutherford, who admitted to be of little use with a needle, would have provided moral support.

Completed in just nine weeks, the film went on to become one of the biggest grossing films of 1950. *The Times* described it as, 'A genuinely hilarious farce . . . Miss Margaret Rutherford sets before her audience a character well enough drawn to survive even the most preposterous demands of farce. Mr Alistair Sim endows the headmaster with the exact qualities appropriate to the part. He is dignified, pompous and ludicrous in turn.' Sim, Grenfell and a few others returned in similar roles in the unofficial sequel, *The Belles of St Trinian's*, in 1954.

In addition to film and theatre work, Rutherford also worked on the occasional radio broadcast in children's serials. She played the part of Miss Price in *The Magic Bedknob* and was offered the part of Miss Dollit in *Worzel Gummidge at the Treasure Ship*, to be recorded live for *Children's Hour* on the Home Service. The contract was returned with a letter from agent Dorothy Mather stating that, 'Miss Rutherford does want to take part in more broadcasts but unfortunately does not feel that this is quite the part for her.'

A more interesting offer from the BBC arrived in April 1948 in a letter from Anthony Derville (Home Talks Dept): 'I wonder if you would be interested in the idea of broadcasting in our *Woman's Hour* programme – a daily programme which has achieved an audience of some five million housewives – normally consists of 5 minute talks on such topics as 'How to bottle tomatoes' 'How to bring up your children.' We would like you to talk about your profession (previous guests have been Peggy Ashcroft and Celia Johnson). If you are interested come and have lunch one day.'

Lunch seems to have been declined, but Margaret Rutherford went to a meeting on 13 May 1948 at 4 p.m. to discuss the production. The subject of the talk was 'It's never too late to be happy' and her fee, ten guineas. Margaret sent a draft of what she was going to say with a note: 'Let me have the copy back so I can further polish it . . . my chief idea is to cheer those who are not happy.'

Anthony Derville replied: 'I would be grateful if you could let me see your final altered version by Saturday and also a copy of the poem you will be reading. There are certain sentences in this talk which some of our listeners might call whimsy . . . I do believe the more matter-of-a-fact this talk is – the better it will go over. The Editor of *Woman's Hour* further feels that you are telling people that it is virtuous to suffer but that you are not pointing out the gain there is to be got from suffering.' He obviously thought he was being a little presumptuous for he added: 'Please only accept any of these comments you think are helpful and ignore the rest.' The programme was subsequently broadcast on 31 May 1948 and must have gone well because Mr Derville wrote to Margaret a few days later, thanking her again for 'the delightful talk'.

In her discourse, 'It's Never Too Late to Be Happy', Rutherford began by saying, 'A bold statement on the face of it, but I am encouraged to make it the subject of my talk to you, because my own happiness has come late, both in my work and in my domestic life.' The actress recounted the time when as a child she played the 'Bad Fairy' and continued: 'Suddenly I knew an intoxicating happiness – a little flame lighted up inside of me and kept burning until, twenty-five years later, I walked on stage at the Old Vic, in a lovely Venetian dress as Lady-in-Waiting to Edith Evans, who was playing Portia in *The Merchant of Venice* – it was happiness beyond all imaginings – the greater because, in that long waiting time, the little flame had burnt very low, but it had never quite gone out. A little flame, I like this as a symbol of happiness. It is in the heart of the black coal, buried deep in the earth for hundreds of years, waiting to be set free. Then suddenly we meet the right person, perhaps a friend, perhaps a husband, or we find the right work. Our imagination is kindled and the spark bursts into life – we are happy. We may have passed through long periods of darkness, of hopelessness, waiting for this to happen, and when it does it is all the more wonderful.'

Rutherford then describes her depression towards the end of the run in *Rebecca* and Noël Coward's part for her in *Blithe Spirit*. 'I was able to embrace with all the more joyousness the part of Madame Arcati – I hold the belief that any sense of happiness I may succeed in giving in my work has sprung directly from the unhappy times in my life. Light and shade, contrast and even conflict. That is life, isn't it? I firmly believe that if we have faith, the little flame of happiness that's there within us all will eventually be gathered up into the life of the sun from which it sprang.'

SIX

In the Name of Thespis

'The theatre is a meeting place between imitation and a transforming power called imagination, which has no action if it stays in the mind. It must pervade the body.'

PETER BROOK

THE 1950S BEGAN WITH the offer of a most exciting theatrical project: *Ring Round the Moon*, a play by Jean Anouilh, translated by Christopher Fry, which Margaret described as 'a piece of French flummery'. Her role was to be Madame Desmortes, an elderly aristocratic aunt. The director, Peter Brook, had been engaged by H.M. Tennent. Described as 'without doubt the contemporary theatre's greatest inventor' by writer and critic Michael Billington, Brook has become one of Britain's most respected and visionary theatrical directors, as well as distinguishing himself in opera and film and as a writer, but this was to be his first West End production

Brook was delighted with his cast. The production team included Binkie Beaumont and casting director Daphne Rye and, according to Brook, 'H.M. Tennent knew every actor in London and every actor wanted to work for them.' Paul Scofield was asked to play a dual role as twin brothers Hugo and Frederic – blue-blooded siblings with diametric characters. 'Paul was already recognised as the most extra-ordinary young actor of his time,' wrote Brook in his autobiography, *Threads of Time*, 'so although his movements were awkward and his voice grated and exploded controllably, I went against all the rules of stereotyping and asked him to play an elegant Edwardian gentleman.' To help Scofield acquire grace in his movements, Brook requested that he take ballet lessons. Scofield refused, asking the director to explain what was required so that he could act it. Brook demurred, and reported that 'although his characteristic movements did not change, by a mysterious alchemy of the imagination, they ended by expressing the essence of the refinement that the part required . . . a seemingly abstract word, "incarnation", suddenly took on a meaning.'

Claire Bloom played the waif, Isabelle, a penniless young dancer and sort of maltreated Cinderella, who is brought to a country house and involved in a plot contrived by one of the brothers to seduce his innocent twin. Rutherford described her as 'flitting through the scenes like a pale shaft of moonlight'. When Bloom initially read for the part, she recalled that Peter Brook hardly said a word afterwards, and when she left the audition she had no idea how it had gone. 'I heard nothing about the play for over a month and only in the fifth week did I hear that I had got the part.' The cast was reinforced by the talents of William Mervyn, Mona Washbourne, Cecil Trouncer as a melancholy millionaire, and Richard Wattis – who else? – as a taciturn secretary.

Rutherford felt that the production possessed 'a strange fey quality', due in part, no doubt, to Oliver Messel's enchanting set – a Winter Garden of a grand country house in France, a mini Crystal Palace. She was also delighted by Peter Brook's light touch as director: 'Each evening became an experience as one entered this fairytale with its delicate overlay of Oscar Wilde cynicism.'

There were many challenges in playing this controlling yet intriguing old battleaxe, and initially Rutherford admitted that the part didn't come to her when she first read it. Peter Brook agreed: 'It was a totally new form of writing by Anouilh and even more so in

Christopher Fry's always unexpected word-play. Margaret was used to mainstream West End plays. She was a real actress – of course she was usually typecast – and this role of a witty French Countess was a breakthrough.' Rutherford found herself dripping in jewels and sporting a white aigrette in her hair. She had to puff on a cheroot 'with contempt' and partake regularly of a pinch of snuff while commenting acidly on passing events. 'It was a part with a sting in the tail, but this again I enjoyed as astringency combined with eccentricity calls for a balance of acting.'

A less esoteric hazard in undertaking the role was of a physical nature. Rutherford's character was immobile, so she spent the entire performance seated. She rather enjoyed the idea of sitting throughout the action and watching all the other actors rushing around madly. But when she discovered she would have to manoeuvre a Bath chair around the stage with some agility, she realised that further preparation was required. In the same way that her cycling experiences had served her well as Madame Arcati, her years spent pushing Aunt Bessie around Wimbledon in a Bath chair now gave Rutherford some knowledge of this occasionally temperamental mode of transport. 'I never leave anything to chance when I am acting. Even the most careless gesture has been rehearsed and thought out. I went to a shop and tried out several Bath chairs before I found one that exactly suited my purpose.'

Even this exhaustive preparation didn't assuage her worries, however: 'I was always frightened of going over the edge of the stage into the orchestra pit. One day I cried and said that I simply couldn't do it, this running over everyone's feet.' She approached Peter Brook, who was most understanding and took her out to lunch to discuss her disquiet: 'We went out and had a nice little lunch – a scrumptious meal of roast pork and apple sauce. Stringer was duly despatched to procure another more reliable Bath chair.'

Years later, Peter Brook couldn't remember the menu but confirmed that the rake on the stage did create difficulties with the chair: 'It did cause her problems. It was alarming and could run away with her until she became more expert. In the end, the chair became as expressive as her hands!' Brook also found Stringer to be very endearing. 'He adored Margaret, was in the dressing room or in the wings for every performance and each time I saw him he would wax lyrically about her. For him, she was not only a great talent, but above all a beauty.'

Following two weeks in Brighton, *Ring Round the Moon*, described in the programme as 'a charade with music', opened at the Globe on 26 January 1950. The *Telegraph* was fulsome in its praise: 'Miss Margaret Rutherford appears as an indomitable and witty old aristocrat who from her Bath chair doubles the parts of fairy godmother and wicked fairy, with some assistance from a cheroot as long as her romantically snobbish memory.' The critic in the *Tatler and Bystander* agreed: 'Margaret Rutherford is a formidable dowager in an extremely mobile invalid chair and she is grand fun with her tart comments on the passing scene.' Kenneth Tynan called the play 'a complete wedding cake, traced with an icing gun on gossamer'. Indeed Oliver Messel's conservatory set was so enchanting, and the fireworks so dazzling, that Tynan reported that audiences simply couldn't stop applauding. Yet not all the reviews were flattering. Ivor Brown in the *Observer* wrote: 'The English title bespeaks, I suppose, the lighter lunacy, and that is all there is to it . . . to me it is a Variety Entertainment which never combines in one satisfactory pattern. What does it amount to? Here is a pretty masquerade for admirers of Oliver Messel's decoration, one of Peter Brook's less exhibitionist productions, an agreeable concert of Richard Addinsell's light music. Drama? No . . . this charade was knocked up to be immediately enjoyed; it can hardly be remembered.' Harold Hobson was critical of the translation, but Peter Brook commented that, 'Fry's work was massively admired. He took many liberties with text and was very afraid when the author came to see the play but Anouilh adored it.'

Claire Bloom felt that the story worked beautifully from the first moment and that it was obvious the production would be a success.

She also enjoyed being part of the West End theatrical scene. It was an era 'when Soho still possessed some charm, it was a pleasure to go to your evening's work by way of Old Compton Street, passing the Italian grocery shops. Most of the company used to stop at a coffee shop called Taylor's.' It was also during *Ring Round the Moon* that Claire Bloom auditioned for a part in Charlie Chaplin's *Limelight*. She was allowed a week off for her screen test, and met Chaplin in New York. She then had to wait several months to find out if she had been given the part. When she returned, she couldn't wait to tell her friends in the cast about her adventures in America. However, she discovered that most of them weren't very interested in her adventure: 'Everything in my dressing room had been moved to make room for my understudy, and when I heard that she had given a lovely performance, I realised that I hadn't been missed very much. Then when I started to talk about New York somebody changed the subject. Only Margaret Rutherford took me aside and asked to hear every detail.' On Bloom's nineteenth birthday, Margaret presented her with a bunch of tulips at the curtain call: 'They were "parrot tulips", multi-coloured with serrated edges, the first I had ever seen, and they remain in my mind as the most beautiful. She was divine to act with, always thoughtful about her colleagues, an altogether enchanting woman.'

Margaret Rutherford's performance onstage was – again – truly memorable. Eric Keown wrote: 'In a woman essentially so gentle, and in an actress who took such pleasure in the simplicities of *Perchance to Dream*, this ability to sting may seem a surprising weapon; but as she employs it, it is never ugly. It governs much of her best comedy, lending it astringency and holding the balance of eccentricity.' Peter Brook described Rutherford as a joy to work with, and stated that her theatrical achievements were not simply a result of her unusual looks: 'Margaret's success was that she was a true born actress and could either exploit or transcend her physical appearance as the part required.'

She was the toast of the West End, and enjoyed the patronage at performances and the company of a number of fans afterwards: 'I remember Odette, whose courageous war effort filled me with admiration; Sir Malcolm Sargent was a regular and Mr Atlee. When Queen Elizabeth, the Queen Mother, came, I zoomed backstage in my Bath chair telling everyone, "Such an honour and the audience are working like Trojans."'

While playing in *Ring Round the Moon*, Margaret also appeared in a couple of film releases: *The Happiest Days of Your Life* and *Her Favourite Husband*, known as *The Taming of Dorothy* in the USA, an amiable genial gangster romp which featured Robert Beatty in a dual role as tough hoodlum and meek bank clerk. Rutherford played the assertive Mrs Dotherington, admitting that the film wasn't very good. She could recall just one scene, when Robert Beatty had to give his love interest, Jean Kent, a smack on her bottom: 'The censor allowed that to stay in the film but insisted that the sound of the smack be cut out.'

The Magic Box is a rather poignant Technicolor biopic made at Elstree for the Festival of Britain in 1951. Robert Donat puts in a very moving performance as film pioneer William Friese-Greene, a man who devoted himself obsessively to his work, sacrificing family relationships along the way. Directed by John Boulting, with a screenplay by Eric Ambler, *The Magic Box* features a plethora of Britain's most celebrated acting talent: Richard Attenborough, Glynis Johns, Michael Redgrave, Joyce Grenfell, Joan Hickson, Peter Ustinov, Sid James, Harcourt Williams and many more. Laurence Olivier plays a passing policeman inveigled by Donat to view his moving image. Margaret Rutherford was cast as a disgruntled customer swathed in black. She had just one brief scene in which to make her mark but did, as usual, deliver a perfect cameo, despite being unsatisfied with the experience: 'It was overloaded with far too many stars with nothing to do. Robert Donat and Maria Schell in the role of his first wife did manage to produce something real and romantic. All the same it was like a meringue hidden under layers of whipped cream. None of us liked the taste much.'

Rutherford's next screen appearance was in *Curtain Up*, made in the autumn of 1951 and based on the play *On Monday Next* by Philip King. She received top billing alongside Robert Morley, with other parts played by Kay Kendall, Joan Hickson and Michael Medwin. Stringer played another clergyman. The voiceover introduction promises some fun: 'Where is the centre of culture? Where indeed if not in the temple of Thespis, the local repertory company? Repertory never rests – its gallant company striving for the triumphs of tomorrow while achieving the glories of today. Within the span of a single month it can scale the heights of poetic drama, plunge into the lowest depths of farce or gaily flirt with comedy.'

Sadly what follows is lightweight, parochial and contrived. The action, if you can call it that, takes place within the Drossmouth Rep Company and recounts backstage dramas and romances. *All About Eve* it isn't. Rutherford is the playwright, whose corny melodrama 'Tarnished Gold' is being produced. She likes to attend rehearsals in case there is a 'knotty problem' and begins to give the actors inane notes and mawkish stage directions, much to the annoyance of director, Robert Morley. Of course, these two old pros work well together, and their performances make it just about watchable, but even they struggle with the dire dialogue. Rutherford later commented that she had to make the part out of nothing, but was of the opinion that this film made her better known across the pond – mainly due to a review in *The American Star*. 'This film will be greeted with wild enthusiasm by the growing membership of the Margaret Rutherford cult.'

The film premiered in the UK at the Odeon Marble Arch in May 1952. A critic later reported that, 'The repertory company stands up badly to magnification on the screen. Everybody tries to be screamingly funny. Robert Morley and Margaret Rutherford sometimes succeed . . . however the wave of laughter that comes up from the audiences is as solid as a wall and it would be stupid to ignore it.'

Curtain Up was closely followed by *Castle in the Air*, based on a play by Alan Melville and filmed on location in Guildford. Initially,

Rutherford was not that keen on the project and needed some persuasion to agree to the part. The film starred David Tomlinson as an impoverished Scottish earl who discovers that his decaying castle is haunted by a beautiful woman. He opens the castle as a guest house, using the ghost as a tourist attraction. Margaret Rutherford played one of the guests – the troublesome Miss Nicholson, who is certain that one of her fellow holidaymakers is the rightful King of Scotland and attempts to call the clans to support the claim. Margaret had real difficulties with this scene, as she actually had to blow a horn. She had never done this before and, professional to the end, wanted to make it realistic: 'There were some astonished looks on the faces of the technicians as I walked up and down for several hours blasting my horn to get just the right sound.'

The *New York Times* described the film as a 'slender but good natured little British comedy . . . all told, however, the overall capability would be significantly lacking in spice without the presence of Margaret Rutherford. As a kilt-clad historian bent on proving the hero's right to the throne, this lady does a flamboyant, hilarious repeat of her *Passport to Pimlico* role, thundering through the picture like a dedicated rhino. Spectators who merely abide by the kind of urbane drollery that *Castle in the Air* typifies won't have to wait too long for Miss Rutherford's own personal earthquake.'

Margaret took to the stage in the summer of 1952, although she may well have wished she hadn't: her return to the boards was not triumphant. *Miss Hargreaves* opened at the Royal Court Theatre Club on 29 July 1952, after a two-week try-out in Brighton. Margaret starred in the title role as Constance Hargreaves, whose character begins as a figment of the protagonists' imaginations but then comes to life, 'with all the trappings that idle invention has devised for her'. The idea was interesting: author Frank Baker had come up with the story of two men on an Irish holiday who conjure the persona of an eccentric elderly lady but are subsequently hounded by their preposterous creation. Unfortunately, Baker had explained at length how the phenomenon had happened, and thus destroyed much of the imagination in the concept.

'The pity of it is,' wrote Harold Hobson, 'that, but for Mr Baker's need for rationalisation, we should have accepted his entire story, just as we accept the square root of minus one, and other things that are manifestly absurd and illogical, for the sake of what they bring us. In this case, they brought us Miss Margaret Rutherford and a character, ridiculous, pathetic, poetic and irresponsible, which, had it been worked on with half the zeal the author has given to philosophy, would have yielded rich and rare pleasures.'

Frank Baker had originally sent Margaret the bestselling book on which the play was based. She immediately liked the character and invited the author to lunch at Pinewood studios, where she was filming at the time. Frank Baker takes up the story: 'When I arrived at Pinewood the gatekeeper said, "Oh Miss Rutherford. You will find her down there." He pointed to some sheds. Suddenly I saw her coming out and then turn quickly away from me. She was wearing a long sweeping black Victorian gown and this was so like my Miss Hargreaves that it was extraordinary. I had the curious illusion that she would disappear at any second. I chased this elusive figure around the side of the shed, caught up with her and stammered out, "Miss Hargreaves . . . no, I mean Miss Rutherford." From that moment there could be no doubt in my mind that she was my Miss Hargreaves . . . it was the forthrightness of manner, coupled with a far-away vagueness, which made the two ladies one in my mind.'

Rutherford loved the part and recognised in it many of her own traits: 'She was a very imperious lady, very commanding, autocratic, eccentric with very definite likes and dislikes. She was also very erratic. If she gave an order it had to be done at once. But there was also a great sense of innocence and mischief in her which could suddenly come to the surface and you could be whipped away into a totally unexpected adventure. She was neither real nor imaginary, something between the two.'

But there were problems, one of which lay in difficulties Margaret experienced with her friend, director Joan Kemp-Welch. The director wanted the cast to 'clown' in the last two acts, but Rutherford fundamentally disagreed, feeling that it was not the mood the play should take. The director also became over-involved in stage directions, asking Margaret, 'Could you make a useful move there, dear?' Margaret stopped in her tracks and bellowed, 'I do not make useful moves.'

The reviews were poor, although Rutherford was mainly spared the critics' disapproval. The *Daily Mail* recounted: 'No comedy with Margaret Rutherford, a butterfly net, a solemn bulldog and a cockatoo among its equipment could fail entirely to be funny; but for me this one failed far too often.' Several of the critics noted the importance of Rutherford's contribution, with the *Observer* subscribing that, 'Margaret Rutherford, with a rich offering of mannerisms, turns this little fiction into a substantial solo.' Margaret was much disappointed, and described the production as a gallant failure, 'I could never understand why the critics were unkind to the play. They liked the first act but not the second or third acts. Perhaps if we had been able to play them as we saw them they may have seemed more feasible.'

On a happier note, she and Frank Baker became close friends, and remained so for many years. She also formed an acquaintance with Charlie, the cockatoo, who had been loaned from London Zoo for the production. Charlie lived in the men's dressing room throughout and Margaret became so fond of him that, at Christmas, she asked the keepers if she could take him home as a treat. She told the zoo that, 'Stringer is keen about birds in every shape and form,' and convinced them that they would look after Charlie properly. According to Margaret, 'We all had such a lovely time.'

Theatrically speaking, 1952 may have been a sparse year for Margaret Rutherford, but she was still very much in demand for film work by a number of studios. *Miss Robin Hood*, directed by John Guillermin, was released in November of that year. Margaret Rutherford, with hair bobbed like a cockatiel, played Miss Honey, the owner of a Hampstead children's home. She is full of energy and dutifully dotty, but even she fails to save this mish-mash of a film. Miss Honey's family have had their whisky formula stolen by a rival distiller's some years ago. She thus enlists the help of Henry Wrigley (Richard Hearne), a shy writer and creator of a comic-strip character called Miss Robin Hood, to recover the recipe from 'The Macalister' (James Robertson-Justice) by raiding his premises. Comedy stalwarts Kenneth Connor, Peter Jones, Ian Carmichael, Dora Bryan, Reg Varney and a moustachioed Sid James all crop up during the story.

Innocents in Paris, released the following year, was even more disappointing. A group of disparate passengers travel to Paris for the weekend. Rutherford is Gwladys Inglott, an artist who visits the Louvre and purchases a copy of the *Mona Lisa* from a fellow artist (Stringer Davis). He has painted the famous painting 338 times, but this is his first sale. British officer Captain George Stilton (Jimmy Edwards) spends the whole trip boozing in a bistro, Claire Bloom is romanced by a local Lothario, Ronald Shiner is in a Marine band that is performing in Paris and James Copeland is a kilted Scot who falls for a young Parisienne. Alistair Sim completes the cast as diplomat, Sir Norman Baker. The script, by Anatole de Grunwald, fails to deliver many laughs, despite lots of jokes about the French, including men kissing men, the eating of snails, money-grabbing taxi drivers and sexual favours with room service.

On a personal level, Margaret found the experience much more pleasing. This was her first time in Paris – a stay which she described as a second honeymoon. Margaret spoke excellent French, and she and Stringer explored the city and its environs on their days off. They visited the gardens at Versailles, and Margaret was surprised to discover that the Eiffel tower was what she described as 'openwork'. They ate out in cafés and were delighted to discover that food was more plentiful, if more expensive, than in England.

The Davises were also keen to see the *Mona Lisa* but they were denied the honour, as the masterpiece had been sent for cleaning. However, while roaming through the Louvre, Stringer admired a statue which he thought he recognised. He checked the label and saw that the sculptor's name was Catal. Further on they came across a painting they both admired. The style was completely different from that of the previous bronze figure but surprisingly the picture was also by Catal; the couple found a number next to the name which they presumed was the date of origin. They then entered a room full of the most beautiful blue pictures. Margaret picked her favourite and discovered to her astonishment that it was also by Catal. 'We next turned into a room where the whole of one wall was given up to a full-sized painting of the Last Supper. As we approached, Stringer said, "Don't tell me, I know who painted that – It's a Catal!" And so it was.' The bemused couple needed an explanation and asked a commissionaire, who clarified that, of course, 'Catal' followed by a number referred to the Catalogue and its reference therein. Rutherford described the denouement as extremely funny and that, 'We all had a good laugh.'

Margaret's next project in front of the camera was much more successful. The screen version of *The Importance of Being Earnest* was released in the UK in June 1952. Adapted and directed by Anthony Asquith, the film is pretty faithful to Wilde's 1895 text and begins in the interior of a theatre with a curtain going up on proceedings, before taking on movie dimensions. Michael Redgrave and Michael Denison are the two eligible bachelors who adopt 'Earnest' as a pseudonym to conduct their respective romantic intrigues, Edith Evans is Lady Bracknell and Gwendolen Fairfax is played by Joan Greenwood, whose voice was once described as 'the aural equivalent of framboise liqueur'. The ubiquitous Richard Wattis is the manservant, Seaton. Rutherford is, of course, Miss Prism and the lovely Dorothy Tutin is her charge, Cecily Cardew.

Some of Rutherford's best moments are with Doctor Chasuble (Miles Malleson), with whom she flirts coyly: 'You do not seem to realise, my dear Doctor, that by persistently remaining single, a man converts himself into a permanent public temptation. Men should be more careful, this very celibacy leads weaker vessels astray.' She also gives the Minister advice on relationships: 'Maturity can always be depended on. Ripeness can be trusted. Young women are green.' As Dr Chasuble attempts to interrupt, she adds hurriedly, 'I speak horticulturally. My metaphor was drawn from fruits.' It is a delightful film, peppered with bons mots, and the performances from the fine cast match the razor-sharp dialogue.

At the Venice Film Festival critics praised the film, although some found that 'the sharp realism of the camera' diminished the 'airiness of the story'. More importantly however, as writer, Paul Dehn pointed out, the film preserved 'six succulent performances, as though in aspic, for posterity'. He went on to applaud 'Miss Margaret Rutherford's Miss Prism, just sufficiently in control of her romantic longings to snap them back into their proper place as cleanly as she snaps the pince-nez back to her bosom'.

Dorothy Tutin, who was nominated for a BAFTA as Most Promising Newcomer in the film, recalled her relationship with Margaret Rutherford some years later in a letter to Rutherford archivist, Mark Whiston: 'She was very special and I adored her – I'm only sad I only worked with her once . . . it was my first film role and I was very nervous – it wasn't that she said or did anything 'special' – she just made me feel that we were in it together – and I suppose she was so totally, completely Miss Prism – I thought of her like that and when she did the last scene – recognising the handbag, in only two absolutely perfect takes – so funny and so true – it was quite hard not to cry. Later, when I met her, she always seemed like a sort of guardian angel – once it was outside the Aldwych and she asked that I was doing and I said I was going to America and she said, 'Oh dear,' and looked aghast. Then she took me in her arms and said, 'I'll pray for you!' I believed her and I loved her – she was above anything petty and tiresome.'

Rutherford interspersed her film work with regular radio appearances. In May 1950, she was interviewed by Leslie Mitchell for the *Filmtime* programme on the Home Service and in the same month appeared in a radio version of *Miss Hargreaves*, also on the Home Service. She was paid fifty guineas, with five guineas for a repeat and two guineas for each subsequent broadcast. Margaret wrote to the BBC, referring to the radio play: 'We have had quite a few chance reactions from complete strangers about our "Hargreaves" transmission. Particularly the artisan class seem to have been really held by it.' Not content merely to enjoy her own success, Rutherford, in a typically selfless gesture, also recommended that the BBC employ several actors she had successfully worked with – these included Mary Ure, Joan Hickson and Beatrice Kane.

There is also an intriguing correspondence from Margaret to Cecil McGivern, Controller of BBC Television Programmes. He had apparently provided Margaret and Stringer with a television set to watch a BBC drama starring Virginia McKenna. Margaret thanked him profusely and praised McKenna's 'exquisite performance'. Mr McGivern replied to her: 'Please get in touch with me if you ever want to see any special TV programme – I should be delighted to help.'

Despite the lack of further dramatic work on the radio (Rutherford's agent had inquired of the BBC about further roles following her departure from *Ring Round the Moon*, but had been told her inquiry was made 'at rather short notice'), Margaret recorded the celebrated BBC radio show *Desert Island Discs* on 12 December 1951, for broadcast three weeks later. It is – and I suppose one should not be surprised – a rather odd edition. Rutherford seems to have been over-influenced by the lilting signature music, 'By the Sleepy Lagoon', as the whole show has a nautical theme. Her selections are 'La Mer' (Debussy), Dame Myra Hess playing 'Sea Pieces', 'Pedro the Fisherman' sung by Richard Tauber, Dame Ethel Smythe's overture 'The Wreckers', Elgar's 'Sea Pictures – Where Corals Lie' and inevitably 'Fingal's Cave'.

More bizarrely, however, is the mermaid motif which glides throughout the carefully scripted broadcast. When Roy Plomley asks Margaret, 'How does the prospect of being marooned on a desert island appeal to you?', Rutherford replies, 'Oh, I wouldn't stay there . . . solitary existence on a desert island is unthinkable. That way madness lies . . . I'd become a mermaid . . . they are fascinating creatures. They have tails and long hair, and are most graceful.'

A coy Plomley pretends to be flummoxed, 'I . . . I. . . know. And you are going to become one?'

'Yes,' responds Rutherford. 'I think it would be an efficient and reasonable way out of my quandary. Indeed I have in fact, for some years, nourished a vague desire to become a mermaid. And mermaids I have spoken to have told me that the best place to be a mermaid is near a desert island, where the coral reefs and caves beneath the sea are quite indescribably beautiful. You just wouldn't believe, they say, the brilliance of the colours.'

Plomley feigns amazement: 'They told you this?'

Rutherford continues undaunted: 'I'd never be lonely if I was a mermaid – with all the other mermaids and mermen, of course.' Margaret states that she proposes to turn into a mermaid by the use of magic, which she says she is very good at, having played Madame Arcati and Miss Hargreaves. She does reminisce on how she became an actress and talks about some of her work, but the mermaid motif returns. 'Mermaids have our uplifting moments even down below, as when we hear this lovely piece of piano music by Debussy called "The Submerged Cathedral". There are many fine buildings for our use on the seabed, as well as our own coral sea-halls . . . especially round Atlantis. That's a beautiful place where many mermaids go for their summer holidays.' Rutherford's luxury item is a 'golden comb with a jewel in every prong to comb my long golden locks.' I'm not sure whether this flight of fancy was the brainchild of an over-enthusiastic producer or dear Margaret suffering in the throes of a manic breakdown but, in any case, she enjoyed the experience because on the script is a scribbled note from her: 'Thank you for a lovely occasion.'

*

During this period, Margaret also became more involved in charity work. In addition to performing in galas, opening fêtes and attending bazaars for various organisations such as 'Mothercraft' and 'Spastics Society' (at a fair in south London, she posed with a tuba owned by the Croydon Territorial Army Band), she also committed herself to other causes with which she felt some spiritual link. With much gusto, she threw herself into visiting prisons and borstals and told a newspaper journalist, 'If I am interested in a person or a cause, I fight and work. After all there's not much use going through life and doing nothing for a soul, is there?'

Margaret was introduced to the penal world when she was invited to Feltham Borstal in Middlesex. A group of offenders, who belonged to a recreational club within the institution called the Compass Club, asked her to give a talk about her work. She and Stringer were immediately impressed by the spirit of the boys and were sympathetic to the aims of the group and the understanding nature of the volunteers running it. 'I do not feel the lads to be sinners, although, of course, they do wrong. Their wrongdoing, I think, is largely in consequence of their home background and mental disability.'

She was thus delighted, in due course, to accept an invitation to become a Patron for the Compass Club and an informal 'mum' to the boys. She duly received grateful letter from the club's leader, John Hibberd, with whom she was to remain in contact with for many years: 'My dear Miss Rutherford, I am writing to thank you once again for giving up your Sunday evening. We all enjoyed your visit immensely and the boys are as proud as peacocks about you. All I can hope is that both you and your husband really did enjoy yourselves too, and that in time you will become proud of your naughty sons.'

Rutherford was touched by the candidness of the boys about why they had ended up incarcerated. 'In so many cases the story always begins in the same sad way – they were children from a disturbed or unhappy home and therefore had turned to crime as a protest against present day society, which they felt had let them down. Many of them were not criminals, merely unhappy lost children who needed love and guidance.' She was also made aware that many of the young men were in a spiral of unemployment and poverty and victims of family history. 'Many of these boys have been married as teenagers to a girl just out of school and have been unable to cope. Often there is a baby and money is short, or the marriage has broken up after a few months. The boy is sad, puzzled and disillusioned, and in this state is vulnerable to any influence.'

Whenever Margaret was in a West End production she used to arrange for half a dozen tickets to be sent to Feltham so that some of the lads, accompanied by warders, could attend the show. After the performance, she would invite them backstage for a chat. The boys would sometimes bring a box of chocolates for the cast, which Margaret always found particularly touching. She was keen to encourage them to turn their backs on the delinquent lifestyle, and 'to help them, by sensible thinking, to stress the stupidity of crime which if pursued would bring only misery and unhappiness not only to themselves but to those dear to them. If only the good work that is done in these institutions could be followed up in the world outside perhaps there could be less crime'.

It's warming to reflect that these days when a number of people consider prison to be something of a soft option, just a few kindly words from Mr and Mrs Stringer Davis in the 1950s could make future Krays turn their backs on a life of crime. Of course it may well have been that a trip to see the universally panned Miss Hargreaves proved an effective deterrent.

SEVEN

A Banquet of Acting

'How hard a thing 'twould be to please you all.'

WILLIAM CONGREVE

MARGARET AND STRINGER were now living at 5 the Old Hall, South Grove, Highgate. They occupied the first floor flat of the historic building, a William and Mary period mansion where the states-man and philosopher Francis Bacon had died in 1626. With its grand, scrolled iron gates and paved walk framed by beautiful standard roses, the property enjoyed a spectacular view of the city of London. The back door led directly into the renowned Highgate cemetery.

The interior of the charming flat, with elegant panelling and bow windows overlooking a lovely garden, could have been the drawing room of a country house. The parquet floor was covered with Persian rugs, while chintz covers and antique furniture added to the décor. A Dresden vase adorned the piano. Margaret's white bedroom, which also faced the garden, was embellished with colourful printed linen curtains, and one of her treasured possessions was a china figure of Pan, left to her by Ivor Novello. Near her bed was a framed needlework panel featuring the signatures of all the cast in *Ring Round the Moon*. Signed photographic portraits of Ivor Novello and Robert Donat and a framed play-bill of *The Way of the World* added to the theatrical atmosphere.

The Way of the World, by William Congreve, opened at the Lyric Theatre, Hammersmith, on 19 February 1953 and was directed by John Gielgud, who also starred. This Restoration comedy of manners, which James Agate described as 'the greatest prose comedy in the English language', was first performed in 1700 – albeit to a cool reception. The cast at the Lyric featured Paul Scofield, Eric Porter, Peter Sallis and Margaret Rutherford as Lady Wishfort, in what was arguably her greatest stage triumph. She described it as one of her most rewarding parts but also 'an exacting and a supremely difficult play because all the characters are required to speak in a stunning mixture of crazy poetry and Billingsgate. It is terribly trying on the vocal chords.'

Rutherford took to the role with great zest and was confident that her grounding in elocution would assist her with the troublesome dialogue. 'I love this role. I love the language of the play, to study it and to speak it,' she said in an interview for the magazine *Theatre Arts* at the time. 'And I love to wear all those furbelows and this gorgeous auburn wig. You know, as a girl, I always wanted auburn hair and violet eyes. Well, I can't do much about my eyes – they're hazel. But the wig does solve the problem of the auburn hair.'

Kenneth Tynan, who was to replace Ivor Brown as drama critic of the *Observer*, was an unequivocal aficionado of *The Way of the World*'s author. 'Congreve is the only sophisticated playwright England has ever produced and, like Shaw, Sheridan and Wilde, he was brought up in Ireland.' He was equally fulsome in his praise of this particular production and wrote eloquently: 'At the heart of the "quadratic equation" of the plot is Lady Wishfort, to whom nearly everyone in the play is related and in whose money everyone has a consuming interest ... Mr Gielgud is at the helm, a crowd of deft character actors like Eric Porter are manning the rigging, to pipe us aboard is Paul Scofield. Gielgud's galleon would not be complete without a figurehead, and there, astride the bow, she triumphantly is. Margaret Rutherford, got up as Lady Wishfort, the man-hungry pythoness. This is a banquet of acting in itself. Miss Rutherford is filled with a monstrous vitality: the soul of Cleopatra has somehow got trapped in the corporate shape of an entire lacrosse team. The unique thing about Miss Rutherford is that she can act with her chin alone: among its many moods I especially cherish the chin commanding, the chin in doubt, and the chin at bay. My dearest impression of this Hammersmith night is a vision of Miss Rutherford, clad in something loose, darting about her boudoir like a gigantic bumblebee at large in a hothouse.'

Sadly Tynan was almost alone in his positive appraisal of the production. Rutherford, with phlegmatic understatement, felt that the critics were 'on the whole a little unkind about the production'. Indeed they were, although her performances were almost universally admired: the *Daily Mail's* critic complained that 'The plot has grown no clearer with the years . . . but the important thing is that Margaret Rutherford should play this patched-up old ruin – this "antidote to desire" – and sweep gustily through the maze of wooings and deceptions.' *Punch* subscribed that, 'Top marks must go to Miss Margaret Rutherford, most happily cast as Lady Wishfort, whom she plays with enormous gusto in the grand manner, waving her jaw menacingly at her enemies and behaving like a splendidly paddled windmill.' Harold Hobson in the *Sunday Times* reported that, 'Margaret Rutherford achieves a comic triumph in her trembling rages . . . here is a performance that moves the imagination.' However, T.C. Worsley wasn't convinced: 'Miss Rutherford cannot get that formidable jaw of hers round half Congreve's phrases. Comic business is not enough here. She is drowned in a welter of unprojected sentences. She goes down with all guns firing; but she goes down.'

Gielgud later admitted to some of his directorial difficulties: 'Although I managed to arrange the text a little better than usual to simplify the rather boring complications, I could not find much to do with Mirabell and was haunted by the memory of Edith Evans' performance as Millamant, which was perhaps why I failed to help

Pamela Brown, whom I loved . . . the success of the production was chiefly due to Margaret Rutherford's splendid Lady Wishfort.'

Another member of the cast was Peter Sallis, who, in a career spanning six decades, remains best known for the BBC comedy *Last of the Summer Wine* and as the voice of Wallace in Nick Park's series of *Wallace and Gromit* animated films. Sallis remembers Margaret Rutherford with great fondness: 'Margaret was already a star although she never expected to be treated differently from the rest of the cast. She was always very friendly and helpful, but it was when she donned her wig and costume and assumed her character as Lady Wishfort that she really came to life.'

Although Gielgud could be a ruthless director, Sallis liked his honesty and directness. 'When he was casting for *Richard II*, Gielgud admitted that that he had two beautiful men as servants to the King and needed me because I would be a perfect balance to them. In other words I was ugly – and he was right!' In later years Peter Sallis was acting in *Wait Until Dark* in the West End with Honor Blackman. He bumped into Gielgud outside the theatre. They exchanged pleasantries and Sir John asked him what he was doing. Sallis proudly pointed to his name in lights. 'Ah yes,' Gielgud replied, 'I hear the girl's very good.'

Rutherford reprised Lady Wishfort for a limited revival at the Saville Theatre in December 1956. In this production, by John Clements, who also appeared as Mirabell, Kay Hammond was Mrs Millamant and Harry H. Corbett and Rosalind Knight also appeared. Rutherford felt much more confident than in the original production, and it showed. She was described by the critic in *Plays and Players* as 'a gaudy galleon of lecherous womanhood ploughing her way through a sea of amorous troubles . . . played with vigour but never overdone'. The *Illustrated London News* critic J.C. Trewin wrote: 'Rutherford's is an extremely comic performance, much funnier and firmer than it was at Hammersmith. She looks now like one of those portentous decorated balloons of the Classic period.' 'It is a brilliant performance,' wrote a third critic, 'a real interpretation of depth and feeling, alight with vitality, every line given a true, full measure of wit or rich comedy, and, at the end, having a pathos untinged by sentimental appeal yet genuinely moving. Miss Rutherford tackles the part in grand style . . . we forget the actress and live with the woman. Miss Rutherford's technical resourcefulness has increased and the artist has come to the fore as never before . . . you believe in her heart's longing even though you laugh heartily at her absurdities . . . she lights up the stage.'

Alice Through the Looking Glass was produced at the Prince's Theatre in February 1954. Michael Denison played the White Knight and Binnie Hale appeared as the Red Queen. Margaret was the White Queen, a part she thoroughly enjoyed: 'It was all so joyous. I loved each magical moment from my entrance with a brush caught in my hair, to the end when I went to sleep in Alice's lap. One of my favourite scenes was when I turned into a woolly sheep and sang, "Jam, jam tomorrow and jam yesterday but never jam today," to the tune of the Eton Boating Song.'

Eric Keown described Rutherford as 'fluttering with moonbeam futility while wearing a marvellously scalloped hat with crown attached'. He did feel, however, that, 'Occasional whiffs of pure Carroll came across but one was left with the disappointing feeling that it was only very mild entertainment.' The *Observer* was more scathing: 'A result so dim as to be almost dull. Margaret Rutherford flaps and flutters in the best manner of bewilderment . . . and why are the Tweedles cockney?'

Jean Anouilh's romantic comedy *Time Remembered* opened at the Lyric Theatre in December 1954. The play is a fantasy about a young prince still infatuated by his memory of the dead ballet dancer, Leocadia. Margaret Rutherford played the Duchess of Port-au-Branc, and Stringer was the butler. There was a feeling that the play, which had some of the charm of *Ring Round the Moon*, was a little lightweight and lacked dramatic interest. 'One felt that it was an entertainment rather than a play,' wrote Eric Keown, 'and so detached in spirit that we were never quite allowed to lose ourselves. Visually it was beautiful, verbally sometimes a little flat.'

Rutherford's part as the Duchess was the closest she would come to portraying madness rather than eccentricity. In Anouilh's play the elderly French aristocrat reconstructs, in her Breton park, all the trappings and background of her adored nephew's tragic love affair. Her first entrance sets the tone for the evening: 'A fluttering mauve veiled moth, bobbles on her hat nodding like antennae, lifting a lorgnette for closer inspection, reassures us that she is free to play herself.' Rutherford had to be both slightly deranged and curiously romantic, and this Eric Keown felt she achieved: 'It was Margaret who took the burden of the evening . . . she fluttered, she twittered, in her nervous restlessness. She was preposterous, and also deeply touching. I cannot think of many other actresses who could have fitted this moonstruck fairy godmother so perfectly into Anouilh's artificial Cloud-Cuckoo-Land. Her clothes had been carefully chosen. In the drawing room she wore a hat which might have served for a seedsman's catalogue; out shooting in the park she carried a gun.'

Rutherford admitted that acting in an Anouilh play wasn't easy: 'It was a typical fantasy – the story is about a hat shop midinette who suddenly finds herself in a noble home with the job of distracting a young prince from his grief over his dead love. The handsome and accomplished Paul Scofield played the young man. It taxes every piece of nervous energy and concentration that you can muster up . . . for me the part of the duchess was a heavy one but one I like – strange, intangible yet with a hard crisp core that needed attack.' One of her favourite moments was when she had to break into a few gentle ballet steps. Rutherford often stated that she would have loved to have been a ballet dancer and this one brief situation gave her an opportunity to fantasise. She wrote at the time: 'At one time I wanted to be Pavlova and nowadays I would love to change places with Margot Fonteyn. Apart from being a great star in an exquisitely beautiful form she is equally popular here and in America which must be gratifying. I think the wonder and romance of the ballet must compensate for all the hard work and dedication.'

The play didn't make it to America but it did enjoy a long run at the Lyric and subsequently transferred to the New Theatre. It also went on tour around the United Kingdom; in Edinburgh some of the dialogue was censored by the Lord Provost. Rutherford's line to Mary Ure, 'If you were my daughter – but I have no daughter, I could never have a child. Was it poor Gaston's fault, or mine? I never knew. And when he died it was too late for me to find out,' with its discreet reference to impotence, was obviously too much for the sensibilities of the Morningside crowd and was thus cut from the play. Mary Ure, who Margaret had tried to help find work with the BBC, made her stage debut to wonderful reviews: 'decorative and cool'; 'natural, grave and enchanting'. She died tragically at the age of forty-two of an accidental overdose, following a battle with alcoholism.

The critics were divided by both the play and Rutherford's performance. 'Much of the play is quite breathtakingly beautiful,' remarked Harold Hobson. 'Miss Rutherford's performance as the half mad yet wholly wise Duchess, fluttering tremulously, is of the highest class.' Milton Shulman, who was never a great fan, decided that, 'Margaret Rutherford, as a mad aunt, all violet and pearls, achieves eccentricity but misses the subtler, ethereal nuances of her role.' The *Daily Telegraph*'s critic felt that, 'The play lacks heart. The Duchess is a close relation of Tennent's White Queen and so has to be played by Rutherford.' The *Illustrated London News* declared: 'The play is as tenuous in the memory as the morning haze. Rutherford flickers about like a coloured balloon in the light of evening airs. Beneath her the slithy toves are gambling.'

Despite the mixed reviews, *Time Remembered* did win Rutherford new fans: the play marked the beginning of a long relationship with theatrical historians Joe Mitchenson and Raymond Mander. The couple attended the first night of the play, and from then on never missed one of Rutherford's opening nights. The Raymond Mander &

Joe Mitchenson Theatre Collection, now based in Greenwich, is an extraordinary theatrical archive.

Two years later Margaret Rutherford revived the part of the Duchess of Port-au-Branc on television. Natasha Perry was Leocadia and Paul Scofield's part was played by Paul Daneman. Margaret never particularly enjoyed the small-screen medium, which she found 'most restricting', missing the camaraderie of a theatrical run and the contact with the audience, and, while this production was mainly well received, the *Wolverhampton Express and Star* critic appeared to identify her reluctance: 'Eccentricity is Margaret Rutherford's forte but her ebullient characterisations belong to the stage or the wide cinema screen, not to the narrow confines of the television screen.'

Margaret returned to the cinema in 1953 with *Trouble in Store*, which was filmed over fourteen weeks at Pinewood and gave her and Norman Wisdom equal star billing. The film's background had been somewhat troubled: Jill Craigie, a documentary maker and the wife of future Labour leader Michael Foot, had written the script, but the Rank Organisation, following a falling out with original director, Ronald Neame, had cancelled the film. Rank, who had Wisdom under contract, had yet to unleash him on an unsuspecting British public, and were determined that his debut starring role should be an unqualified success. They were concerned that this slapstick farce set in a department store would not come up with the goods. Neame was replaced by John Paddy Carstairs and a new creative team was brought in.

Bumbling Wisdom works as a stockroom assistant at Burridges, a prestigious West End department store. His ambition is to become a window dresser and win the heart of Sally (Lana Morris), who works in the record department. He soon falls foul of the arrogant new general manager (Jerry Desmonde) and is under constant threat of being sacked. In a sub-plot, he also manages to foil a robbery attempt by a gang of thieves. Margaret Rutherford is Miss Bacon, an aristocratic shoplifter: 'Is this Burridges? Could you direct me to suitcases?'

She selects a large, sturdy suitcase and, with much luxuriant licking, sticks labels from all over the world to give it the appearance of being her own well travelled piece of luggage. She later tries on and rejects a number of hats while being attended to by sales assistant Joan Sims. Miss Bacon is provided with a millinery monstrosity, a bird's nest, complete with bird peeping out, and responds with probably the most comical line in the film: 'Haven't you got something more seductive?' Decked out in chequered coat and feathered hat, Rutherford is finally apprehended by the store detective. Meanwhile Stringer has one line as a sales assistant trying to stop the aforementioned gang from removing his cash till. It's really not a very good film, and the most inspiring acting comes from Lana Morris and several extras who have to look admiringly at Wisdom as he sings 'Don't Laugh at Me 'Cos I'm a Fool'.

Initially the atmosphere on the set was described by Wisdom as 'tense as a bow string from the director down to the clapper boy'. However, after initial difficulties between Wisdom and the temperamental John Paddy Carstairs, the two of them managed to forge a successful working relationship, which was to produce a further five films. Rutherford recalled Wisdom's lack of confidence while working on *Trouble in Store*: 'After being signed up he was then made to take a screen test which turned out to be a colossal flop – the poor boy was therefore very uncertain as we began shooting – his confidence had been stripped from him and he was completely unnerved.' According to Rutherford, she invited Wisdom to her caravan, whereupon he admitted all his fears and apprehensions. She cheered him up and suggested they just have fun together on set. 'From then on it was easy . . . whenever he was a little stiff, I would tell him to be more natural and loosen up. I encouraged him all the way. We became a great double act . . . I did enjoy myself on that film – to this very day Norman always says that he needed me for that film. It was as if I had been specially sent to him.' Unfortunately there is no mention of the great actress's support in Norman Wisdom's autobiography . . .

Film critic Virginia Graham wrote: 'Although it is unfair to compare the two, coming from such different schools as they do, Mr Wisdom could learn much from her [Rutherford]. Her timing is exquisite, there are no loose ends, her humour is a blend of tones and half-tones blended with infinite cunning.' Norman Wisdom did, however, win a BAFTA award for Most Promising Newcomer to film, and this was by no means the only success that *Trouble in Store* achieved. 'Don't Laugh at Me' was a top-twenty hit, spending fifteen weeks in the charts, and, despite the misgivings of the Rank Organisation, the film was a massive box-office success. According to Matthew Sweet's *Shepperton Babylon*, 'When it opened in thirty Gaumont cinemas in suburban London, it took £9,000 more in its first week than any of their previous presentations.'

The Runaway Bus, released the following year, was written and directed by Val Guest and filmed at Southall studios. The comedy thriller was a yet another debut vehicle – this time for comedian Frankie Howerd. Val Guest went to see the comic in a show at the Palladium and told him about the project backstage. The ever-anxious Howerd agreed to do the film – but only if he wasn't the star. 'I don't want to take all the blame!' Howerd added, however, that he would love to work with Margaret Rutherford. Mr Guest duly sent her the script, which she liked very much, and she agreed to take the part of harridan Cynthia Beeston. Early in the filming, having seen some rushes in the projection room, Rutherford approached Guest: 'I'm not taking top billing over him, he's wonderful. I'm not going to star over him. It would be ridiculous!' Guest was somewhat perplexed. 'The person who had a contract to be the star didn't want to be the star and the other star, who was brought in to take pressure off the first star also didn't want to be the star!' Whatever the billing problems, Frankie was delighted to have the fine actress on board: 'The great advantage I had,' he said, 'was having Margaret Rutherford, who became a great friend of mine.'

The film begins at London Airport, where hundreds of travellers are stranded, the whole country blanketed by thick fog. Rutherford, as determined termagant Cynthia Beeston, purporting to be the chairman of the 'Positive Thought Movement' and attired like an ageing Mary Poppins in a porkpie hat, excitedly brandishes an umbrella at a stewardess: 'Young woman, when does all this nonsense stop?' Howerd plays Percy Lamb, a relief bus driver who has to transport half a dozen characters from London to Blackbush airport. Once on board he is advised via his radio that somewhere in the bus has been hidden some stolen gold bullion. The heist's mastermind, known to the police only as 'the Banker', is probably one of his passengers.

Rutherford and Howerd, the film's reluctant stars, were fortunate that Val Guest also assembled an experienced and talented supporting cast. A young Petula Clark is excellent as an unflappable stewardess; Terence Alexander is appropriately suspicious as a suave airline pilot; while Hollywood heavy George Coulouris is a shifty foreigner. Rutherford flirts with an uncomfortably twittering Toke Townley and refers to him throughout as 'my sweet little man'. Stringer is, of course, present and correct as 'Second Transport Officer', grasping a selection of clipboards, files and papers.

Made on a very low budget (£45,000) at Southall Studios and shot in less than five weeks, *The Runaway Bus* is fairly predictable and not hugely funny, but enjoys some noirish elements in its photography and atmosphere. Margaret Rutherford felt that Howerd gave a good account of himself, and his comic persona is already established, with much snorting and harrumphing and 'Please Yourselves'. The film received fairly positive reviews and did quite well at the box office.

Petula Clark recalled that it was a traumatic film to work on because the studio was constantly enveloped in an artificial fog which made all the cast ill. The technicians tried different chemical concoctions, but the result was always nauseous actors. They were advised to drink milk before the days' shooting to reduce the feelings of sickness, but this made them even worse! The crew all wore masks, but of course the actors weren't able to benefit from such protection.

Miss Clark, now a much celebrated international star, has a poignant memory of that period. In November 1953 she had been seriously ill, having undergone an appendectomy the previous month. She had contracted peritonitis and complications had set in, requiring emergency surgery. One night, some weeks after the immediate danger was over, but having spent several weeks in and out of consciousness, she was woken and told there was a visitor who had been waiting a for a considerable amount of time to see her. 'Although I was very drowsy and had been bedbound for some time, the news encouraged me to get up and see this visitor. I begged the staff to help me and eventually two nurses agreed to help me walk to the end of the corridor.' At the end of the passage, sitting on a wooden bench and clutching a bunch of violets, she saw the outline of an elderly woman she vaguely recognised. As the nurses helped Petula along the corridor, she heard the unmistakeable voice of Margaret Rutherford: 'My dear how wonderful to see you on your feet!' The recovering Miss Clark described the moment: 'The hands went up, the flowers went around me, and I found myself looking into a lined and whimsical face which mirrored all the kindness and pleasure in the world.'

Margaret had travelled all the way out to the South London Hospital for Women in Clapham, late on a foggy November night, and had waited there for nearly three hours on the off-chance of seeing the stricken singer. Petula was staggered that this 'adorable and legendary actress', whom she hardly knew personally and with whom she had only ever shared a few scenes professionally, having heard that how ill she had been, had made a special effort to see her. 'When I told her it was my first time out of bed she rammed her hat firmly on her head in a characteristic gesture and went into her act, "My dear, what a chance to celebrate. Saunders, please bring the champagne!" As there was, of course, no "Saunders" and no champagne, she rushed out into the fog, calling over her shoulder to the delighted nurses that I should get back to bed and that they should have the glasses ready for us. Late as it was, she returned, beaming, two bottles tucked triumphantly under arm. Heaven knows where she found them in the middle of foggy Clapham at that hour! To me such incidents of giving from one person to another are the lamps in life, lighting the dark stretches. And I have found that they never go out, no matter where you are.'

Margaret Rutherford and Frankie Howerd worked together in several projects as a result of *The Runaway Bus*. She appeared with him in a radio recording of *The Frankie Howerd Show* at the Camden Theatre for *The Light Programme*, and some years later joined him in a television sketch show, written by Eric Sykes and featuring Michael Denison and Sabrina. The most idiosyncratic enterprise on which Rutherford and Howerd collaborated was the recording of a 1954 record. The A-side is a choral rendition of 'Nymphs and Shepherds', allowing Frankie Howerd to interject with typical innuendo, 'Oh naughty Nymph' and 'Take yer hand off my crook!' It was all rather risqué for Margaret and one wonders quite how much she knew what was going on. Nevertheless, it does sound as if she is enjoying the fun. Th B-side is a sketch – a telephone conversation in which a holidaying Lady Montmorency (Rutherford) attempts to ascertain the plight of her estate from butler Howerd. She becomes more and more concerned, as Howerd's attempts to reassure her are punctuated by accidental revelations of disaster after disaster. His repetitive response of 'All's going well, my Lady Montmorency' becomes more desperate. At the end of the conversation we learn that the estate is destroyed – although Lady Montmorency's main preoccupation remains the predicament of her prize pumpkin!

Margaret also appeared with Howerd in a charity event – a midnight cavalcade at the London Palladium on 18 March 1954. This was a gala night in aid of the Actors' Orphanage, organised by its president, Noël Coward, the charitable funds of the Grand Order of Water Rats and the Jewish National Trust. John Mills and Margaret Lockwood did a musical number, 'We're a Couple of Swells', Ralph

Richardson played a busker in a scene from Coward's 1936 revue *Words and Music* and Hermione Baddeley and Rex Harrison performed 'Mad about the Boy'. Margaret and Frankie performed a sketch by Arthur Macrae in which they portrayed two gossiping English ladies aboard a cross-Channel steamer.

In his informative biography, *Frankie Howerd, Stand up Comic*, Robert Ross recounted an incident between Margaret Rutherford and Howerd's dog, 'a large slobbering boxer, called Red'. Enjoying a party at Howerd's Holland Park Villas residence, Rutherford turned from her plate of roast chicken to 'deliver the punchline to one of her theatrical anecdotes', and was 'startled by Red leaping on to her lap and gobbling up all of her dinner'. Complaining to her host, Rutherford was told by Howerd, 'Oh . . . don't stop him, dear, he's enjoying it!' I'm not sure Miss Rutherford would have been quite so understanding. She was, after all, quite a stickler for good table manners.

Margaret's next film, *Aunt Clara*, released in November 1954, gave her one of her favourite screen roles. Rutherford plays the eponymous lead, social worker Clara Hilton, all straw bonnets and white lace collars, who is remembered in her swindling uncle's will. She inherits a dodgy pub, doped greyhounds and a brothel, and vows to rectify the situation, while assisting a young couple whom she has 'steered into the path of true love' along the way. Jill Bennett and Sid James, as 'Honest Sid', also appeared in this film based on a novel by Noel Streatfeild. The sympathetic character of *Aunt Clara* appealed a great deal to Margaret, and her work in the scenes with Ronald Shiner, as her uncle's valet, is particularly enjoyable.

Mad about Men (1954) was filmed at Pinewood and produced by Betty Box as a sequel to *Miranda*, made six years previously. Set in Cornwall, the film again features Glynis Johns as the alluring mermaid, but also as her games mistress cousin. The two swap lives for a fortnight's holiday and encourage each other's romantic adventures. Margaret Rutherford also returns in the guise of Nurse Carey and is quite marvellous. She first appears in a hideous mud brown cape and

Afrika Korps-style desert cap, before donning a nurse's uniform with cotton bonnet pressed tight to her skull, from which several silver curls protrude. She is barely off the screen and gives a physically extravagant performance in a Madame Arcati-ish manner, even indulging in some slight slapstick in one scene when she has to crawl around an orchestra pit to procure a microphone for Miranda.

It is a quite charming, terribly English film with some witty dialogue. No opportunity is lost in cracking jokes or creating puns that allude to Miranda's true nature – 'making quite a splash', 'drinks like a fish', 'all a bit fishy' – and it includes a lovely reference to the mermaid's tail as her 'piscatorial extremity'. A startlingly handsome Donald Sinden completes the principals, and other cast members include the underrated Dora Bryan as a tone-deaf siren with kleptomaniac tendencies, Joan Hickson, the Cowardesque Ronald Baker and the marvellous Irene Handl. There is also a terrific revue-style musical number, 'Mad about Men', sung by Glynis Johns.

As well as the mermaids, Nurse Carey also had to dive into the water, fully clothed. When director Ralph Thomas assumed that a double would be needed for Margaret Rutherford, he was clearly unaware of the actress's passion for swimming and her doughty addiction to an early morning dip in Highgate Ponds. She naturally declined his offer of a substitute swimmer and, when Dora Bryan stole her nurse's cap, swam out to sea and taunted Margaret's character, 'Come in and get it you old trout!' Rutherford described the ensuing action: 'I performed my best swallow dive for the occasion. In I went with a swoosh. My cape flew behind me like great wings and I hit the water with a loud splash. As I surfaced smiling, the whole camera crew broke out into spontaneous clapping.'

In fact, she only had to swim a few strokes in the 'lagoon', but Donald Sinden takes up the story: 'A special lake had been built at the studios and Stringer, who was playing a local vicar, stood next to the cameraman, attired in a long overcoat. When the scene was completed and Ralph Thomas called, "Cut!," Stringer relaxed and took off his coat to reveal that he was wearing bathing trunks. He was obviously ready to leap into action in case Margaret got into any difficulties in the water.' Sinden described Margaret Rutherford as a consummate professional, totally confident in her work, and remembered that Stringer, who only had one line in the film, was on hand for all of his wife's scenes. He was also greatly amused about Stringer's entry in *Spotlight*, the actors' directory. Most actors or actresses listed their achievements or latest work. The text under Stringer's photograph read, 'Have you thought of Stringer Davis?'

Donald Sinden also starred with Margaret in *An Alligator Named Daisy* the following year (Rutherford is billed as 'Our Guest Artiste'). It is altogether a rather silly film in which Sinden is lumbered with an alligator on an Irish ferry. He is engaged to the excellent and glamorous Diana Dors but becomes romantically entangled with zoo worker Jeannie Carson, who bursts into a song and comedy dance with 'I'm in Love for the Very First Time'. Sinden smuggles Daisy into his eccentric family's house – without hilarious consequences. Despite a strong cast including the likes of James Robertson Justice, Stanley Holloway, Joan Hickson and Richard Wattis, the comedy just didn't work.

Margaret Rutherford has only one scene. As the owner of a pet shop, she examines the very lively 'Daisy' and attempts to communicate in the animal's own language, using a homemade trumpet and an extravagant stethoscope. Donald Sinden described the alligator as 'highly dangerous with swift lateral movement. During the last week of filming the alligator snapped at its keeper and broke her arm in four places.' Sinden wasn't in the pet shop scene but was watching the proceedings. As in the aquatic scene in *Mad About Men*, Stringer was again in evidence and still wearing the same long overcoat. On completion of the filming Stringer produced a large claw hammer from within his coat. He had obviously been prepared to deliver a lethal blow, should the moody reptile have misbehaved. Good old Stringer left nothing to chance when it came to the welfare of his precious wife.

*

Mrs Stringer Davis had packed in a huge amount of work in these last few years, in many varied roles. Although she maintained that she was choosy about the parts she played, she loved to work and was never happier than when professionally engaged. Rarely satisfied with her performances, she was always trying to improve her craft. From her early days in rep, she described herself as a squirrel, 'hoarding and cherishing to myself each of the acting experiences'. On first reading she would consider a character's traits: 'I never consciously work out what I am going to do with the role. I just play it as I think and have no "picking up" tricks. People say that I am a natural actress. I merely play a part as truthfully as I can. I have always been told that I can manipulate each part of my face with precision while the rest remains homely and normal. That is true, because like any trained and experienced actress I do have every twitch and ripple of my body under control. I have always known how to make it obey my mental image of a part.'

When Rutherford was interviewed for the BBC radio programme, *In Town Tonight*, the presenter, Alex Mackintosh, asked: 'How far do you allow yourself, Margaret Rutherford, to go along with you in a part. How far can she come into it?' The actress paused momentarily and then replied very firmly, 'I turn her out at once if ever I see her anywhere, but then I don't always know when she's about, you see. My great delight in being an actress is to escape from myself into some other person. It's a sort of translation and it fascinates me.' Mr Mackintosh asked about her depressive illness and the difficulties she had endured during her career, to which Rutherford responded: 'Every great clown has been very near to tragedy, you know? Comedy springs from it, I think. There I am reminded of a dictum that came from a very much loved director of my early days. His name is Gerard Neville. He once said to me when I was playing in farce in repertory: "You must play this as if it was tragedy."' Although she wanted to play more dramatic parts – 'I always wanted to play Cleopatra, I was fascinated by her power' – it was comedy in which she excelled and had been typecast.

An insight into the Rutherford comedy style was offered by actor George Howe, who played stage roles with her in *The Happiest Days of Your Life* and *The Importance of Being Earnest*: 'She did not know how funny she was being. She never strove to be funny and was always sincere in her approach to a comic part. She was an unconscious comic and could just not help being amusing. She had nervous tricks – she wrinkled her nose like a rabbit and she gobbled – and these mannerisms were encouraged by directors – much to the delight of the public.'

Jack Lemmon visited the actor Edmund Gwenn when he was terminally ill and asked him how he was feeling. The dying man replied stoically: 'It's not as hard as doing comedy.' To Rutherford, it seemed easy, as long as the part was well written and 'in good taste'. Rutherford spoke of trying to give an extra dimension to comedy. 'I always try to under-act. In my view, good timing can only be achieved by instinct – it all depends on the actor's judgement. Good timing is, I think, more vital to comedy than to tragedy. In tragedy the 'emotional colours' are more distinctly black and white, but in comedy they often cover the whole spectrum. This to me is what makes comic acting so compelling. And the sound of an audience laughing is quite wonderful, like nothing I'd ever experienced before.'

Her peers, critics and writers loved her work. Brendan Gill wrote in *The New Yorker*: 'That great face with its beguiling assortment of crags and valleys, and that plump, ramshackle and yet quick moving body dominate any setting; moreover by the authority of her style she breathes life into roles that without her would betray themselves as literally paper thin. On the occasions when she gets her teeth into something substantial what a high old rollicking time she has with it! Then we laugh not merely because she is audaciously droll but because, contriving to be at once inside and outside a given character, she permits us to share her delight in the practice of her art. Plainly she loves to act and isn't afraid to let us see that it costs her no anguish.'

Although it was theatre in which she had first made her mark, and which always remained her first love, the critic James Agate saw her strengths as a screen actress: 'Her art knows no poster work. It is all delicately pointed, often taking its biggest dividends from some excess of behaviour so slight that only perfect timing draws attention to it. Her face with its round small mouth, expressive jaw and thoughtful eyes has a basic innocence that needs no more than a tiny injection of mild cunning, of the domestic variety one has been pleased to detect in the features of one's nicer aunts, to make it immediately dynamic. Coupled with her beautiful speech and her ability to tincture her voice with precise degrees of irony, this is one of the main reasons why she is such a boon to the cinema, bringing to it a facial technique proof against the most lethal close-up.'

Margaret Rutherford needed to perform. It gave succour during illness and loneliness and warded off her fear of madness. As she admitted, 'To me acting is my life. It is as necessary for my survival as breathing.'

EIGHT

A Most Refreshing Hobby

How pleasant to know Mr Lear!
Who has written such volumes of stuff!
Some think him ill-tempered and queer,
But a few think him pleasant enough.
When he walks in waterproof white
The children run after him so!
Calling out, 'He's gone out in his night-
Gown, that crazy old Englishman, oh!'
He weeps by the side of the ocean,
He weeps on the top of the hill;
He purchases pancakes and lotion,
And chocolate shrimps from the mill.
He reads, but he cannot speak, Spanish,
He cannot abide ginger beer:
Ere the days of his pilgrimage vanish,
How pleasant to know Mr Lear!

AN EXTRACT FROM 'HOW PLEASANT TO KNOW MR LEAR'
BY EDWARD LEAR (1879)

MARGARET RUTHERFORD HAD a lifelong love of poetry, to which she was first introduced by Aunt Bessie in Wimbledon. She found comfort and inspiration in verse and would often retreat into the world of her most favourite poets at times of stress. She would read aloud at home by her fireside, but also involved herself in public recitals and performances. Margaret's involvement in the Chelsea Poetry Society brought her into contact with its president, John Carroll, who was to become a close friend.

Margaret described a visit to Walter de la Mare's house in 1950 as one of the most memorable days of her life. She was accompanied by Paul Scofield, his wife Joy and John Carroll. The idea was to meet the celebrated poet in order to discuss a programme that Rutherford and Scofield had planned to celebrate the 1951 Festival of Britain. When the group arrived, Mr De la Mare's housekeeper, the faithful Miss Saxton, showed them up an elegant staircase to a room on the first floor. 'As I was admiring the collection of silver tea caddies, which had once belonged to Queen Charlotte, and the cabinet of fine jade figures, Mr De la Mare came into the room. He was a small, striking looking man; he had a fine aquiline nose and a cap of grey hair. He greeted us in a gentle, friendly matter.' Tea was evidently a lively affair, with the five of them discussing the joy that poetry brought to the world. Walter de la Mare praised Margaret for the freshness she brought to his work in recitals, and professed that it was as if he was hearing them for the first time. She was naturally flattered and delighted when he told her that she read his poetry 'like no other woman he had ever heard'.

As well as De la Mare, Margaret was particularly fond of the poems of Edward Lear, whose work she found to be timeless. *The Owl and the Pussy Cat* was one of her favourite poems. In fact she lent her name to a book of Lear poetry, *Margaret Rutherford Says, How Pleasant to Know You, Mr Lear!*, an anthology of his works specially chosen by the actress and with an introduction by Frank Baker, author of *Miss Hargreaves*.

Rutherford also treasured 'Mrs Malone' by Eleanor Farjeon: 'It is so beautiful that it is almost unbearable. Mrs Malone is a little Irish woman who lives all by herself with virtually no money. But she does have enough to produce crumbs for the birds and saucers for the stray animals. Eventually when she dies the birds and animals are the only ones who really care.' The writer, Rumer Godden, spoke warmly of the truthfulness and emotional depth in Rutherford's frequent renditions of 'Mrs Malone'.

One of the more unusual readings that Margaret Rutherford gave was at the London office of the Phoenix Insurance Company. Margaret's cousin Ernest Benn, who ran a publishing company, owned the rights to the books of author and poet Edith Nesbit, most famous for *The Railway Children*. Another of Nesbit's novels, *The Phoenix and the Carpet*, features a sequence where the Phoenix insists on visiting one of his temples – 'his finest temple' – which transpires to be the head-quarters of the Phoenix Insurance Company. Ernest Benn had the unusual idea of inviting Margaret to read the relevant chapter of the book at the opening party for some new Phoenix offices. The reading was, by all accounts, a great success – according to Miss Rutherford, 'the showpiece of the event'.

In February 1950, in an attempt to find opportunities for Margaret to perform more poetry readings, Dorothy Mather wrote to writer and broadcaster John Arlott: 'I see that you have now re-introduced the programme, *Book of Verse*, on radio. My client would very much like to be invited sometime to read some poetry on air. You probably know that she reads a great deal for the Poetry Society.' But Rutherford's agent seems to have got her wireless crossed: a rather terse reply from Arlott stated that the BBC had not in fact reintroduced his programme but that there was now a new poetry programme, *Time for Verse*, in which he was not involved but 'is produced, I believe, by Mr Patric Dickinson'. There is no evidence that either Rutherford or Mather followed up this lead although in the following years she did participate in a number of BBC radio programmes of poetry and music.

John Carroll involved Margaret in a variety of recitals in some surprising venues, and on occasions she combined these readings with her prison visiting. She was once invited, with others, to give such a recital at Pentonville Prison. She recalled that it was 'a full house' with about 950 prisoners, and rather quaintly expressed the feeling that, 'The Governor had popped in all the worst offenders. It was a very tough, grim audience who were obviously wondering what they were going to get . . . I had put on one of my favourite dresses and a little bit of jewellery as I wanted to look my best for this audience . . . you could have heard a pin drop during my recital of "Lady of Shalott".'

Another captive audience was to be found at Holloway Prison, where Margaret gave recitals over many years. On one occasion, the governor asked what she was going to perform. She replied: 'A poem by Robert W. Service, "The Shooting of Dan McGrew".' She felt that, 'It was a good blood-curdling piece which I thought the women would enjoy as they must have been a little disillusioned by the men in their lives.' The governor pointed out that this particular poem might not be entirely suitable in view of the surroundings and specific audience. Miss Rutherford reconsidered and reverted to Tennyson's romantic poem that had gone down so well at Pentonville.

Fortunately she also appeared at other, less austere, locations, mainly for charity. These included the Royal Festival Hall for the Apollo Society, where she read works by Wordsworth, Keats and Auden, and at the Theatre Royal, Brighton, where she was joined by Paul Scofield. Rutherford was also a regular visitor to Stratford-on-Avon to give one-off readings at Hall's Croft, the house, where Shakespeare's daughter, Susanna Hall, lived, very close to his burial place at Holy Trinity Church. Rutherford once gave an Edward Lear recital at the Old Vic with John Neville. At the end they marched down stage, 'King and Queen of the Pelicans we'. She wrote that the entire audience 'fell apart in helpless mirth and so did we – because we really did look just like pelicans.' Writer and critic Alan Dent, in the BBC radio programme *The Art of Margaret Rutherford,* was quoted as saying: 'She was fond of taking part in serious poetry – but whenever she appeared there was an audible buzz of amusement when she took to the stage . . . she was "a caution", a sight for sore eyes, and her nose went up and down like a rabbit when she spoke.'

In March 1953, Margaret Rutherford was taking an afternoon constitutional near to her Old Hall home. Malcolm Troup, a young aspiring concert pianist from Canada, was hurrying down Highgate West Hill. The two walkers passed each other with a brief nod of acknowledgment. Mr Troup then heard a loud voice calling, 'Excuse Me. Hello!' He turned to see this elderly lady brandishing an umbrella at him. He thought he had done something wrong and slowly approached her. 'Don't I know you?,' she barked.

'Well, perhaps you've been to one of my concerts.'

'What do you play?' enquired Miss Rutherford.

'The piano.'

'Oh I see. I'm Margaret Rutherford. I'm sorry but I thought I knew you. You're the spitting image of an actor friend of mine. I do apologise. Anyway, I live nearby – you must come to our flat and play for us.'

He did. The following afternoon Malcolm was invited to tea and thanked Margaret and Stringer by playing for them. There followed an immediate friendship. Margaret was always interested in his life and career, and they shared musical tastes. Troup was very impressed by her musical abilities, about which she remained extremely modest, and still cherishes a portrait she gave him of the composer Grieg which she had won as a prize for gaining top marks at a piano examination. She also gained him a part in the film, *Mad about Men,* where his performance of Saint-Saën's 'Le Cygne' is rudely interrupted by a seal and where he was also asked to teach an actress to pretend to play the piano. Malcolm used to go to Pinewood early every morning, and remembers a limousine collecting him from his flat in Lissenden Gardens and delivering him to the studio, where he breakfasted on smoked salmon and sauterne. During the evenings, when he was booked to give a piano recital, Margaret would cause a flurry of excitement by arriving, in Troup's words, 'like a flagship in full sail'.

Florence Nicholson Rutherford, Margaret's mother, who committed suicide in India when 'Peggy' was aged 2 years old. **By kind permission of the Benn family.**

A young William Rutherford (William Rutherford Benn), Margaret's ill-fated father. **By kind permission of the Benn family.**

Margaret's Aunt Bessie, whom she called, 'My adoptive mother and one of the saints of the world.' **By kind permission of the Benn family.**

Form 1, Wimbledon High School (1900). Even at the age of 8, Margaret, second from right in the front row, is unmistakable. **Wimbledon High School**

An early publicity shot, 1930's.
Wimbledon High School

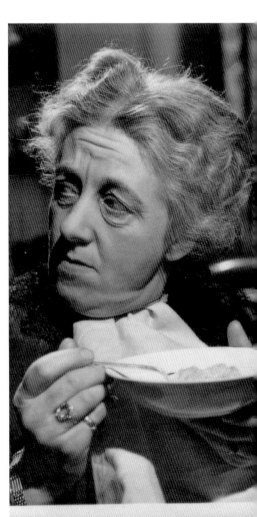

Conquering the gallery as Aunt Bijou in *Spring
Meeting*, 1938. 'I used to look forward to my
nightly bowl of porridge.' **Angus McBean**
© **Harvard Theatre Collection**

As the sinister Mrs Danvers in *Rebecca* at the war-torn
Piccadilly Theatre, 1940. **Angus McBean**
© **Harvard Theatre Collection**

'I see an extremely long and successful run of this production.' One of the 1, 997 theatre performances of *Blithe Spirit*, 1941. **Getty Images**

'Are you ready to empty your minds?' One of Margaret's most celebrated film roles: Madame Arcati in *Blithe Spirit*, 1945, with Rex Harrison and Constance Cummings. **Rex Features**

'Dazed with happiness'. Margaret and 'Tuft', following their 1945 Beaconsfield wedding.

'How dare you, sir!' 'How dare you, madam!' Alastair Sim (Wetherby Pond) and Margaret (Muriel Whitchurch) fighting for the telephone in *The Happiest Days Of Your Life*, 1950.
Rex Features

A cigar and a prize performance in her guise as Madame Desmortes, during Peter Brook's 1950 acclaimed *Ring Round the Moon* at the Globe Theatre.
Getty Images

'The good ended happily, and the bad unhappily. That is what fiction means.' Margaret, as Miss Prism, in a publicity still from *The Importance of Being Earnest*, 1952.
Rex Features

'A monstrous vitality.' Lady Wishfort was one of Margaret's most treasured and praised roles. *The Way of the World*, Lyric Theatre, 1953. **Getty Images**

Margaret and Gordon Langley Hall leaving All Saints Parish church, Old Heathfield, Sussex, 1962. **Duke University**

Maintaining modesty while swimming in the Leeds Parkway hotel pool whilst on *The Importance Of Being Earnest* tour in 1957. **Damaris Hayman**

With mermaid Glynis Johns (fishy tail cunningly concealed under a blanket as she feigns illness) in the charming Ralph Thomas film, *Mad About Men*, 1954. **Rex Features**

Tending the roses in the garden of her beloved 'Elm Close', Gerrard's Cross, September, 1963. **Alamy**

Sporting that 'brute of a hat' in her Academy Award-winning portrayal (Best Supporting Actress) of the impoverished, pill-popping Duchess of Brighton, in Terence Rattigan's *The VIPs*, 1963. **Corbis**

A celebratory peck on the cheek from Stringer while filming *Murder Ahoy* at Elstree Studios. Margaret had just been advised of her Hollywood Oscar success, 1964. **Corbis**

Sid James and Margaret outside the Saville Theatre in 1965, publicising *The Solid Gold Cadillac*. Unfortunately the play received a savaging from the critics and Margaret suffered another breakdown, closing the show. **Getty Images**

'The murderer made one error.' Miss Marple and Jim Stringer researching a killer's modus operandi in *Murder Ahoy*, directed by George Pollock, 1964. **TopFoto**

There is nothing like a Dame. Two are even better. Margaret and Agatha Christie on the Elstree set of the first Miss Marple film, *Murder She Said*, 1961. **TopFoto**

As Jane Marple, working undercover, 'Collecting jumble for the church bazaar' in *Murder Most Foul*, 1963. **Alamy**

1963 was a very good year for Margaret. Proudly posing with her Oscar, Golden Globe, and Variety Club Awards. **Malcolm Troup**

Toasting John-Paul and Dawn Langley Simmons following the blessing of their marriage at Hastings in 1969. **Duke University**

Being presented with her portrait by artist Michael Noakes and Stringer in October 1970 at the Royal Institute of Oil Painters. Margaret's memory and mobility were now failing. **TopFoto**

Margaret quietly celebrates with a cup of tea on becoming a Dame Commander of the Order of the British Empire in 1967. Her Oscar statue always adorned the fireplace mantelpiece. **PA Photos**

When Malcolm bought his first house in Islington, he had no effects beyond his two grand pianos. Rutherford expressed immediate concern: 'You'll need furniture!' On moving from their house in Regent's Park into the smaller Highgate flat, she and Stringer had had to put much of their furniture in store, so decided to help out the young pianist. 'We don't need the chattels now but you can return it one day when we do.' On the appointed day, outside Troup's new home, pulled up a large van crammed full of furniture, lofty Aubusson curtains fit for a chateau, china and silver – all of which the couple insisted Malcolm should enjoy until such time as he could find some of his own. Amongst the items were two ornate Victorian chamber pots. These were surprising keepsakes and, when Malcolm later learned of the grisly story of the murder of Julius Benn, he couldn't help wondering if he had actually inherited the murder weapon! He returned the furnishings to Margaret when the couple moved to Gerrards Cross.

A genuine fondness developed as the actress and pianist spent more and more time together. The strength of feeling between them can be seen in letters such as the one Malcolm wrote to Margaret on 2 December 1953, after Margaret had asked him to play for some friends: 'You cannot imagine how happy I was made by your letter which arrived today. Seldom have I received anything so beautiful nor certainly anything quite so heartening in its effect. Words are for me but poor servants, it is to music that I must turn to express the variety of feelings which came to me upon reading your letter but, in that art, I am now strengthened and inspired by the measure of your kindness and understanding.'

Malcolm was performing in Paris at the end of 1953 and wrote again: 'How much my thoughts were with you while I was in Paris and especially now on the eve of a new year do I think of you and hope that you will go on being made as happy as you make those around you by your unfailing kindness of heart . . . this last year, as I think back over it, has held much for me, not the least of which was my wonderful and so unexpected meeting with yourself.'

In March 1954, Rutherford and Troup were invited to undertake a poetry and music tour of Norway, arranged by the Anglo-Norse Society. On the day that she flew to Norway a *Daily Mail* photographer caught Rutherford at the airport. His picture carried the following text: 'Only one woman can dress so nonchalantly and get away with it. Only one woman can knot a scarf so jauntily, button a cardigan so carelessly, clasp a handbag so ineffectively. When the total result is Margaret Rutherford all we can do is cheer.'

Although not actually appearing, Stringer inevitably accompanied his wife and their new friend, ensuring that Margaret's practical needs were met. He lugged various carrier bags bulging with such necessities as teapots, hot-water bottles, egg-cosies and soft toys. Although the couple were generally inseparable, perhaps he was also a little threatened by his wife's increasing infatuation with Mr Troup.

The tour was beset by some unusual events from the first day. Ruth Plant, the honorary secretary of the Anglo-Norse Society who organised the tour, recalled: 'It had been an incredibly hard winter in Norway and the Oslo Fjord froze over which was incredibly rare. When we arrived there were still big lumps of ice floating about.' Unhappily, the party arrived in the Norwegian capital on 5 April, the very day that heir to the throne, Crown Princess Märtha, died from cancer. The planned recital at the university was postponed while court mourning was observed, and the party was invited to Sandefjord to give a recital at a school. Malcolm Troup still recalls 'the lovely journey down from there, especially where the train skirts the edge of the fjord bending round before Drammen. There was a minor international incident here: Margaret, having the typical English love of fresh air, threw open the carriage windows. The dapper and immaculately mannered train guard politely gestured that he wished us to shut the windows. After much signing, gesticulating and futile attempts at crossing the language barrier, the situation was resolved. Margaret proffered some fine chocolates that she happened to have in her possession and the guard withdrew diplomatically.' The school recital went very well, with the headmaster demonstrating himself to be an excellent host, with funds, according to Ruth Plant, provided by 'Anders Jara, the whaling king, who gave a blank cheque to the local school master, from which he entertained us royally but had a bit too much himself!'

Back in Oslo again, following the cessation of official mourning, the artistes gave a recital at the university. Rutherford read from Spenser, Masefield, Shakespeare and Lear, and Troup, so as not to grab too much attention, played characteristic pieces such as the Grieg Nocturne and the Brahms Ballade, 'Edward, My Son', to complement the text readings. He called to mind her stage presence: 'When Margaret began Masefield's "The Everlasting Mercy" by bellowing, "O, who's that knocking at the door?," the audience literally jumped out of their skins. It may have been that with the length of the readings, they had just been dropping off when her stentorian delivery brought them back to life!' The tour enjoyed great success in Oslo, Bergen and other towns, where the performers were often asked to present special poems that formed part of the English curriculum in Norwegian schools. Margaret Rutherford described the reaction to her performances as 'heart-warming', adding: 'The audiences were informed and appreciative, coming on stage and introducing themselves to us afterwards.'

With the expedition to Norway complete, Margaret and Stringer travelled on to Denmark, where they were guests of the city of Copenhagen, while Malcolm Troup went off to perform a Liszt Concerto with the Oslo Philharmonic. On 2 April, the 149th anniversary of Hans Christian Andersen's birthday, Rutherford found herself in his home town of Odense. From the museum attached to his cottage she made a radio broadcast and, while sitting in the legendary story-teller's chair, read two of his tales, 'Little Ida's Flowers' and 'The Darning Needle'. On her way to Odense, at luncheon taken on the ferry between the islands, she was presented with a group of figures in Copenhagen porcelain from 'The Emperor's New Clothes', which were to adorn her piano for many years.

Margaret had obviously been extremely popular in Denmark, for the link continued after her return to England when she was requested to read two Walter de la Mare poems for the Danish division of the BBC World Service. The following year, at an intimate ceremony in London, she was 'deeply honoured when the Danish Ambassador presented me with a gold medal, the *Ingenio et Arti,* which is reserved for artists of outstanding merit'. She and Malcolm Troup appeared in *Words and Music,* arranged by John Carroll, at the Orangery, Kenwood, London, on 31 May 1954 in the presence of the Norwegian Ambassador. Further readings took place at the Leatherhead and Westminster Theatres.

John Carroll was extremely conscientious in arranging these evenings, providing Margaret with the opportunity to express her love of poetry, which she described as 'a most refreshing hobby'. He became quite devoted to Margaret but could, on occasion, be quite possessive and jealous if he felt he was being usurped by her other friends and colleagues. He was a lonely man who was dependent on Margaret for whatever affection came his way. In later years he occupied accommodation in Stringer and Margaret's house in Gerrards Cross and, according to a number of their friends, became a drain on their resources and kindness.

It was, however, Malcolm Troup who was to be the threat to Margaret and Stringer's marriage. The actress and the pianist had spent a huge amount of time together during the two years they had known each other. As well as their performances and socialising, they opened local exhibitions and fêtes together, and their lives became closely entwined. Troup found Margaret to be 'a great romantic and full of empathy'. They admired each other's work and there is no doubt that they enjoyed an unusually intense relationship.

Rutherford's original crush on her young protégé had developed into a hopeless obsession. Despite the fact that she was three decades older than Malcolm, it seems she had fallen in love with him and misread his fondness and affection as an indication he was equally smitten. Although he knew that Margaret was utterly devoted to him, Troup only realised the true extent of her feelings when her customary weekly letters became increasingly passionate and exigent. So much so, in fact, that in the last she went so far as to suggest that they meet on Hampstead heath and 'run away together'. Troup was about to leave for South America on a tour and she was determined to accompany him, leaving Stringer behind.

Malcolm realised he had unwittingly led her on, and that her feelings for him were far more intense than he had ever imagined. It was now clear to him that their relationship had reached 'a critical stage'. Initially he was at a loss to know what to do. While deeply attached to Margaret, and sharing much in common, he had never thought of her in a romantic sense. He realised that he needed to tell her the truth, but was upset at the thought of hurting her.

Margaret had meanwhile visited actress Damaris Hayman, her close friend and confidante, in Cheltenham to discuss the situation. 'The whole business threatened to get out of hand,' admitted Miss Hayman. 'I had to try and talk her out of leaving poor Stringer for Mr Troup.'

Malcolm and Stringer were on good terms, which made Troup all the more regretful for this unexpected turn of events: 'Stringer was wonderful with Margaret and devoted himself to her. In turn, she helped him maintain his link with the smell of the greasepaint.' Malcolm can't remember talking to Stringer about the situation, but knows that Davis was aware of his wife's feelings. Eventually, Malcolm wrote to Margaret that they could not possibly run away together and that it was best for all involved that they didn't see each other or remain in touch. Malcolm admitted that, 'It broke my heart to tell her that but I didn't know what else to do.' In retrospect, he feels he should have recognised the signs of her true feelings earlier but wonders if, overtaken by a manic episode, her grip on reality had become precarious and her inhibitions liberated. He had often witnessed her bouts of depression, particularly when in a group of friends the conversation seemed to drift over her as she sat quite apart and silent.

When Malcolm Troup returned from South America he didn't see her again, nor did he try to contact her, as he felt it would have been a 'caddish' thing to do. Malcolm has been married since 1961 to his charming Chilean wife, Carmen, and is now a world-renowned concert pianist and judge of international piano competitions. He was appointed Director of Music at the Guildhall School of Music and Drama in 1970 and is currently Professor Emeritus at London's City University.

In the summer of 1955 Margaret suffered another, more serious breakdown and was institutionalised for treatment. 'The actress, Margaret Rutherford, has been ordered to rest by her doctors and so has given up her role in a film, *The March Hare*,' reported the *Daily Express* on 19 August. 'She had just returned to her London home after touring with *Time Remembered* but is currently in a Hampstead Nursing Home. A friend said, "She is simply whacked . . . she is very unhappy about it all. It is the first time for years that she has been unable to work."'

NINE

Melancholia, Mania and Comedy

'The whole of brute force is against me.'

MARGARET RUTHERFORD

MARGARET RUTHERFORD REFERRED to her mental health problems as 'occasional ill health'. The closest she came to any sort of revelation about her mental condition was when she wrote in her autobiography, 'Like many actresses I have periods of elation followed by immensely depressing ones.' She admitted to pushing herself to the limit, but blamed her breakdowns on 'the strain of living on two levels – yourself and the character you are playing each night'. And she felt that the parts she usually played, 'dotty old ladies and eccentrics', were likely to tax her even further. Although she loved to work, she acknowledged that she did sometimes require a hiatus from the stress of performing. 'For some actresses the cure is a change of part. For me it is periods in a nursing home where I can have complete rest and find myself again. Sometimes I bounce back quickly, other times I feel whacked and wonder if I shall ever be able to act again. Shall I ever be able to make that nightly entrance, to remember my lines, to keep my technique fresh and credible?' This admission was purely in the context of the stresses of her professional life. There was no mention of the personal suffering that she endured as a result of her mental illness.

In the BBC radio interview with Alex Mackintosh, she was a little more open about her mental health. He asked her: 'Miss Rutherford, you once referred to the sadness in the world and said, "What I really want to do is to make the world laugh." In this, I think you're very successful, but was it your concern for the world's sadness, do you think, that led to your breakdown some years ago? Had you become saddened yourself?'

'Well I think one only has a breakdown when one feels that the whole of one's object for living has gone,' replied Rutherford. 'One has lost one's roots, one's lost one's bearings. That, I think, is almost the deepest sadness that can be imagined in the world today. And it is for that that I have the most compassion for people who are in that state, I think . . . because I've been in that state myself.'

Mackintosh asked how she had emerged. 'I emerged with the help of the Almighty I would say – through his instruments, people around me who were anxious to give me a hand, people who were skilful, such as my doctors, people who were always at hand – such as my husband and my great friends, though I had a breakdown before ever I met him, so that I'm fairly used to them you know . . . but I think I may perhaps be allowed to say that I used a certain amount of will power. And that is necessary.'

'The reason I ask this, Miss Rutherford,' continued Mackintosh, 'is because one never expects a funny person to become ill.'

There is a perfect pause before Margaret turns inquisitor: 'Don't you really? You with your intelligence?'

Discommoded, Mackintosh nervously remarks, 'Well, we hope that they will make us laugh – we never expect them to be sad.'

'Oh but surely you realise that you never have a comedian who hasn't got a very deep strain of sadness within his nature or her nature. One thing is incidental on the other – if I have the right word.'

'Oh yes, you have.' Mackintosh is clearly relieved to be off the hook.

*

The true nature of Rutherford's breakdowns were never discussed publicly during her life. In the mid-1950s there was – as today – much stigma attached to mental illness. Her melancholia and erratic behaviour were caused by manic depression – now referred to as bipolar disorder. With Margaret's tragic family background, it is not surprising that she was unable or unwilling to admit to such a diagnosis.

The disorder has no known cause, although there is a strong genetic component. A predisposition to bipolar disorder runs in families and usually has its onset in adolescence or early adulthood. Stressful life events or problems can also be triggers. The depressive side of the illness manifests itself in feelings of hopelessness or sadness, fatigue and lack of energy, feelings of serious self-doubt – all of which Margaret experienced often. It can also cause suicidal tendencies. Although a close friend felt there were times when Margaret contemplated taking her own life, there is no evidence she ever attempted suicide. As far as is known, she was never subject to a mental health order or detained against her will.

The mood of someone suffering from bipolar disorder swings between lows and highs – a cruel exaggeration of the phrase, 'Everyone has their ups and downs.' Margaret was at times prone to outlandish ideas and open to engaging in romantic indiscretions and spending money extravagantly on her friends while building up debts – all symptomatic of the manic phase. Often the sufferer can be oblivious of their unusual behaviour during the manic phase, resulting in ideas and feelings which are not based in reality.

As treatment, Margaret would have been prescribed mood stabilisers or anti-depressants, but she also underwent electroconvulsive therapy (ECT) during the 1950s and 1960s. Electric shocks had been used in the treatment of mental illness since the 1930s, originally on patients with schizophrenia. Psychiatrists felt that ECT could also benefit patients with mood disorders, particular in the treatment of depression.

'In a standard ECT session electrodes are attached to one or both sides of the patient's head and something like 80 to 100 volts are applied to the head for up to a second at a time,' explains former GP and writer Vernon Coleman. 'That amount of electricity provides a big enough current to light up a 100-watt light bulb. While being given the treatment patients are usually anaesthetised and given a muscle relaxant. After the electric shock has been given, patients slowly regain consciousness but usually remain groggy and confused for a while.' Margaret Rutherford would have been given an average of six to eight treatments at a time, over the course of several weeks, so usually twice or three times a week. It might have taken two or three treatments before any effect was seen and then four or five treatments to mark any noticeable improvement.

ECT remains a controversial treatment, and the medical profession is still divided in its opinion of it. It is clear that this particular treatment can relieve very severe depressive illnesses when other methods have failed. There is, however, also the feeling that the treatment is inhumane and degrading. There is little doubt that patients suffer from short-term memory loss, and sometimes their ability to recall events from further in the past is clouded. This is certainly true of Margaret, who, as the years passed, had difficulty remembering her lines and, in her final years, could not even recall the most important episodes in her life.

From the middle of 1955 Margaret remained institutionalised for over six months. This was her most serious breakdown yet, precipitated by the end of the unrequited love affair with Malcolm Troup. In typically stoical manner, she wrote of that time, 'I had tried everything to bring myself round but the will to go on had left me.' She had even lost the desire to return to the stage, and it seemed that nothing could extricate her from her depression this time. Her great friend, Robert Morley had other ideas. He was convinced that a return to work would lift her spirits and provide her with an incentive to recover. He had just such an opportunity to help her and proposed, in the beginning of 1956, that she appear with him in a new play, *A Likely Tale*. However,

Margaret's agent, Dorothy Mather rejected the idea, adamant that that her client was far too unwell to take to the stage.

Morley, who had known Margaret for over twenty years, was not to be deterred. He was determined to help his old friend and felt that this play was perfect for her. He had been offered the dual parts of father and son (Oswald and Jonah Petersham) in Gerald Savoury's play, to be directed by Peter Ashmore. It was a tale of a family's inheritance (two sisters, a brother and the brother's son anticipate the division of their father's estate and wait for their father to dispose of his money) and set in Margaret's old stomping ground of Wimbledon. Violet Farebrother was to play one of the sisters and Margaret would be perfect for the other, Mirabelle Petersham.

Taking it upon himself to visit Margaret in the Brighton nursing home, Morley's opening speech in greeting her was pure theatre: 'Now come along, darling, what are you doing here? I have a nice little play with a lovely part for you. So come along. I am going to take you home with me. Pack your bags. We start rehearsing tomorrow.' He convinced the actress, if not her agent or nursing staff, that being on stage was the best place for her. Rutherford was a voluntary patient and so needed no permission to leave other than signing her own release and settling her bill. 'Just as all those years before he had convinced her that she could excel as a comedienne in *Short Story*,' wrote Margaret Morley in *Larger than Life*, 'he now convinced her that she could do this part.'

Robert duly whisked Margaret away to live with his wife, Joan (daughter of Gladys Cooper), and family at Fairmans, the family's beautiful period home near Henley. Stringer, who had been left helpless by his wife's illness, had, for once, managed to procure some employment on his own and was away on a lengthy tour of George Bernard Shaw's *The Devil's Disciple*, with Tyrone Power of all people. Margaret described the experience as an enjoyable kidnapping. 'Robert and I used to drive up to London every morning to attend rehearsals and then return to Henley.' Morley wrote that, 'In the evening and at weekends, she would disappear into the wind on marathon walks, swathed in a billowing cape. She always went to bed after supper with a huge tray of sandwiches – all of which would be consumed by morning.'

Although rehearsals went surprisingly well, and Margaret was of the opinion that 'Robert had done the trick and rescued me from my melancholia', the weeks leading up to the West End opening were far from straightforward. Morley reported that, 'On a pre-London tour with a free morning she occasionally betook herself to a local head-shrinker demanding a release on medical grounds without success, until she managed to find one in Brighton who opined she could do with a rest, whereupon the play's management announced they were going to bring a law suit against him and he revised his diagnosis.'

Against all the odds, *A Likely Tale* opened on 22 March 1956 at the Globe Theatre, Shaftesbury Avenue – with Rutherford in tow. The critics were particularly interested in Morley's dual role. One moment he was Oswald Petersham, fat and sixty-five, and ten seconds later he was Oswald's son Jonah, still fat but only forty-five. Morley recalled later: 'As the father I had grey hair, and as the son I wore a red wig and an eye patch. I was always hoping that someone would remark on the difference in the two performances. But the truth was, I suppose, that there wasn't a great deal.'

The reviews were not kind. The *Daily Telegraph* and *Manchester Guardian* described the action as 'weak' and 'disappointing' respectively. The *Daily Mail* found 'little to amuse. Miss Rutherford goes through the familiar motions of tossing words around her mouth like hot potatoes. The play sadly lacks sugar and spice,' while *Punch* wondered, 'Should one laugh or cry at Miss Rutherford's terrible spasms of childlike grief?' The ever-faithful Eric Keown declared that the play was 'thin but charming – about a family of elderly failures by-passed by life – a play which for all its gentle absurdity has a streak of real sadness . . . Margaret Rutherford is beautifully cast and in a part which, in its mixture of girlish hysteria and telling silences, gives her a chance to exploit the subtle undertow of melancholy she conveys so delicately; even at its funniest it is touching.' Despite the spectacles of Morley's doubling and Rutherford's Mirabelle, 'her curls a quiver and her chin tremulous', the critics concluded that the play just wasn't good enough. Kenneth Tynan called it, 'neither good theatre nor bad; it is simply irrelevant theatre.'

One actress to receive praise as 'a very pretty parlour maid who has taken the old man's fancy' (from the *What's On* critic) was Judy Parfitt. Parfitt had worked with Margaret Rutherford once before, when she was only aged sixteen and an understudy on an eleven-week tour of *Time Remembered.* Miss Parfitt recalled this as a marvellous experience – particularly as she was just embarking on her illustrious career. As the maid in *A Likely Tale,* she shared several scenes with Miss Rutherford and learned a great deal. 'She didn't just play the part, she inhabited the role. When you looked into her eyes, you saw the truth of her performance. She was very generous both as an actress and as a woman. She was also very maternal.' Margaret Rutherford was indeed incredibly protective of the young actress. A member of the cast took a shine to Miss Parfitt and was beginning to be bothersome: 'Margaret called him in to her dressing room and, in stern terms, made it quite clear that he should know better and behave himself.'

The veteran actress had a pair of curved emerald paste earrings which Judy Parfitt admired. Margaret was pleased but commented, 'My dear, you're a redhead – the earrings would look so much better on you.' Judy, of course, demurred, but the following day she found them on her dressing room table, left there as a gift by Margaret. Parfitt has naturally kept the earrings as a keepsake of Rutherford's wonderfully generous nature and a reminder of the time they spent together. She was aware that Rutherford had just come out of a nursing home and that she suffered from manic depression, but felt that Margaret coped remarkably well with the stress of the production. She witnessed only one suggestion of eccentric behaviour, when Rutherford remarked: 'We should stop doing the show and go up the Amazon!' The play was a very happy experience for Parfitt, now a much respected and extraordinarily prolific actress, who also recalled that Robert Morley was great fun to be around and played lots of tricks and practical jokes on the cast.

The adrenalin of appearing on stage provided Rutherford with the motivation to emerge from her slump. 'It seemed that as if by magic every night when the curtain went up I was given an injection of strength.' Unsurprisingly, in view of Margaret's fragile mental state, there were times when she struggled to cope with all the pressures of a long run, and there was at least one night when it all became too much for her. 'I was particularly sad and felt nothing but hopelessness. As I sat in my dressing room I thought, I simply cannot go on. I told Robert, who became very conspiratorial. "Very well darling, if that is the case I will get another actress I have standing by. She will play the part." And then all my professionalism returned and I could bear it no longer. I swept on stage to see my friend Grace Bridges sitting in my chair.' Robert Morley immediately asked Grace to vacate the stage and invited Margaret to take her usual seat. 'I took Grace's place seconds before the curtain went up. It was again exactly what was required and Robert again had come to the rescue.' Morley's plan had worked perfectly. Despite the reviews, the public loved *A Likely Tale* and the play did extremely good business. It ran for a year and was still playing to full houses when Binkie Beaumont took it off so that Robert Morley could appear in *Fanny*.

On 28 June 1956, during the run, Margaret appeared with Robert Morley in the sketch 'Progress in Work' in *A Night of a Hundred Stars*, a midnight review in aid of the Actors' Orphanage whose president was now Laurence Olivier. Hosted by Zsa Zsa Gabor, the show also featured Bob Hope, Cyd Charisse, Vera Ellen, John Gielgud, Olivier himself, Paul Scofield, Tyrone Power, Edith Evans, Peter Ustinov, Alicia Markova and Jack Benny. Not a bad line-up.

Robert Morley's insistence that Margaret would benefit more from appearing in a lengthy West End production than from undergoing some kind of 'rest cure' seemed to have been vindicated. She was in remarkably good spirits at the end of the run and, although fatigued, was ready to return to the studio. Pinewood, in fact.

Just My Luck, Rutherford's second film with Norman Wisdom, was released in November 1957. This time the comedian had the sole starring role. This formulaic comedy had Wisdom playing Norman, a manual worker who lives with a domineering mother and is employed in exclusive West End jewellers alongside Sam Kydd and Bill Fraser. He has a crush on Anne (Jill Dixon), who works in the store opposite, but has never actually spoken to her. He is keen on buying a pendant for Anne but can never afford it, so places a £1 accumulator bet with some dodgy turf accountants (Leslie Phillips, Peter Copley and a sympathetic Delphi Lawrence) in the hope of making a fortune.

Norman is concerned about losing the last leg of the bet and goes to see horse owner and eccentric menagerie enthusiast Mrs Dooley (Rutherford), in an attempt to stop her from running the horse. She ends up giving him the horse as an engagement present. When he arrives at her country pile, there is an elephant on the lawn and a parrot at the front door. Mrs Dooley is giving a chimpanzee (Josephine) a bath. And that's probably the highlight of the scene. Rutherford trains a very dodgy Irish accent on some even dodgier dialogue. Her talents are totally wasted, and one can only conclude that her performance was affected by the leaden lines she had to deliver. It's a film she would surely have wanted to forget.

Yet Margaret's connection with the film did not end with the cessation of shooting. The writer and novelist Rumer Godden, whose books included *Black Narcissus* and *The Greengage Summer*, lived with her husband James Haynes-Dixon on the main floor of Old Hall, and their apartment was linked by an internal staircase to Margaret and Stringer's flat. Miss Godden was aware of Rutherford's fame and, in the knowledge that many people did seek her out, she and her husband decided not to be intrusive and would only bid the famous actress a friendly 'Good Morning' if their paths crossed.

One afternoon, when she was working in her study, the author became aware of Margaret walking up and down outside, obviously in great distress. 'She was wringing her hands as she often did on stage and her face was puckered with worry. At last I dared to get up and go out and talk to her. I said, "Miss Rutherford, is there something wrong? Is there anything I can do to help?" She clasped her hands and said, "My dear, you've lived in India; you must know about monkeys. You see I'm having a chimpanzee to tea." This couldn't have happened with anyone else but Margaret.'

Rutherford explained that she had just finished filming in *Just My Luck* and had invited Josephine, one of her co-stars, to the flat. Rumer Godden attempted to reassure Margaret and told her, 'I did indeed know a little about monkeys as my husband had kept one as a pet when he was a small boy. I warned her that the chimpanzee would probably shake hands with her and that she must not try to shrink at the extreme coldness of a monkey's hands.' In due course the chimpanzee arrived to have tea, walking hand in hand with its trainer. Josephine was about three years old, three feet high and dressed in scarlet rompers with a scarlet hair ribbon. Rumer was duly invited to join the other guests and maintained that the chimp behaved rather well, 'except that every so often she got up to turn somersaults'.

Margaret's next work for silver screen involved neither a monkey nor Norman Wisdom. It was altogether a different experience. *The Smallest Show on Earth*, a delightful and quirky British comedy, written by John Eldridge and William Rose, who also scripted *Genevieve*, was released the same year, 1957, and directed by Basil Dearden at Shepperton. Matt (Bill Travers) and Jean (Virginia McKenna) Spenser inherit the Bijou, a dilapidated cinema nicknamed 'The Fleapit', from an unknown great uncle. They travel to Sloughborough to discover that the cinema is in a terrible state, with trains thundering past and shaking the building to its foundations.

The cinema's staff isn't in much better condition: Peter Sellers is Percy Quill, a dipsomaniac projectionist; Rutherford is Mrs Fazackalee, an authoritarian ticket seller; and Bernard Miles is Old

Tom, the commissionaire/caretaker. As if the fleapit didn't have enough problems, its very existence is under threat from Mr Hardcastle (Francis de Wolff), the owner of the Grand, the town's corporate and palatial alternative cinema. He wishes to put the independent picture house out of business, demolish the building and use the grounds for a car park. Leslie Phillips is the wily young solicitor, acting on behalf of the Spensers, and there is a tiny role for Stringer as Emmett, an assistant to Hardcastle. Sid James makes a cameo appearance as the father of the Bijou's blousy, blonde cigarette girl.

The Bijou mainly shows westerns such as 'The Killer Riders of Wyoming', 'The Devil Riders of Parched Point' and 'The Mystery of Hell Valley' – a scorching drama of the pitiless, thirsty desert, starring comedy stalwart Alec Bregonzi as the unlikely gunslinger. Most of these include scenes of trains rumbling through rocky canyons, in fruitless attempts to cover up the sounds of the real trains which roar past the Bijou.

Apart from the gentle humour and extraordinary ensemble acting, there are some magical nostalgic moments. *The Smallest Show on Earth* is a paean to the much cherished independent cinemas of the mid-1950s, and a snapshot of cinema-going in post war Britain. Sellers runs the 1924 silent film, *Comin' Thro' the Rye'*, for the staff's enter-tainment, to which Rutherford provides musical accompaniment on a battered old piano. Sellers, playing a character twice his age, is marvellous as the curmudgeonly projectionist, driven to drink by his ageing and decrepit machinery. He is ably supported by Bernard Miles, described by Roger Lewis, author of *The Life and Death of Peter Sellers*, thus: 'Old Tom, dressed in fraying brocade, slouched and growling, welcomes people into the Bijou as if they are crossing the threshold into Hell.'

Sellers' scenes with Margaret Rutherford are a joy – two of Britain's most skilled actors playing off each other. Neither is overawed or outdone by the other. 'It has nothing to do with techniques or tricks,' observes Lewis. 'What we notice is that Sellers and Margaret

Rutherford can invest the material with more hush and resonance than perhaps its writers were aware of. There's a drollery about what they do; a fine, intuitive grasp – a clairvoyance, if you like.' When the Spensers visit the premises for the first time, their employees come from behind a curtain, nervous and frowning: 'Mrs Fazackalee, squat in the guichet as if it was a sedan chair, doesn't sell tickets, she accepts poultry or vegetables as barter.'

Attempts at revitalising the cinema are hindered at every turn, including when one night a group of hooligans gains admission. Virginia McKenna, who tries to sell some ice creams, is derided and harried. But then Mrs Fazackalee arrives on the scene, and the hooligans are terrified of this behemoth. 'Stout and imperious,' writes Roger Lewis. 'Clad in black lace and jet jewels, flourishing a pince-nez tethered to her bosoms by black ribbon, she is Madame Arcati, from *Blithe Spirit*, a medium in mourning. The joy of a Rutherford performance is that, always booted, spurred, and costumed in layers of tweed capes and bonnets, she could yet convey spirituality and feyness.'

Virginia McKenna was initially quite daunted about the thought of working with Rutherford. 'I was a young actress and Margaret Rutherford was already a star. She was quite unique and had an extra-ordinary presence, walking in a most stately fashion. Margaret didn't try to be humorous – she just was naturally funny. Her timing was brilliant and was delightful to work with. She was very amenable to any suggestions.' Miss McKenna and her late husband, Bill Travers, had very fond memories of working on *The Smallest Show on Earth*: 'It was the most enjoyable film that we had worked on and we had trouble keeping a straight face with that amazing cast – particularly with Peter Sellers, who was incredibly funny.' Like so many others who had worked with Rutherford, McKenna also noticed how attentive and solicitous Stringer was. 'He was always around carrying her para-phernalia and personal belongings. He always looked after her very well and was always of great comfort to her. They seemed to share a lovely respectful relationship.'

Leslie Phillips was equally enthusiastic about working with Rutherford: in his autobiography *Hello*, he expressed the view that, 'Margaret Rutherford, already in her mid-sixties, was magnificent as Mrs Fazackalee in the box office. She was one of the outstanding female character actresses to emerge since the war . . . she was always warm and wonderful to work with; while appearing with her in this film at Pinewood, she and Stringer would turn up, full of vim and enthusiasm, announcing that they had stopped at some wild, fast-flowing river or placid lake for a bracing swim – probably in the buff, knowing her! Stringer would always keep his pants on, I'm sure, and always have a towel at the ready to rub down his wife.'

TEN

A Question of
Taking Pains

'Truth has a good face but poor clothes.'

PROVERB

B Y 1957 STRINGER and Margaret were experiencing serious
financial difficulties. Margaret had returned to the BBC at the
beginning of the year with an appearance in the radio programme
The Laughtermakers for the princely sum of ten guineas. In a switch
to the cathode ray in March, she played the hostess in a skit for
Carmichael's Night Out, a television special featuring actor Ian
Carmichael. Later in the year she participated in *Place the Face*, a panel
game recorded at the Riverside Studios, in which contestants were
supposed to guess the identity of a mystery guest. Obviously all did not
go well with this particular broadcast, as outlined in this memo from
BBC television controller Cecil McGivern to the show's producer: 'I
felt sad to see Miss Margaret Rutherford put into what was for her such
a ridiculous and undignified situation. This did not redound to the
credit either of Miss Rutherford's illustrious theatrical past or to
the reputation on the BBC Television Service. I wonder what Miss

Rutherford afterwards really thought about this particular journey to BBC Television.' Surely it can't have been that the contestants didn't recognise the dulcet tones or the unmistakable phizog of our Miss Rutherford?

These BBC projects were not, however, going to pay the bills. Despite Margaret being employed in a couple of films and the long-running *A Likely Tale* the previous year, money was growing increasingly tight for her and Stringer. Margaret's nursing home fees gnawed away at their savings, and their lifestyle, although not extravagant, was hardly frugal. The couple were not much good with money. Not only was Margaret incredibly generous to friends and acquaintances, she was also a poor bookkeeper and possessed a certain antipathy and confusion when it came to settling with the Inland Revenue.

It was thus quite a relief when, in the spring of 1957, Margaret was asked to join a travelling production of *The Importance of Being Earnest*, to play the part of Lady Bracknell. Esma Cannon was Miss Prism and Stringer reprised his role as Merriman. Damaris Hayman, whose career began in repertory in the 1950s and who has appeared in numerous television productions, was cast as the parlour maid and Margaret's understudy. 'Of course, initially I called her Miss Rutherford – certainly never Peggy – although very soon into rehearsals we chose the jewellery for the costumes and established a rapport. I then felt I knew her well enough to refer to her as Margaret!' Damaris had always been a great fan of the star and was delighted to work with and get to know her.

The production, directed by Michael Macowan, began its tour with three weeks in Ireland, followed by a week each in Edinburgh, Leeds, Liverpool, Bournemouth and Eastbourne. The party commenced its journey by train and Rutherford described the cheerful departure. 'There is something very infectious about a tour – like a big family outing to the seaside. The management met us with a bouquet of flowers and everyone was gay and excited.' Margaret also wrote: 'Train journeys always remind me of Marie Tempest, who used to have her teapot filled by the engine driver when she was travelling. I always find they are very helpful too when I want my hot-water bottles refilling.'

The troupe sailed on the overnight crossing, and on arrival in Dublin, which coincided with Rutherford's birthday, the much lauded actress was met by a committee of festival devotees (the play opened in Dublin as part of the Dublin Theatre Festival), who swept her off for a tour of Dublin. Margaret had not been back there since 1938, when she had appeared at the Gaiety in *Spring Meeting*.

Rutherford thought the cast somewhat nervous on opening night – only too aware of the tradition of fine acting in the Republic's capital city. But they were well up to their task, and *The Irish Times* was lavish in its praise: 'The play is given an impeccably stylish production at the Olympia this week . . . it is carried through under Michael Macowan's direction into a production mannered and gay, a production that never breaks from its sprightly trot into an unruly gallop . . . the hard work is done by Robert Eddison, a picture of puzzled dignity as John Worthing, and Derek Blomfield is a mischievous Algernon Moncrieff. But many theatre-goers will remember most clearly the magnificent Lady Bracknell of Margaret Rutherford, a man-o-war in full sail; this is a comedy performance of great tradition.'

From Dublin the play moved to the City Theatre, Limerick. Margaret travelled with an enormous pink teapot which she kept in her dressing room. In Limerick, however, there was no gas ring to boil a kettle and the Assistant Stage Manager was ill and therefore indisposed when it came to brewing Rutherford's customary cup of tea in the second act. A teenager, acting as stage hand, was summoned by Margaret with the words, 'Where is the young boy?' She presented him with the pink teapot and urgently despatched him to his mother, who lived nearby. He returned soon after with a full pot for Miss Rutherford. Evidently 'Where is the young boy?' became something of a catchphrase with the members of the cast during the Limerick leg of the tour. Apart from the lack of backstage facilities, some of the company were staying in lodgings which were situated in close proximity to an abattoir which they had to pass on the way to the theatre. 'Apparently these were the second-best digs in the city and were unspeakable,' Damaris Hayman recalled, 'Goodness knows what the third best digs were like!'

The cast were thus much relieved to move on to Belfast, where they enjoyed comfortable accommodation and improved production facilities. The Governor of Northern Ireland, Lord Wakehurst, attended the first night in the city and threw a garden party in honour of the production. Hayman concurred with the generally held view that Margaret didn't possess much dress sense, and instead attired herself in the way that her public expected (Margaret once lent her one of her capes for an appearance in *Dr Who*), but her choice for the Governor's garden party was daring even by Rutherford's standards: she wore a pink and blue chiffon dress and a yellow cape, purchased in Madeira, with detachable wings, fringed in yellow straw and embroidered with butterflies. To set the ensemble off, her feet graced a pair of bright pink sandals, emblazoned with blue flowers. It seems that Stringer shared his wife's taste, as he remarked to Damaris, 'I thought my wife had real glamour this evening.'

The production was now transferring to Edinburgh, so the next part of the journey was to be more complicated for the company. There was no possibility of taking a boat across the Irish Sea, so an aeroplane was chartered to Stranraer. From there the players travelled by bus to Edinburgh, stopping on the way at a hotel in Dumfries, where they all celebrated Stringer's birthday 'with an excellent lunch'. It was, of course, Margaret's treat. Apart from everything else to contend with on the convoluted tour, a fan gave Margaret a large plant in a wicker basket, which she insisted on transporting throughout the rest of the production. Damaris was given the job of keeping the shrub healthy and visited various ladies' lavatories to top it up with water.

Hayman had a number of relatives in Edinburgh, and Margaret offered her understudy the opportunity of appearing in a matinée performance. Damaris was touched by this gesture but felt it would be very unfair on the theatre-goers who had paid good money in order to see the legendary actress, and thus declined Margaret's kind offer. In the second week of June, the show transferred to Leeds, where the company occupied the Grand Theatre and Opera House. The Grand had a star dressing room which was only opened up occasionally for special events or celebrated performers. The management ensured that Margaret Rutherford was able to enjoy special treatment and the room was duly prepared for her.

On the second day in York Stringer and Margaret asked everyone connected with the production to their Parkway hotel to enjoy a party by the swimming pool. 'The weather was not very good,' wrote Rutherford, 'but I had a feeling that a splash round would do everyone a lot of good – tone up the muscles and what not. Damaris said she would like to swim, in spite of the cold wind, and not to be outdone I decided to join her at the deep end and took the plunge. It was so cold that I almost submerged with the shock. I came up thrashing about and blowing water like a friendly walrus. It was then that my shoulder straps broke.' Ever supportive, Damaris immediately procured two safety pins and came to Margaret's rescue, sparing Miss Rutherford's blushes and securing the costume in the water – 'a very difficult business'. The press also happened to be in attendance and a photograph made the local newspaper.

It was in Leeds that Damaris introduced Margaret to Gaelic coffee. 'When I first tried it I thought it was rather curious with that blob of whipped cream on the top and wondered why it was in a glass,' explained Margaret. 'I suddenly realised what had hit me and broke into a smile like the dawn rising over the Alps.' Margaret was not much of a drinker, but was occasionally inclined to enjoy sweet drinks such as cherry brandy. (Ned Sherrin once attended a party given by one of Rutherford's impoverished relatives. Drink was scarce and the only alcohol was madeira. Sherrin reported that, 'Dame Margaret circled the room holding her glass aloft, sipping occasionally and murmuring, "Ambrosia! Ambrosia!"')

Damaris Hayman described Margaret as the kindest and most generous person one could wish to meet. 'She had the most tremendous maternal instinct and always looked after everyone around her. She was terribly extravagant with other people and had no sense of the value of money. She was constantly treating everyone to lunch and dinner at whichever hotel she was staying at and made sure that all members of the company, whatever their role, were her guests at one time or another.' Damaris also confirmed that Margaret Rutherford never did the 'big star thing', although once, staying in Southport, where the hotel staff were difficult about cooking her customary late night bacon and eggs after the show, Margaret responded by saying, 'You're lucky to have us.'

During the Eastbourne run, Margaret decided she wanted to see Emlyn Williams doing a section of his one-man Dickens show at a nearby venue. During the second act there was a period of about half an hour when she wasn't on stage. In full make-up and red wig which she wore for the part of Lady Bracknell, and donning a coat to cover her costume, she nipped out in the middle of the performance and managed to catch a quick glimpse of Williams before making it back on stage in time!

When the tour came to an end, it was hoped that the production would find a home at a London theatre. Unfortunately Perlita Neilson, who Damaris described as 'the best Cecily I've ever seen', had been offered a film, and it was decided not to pursue a West End transfer. The very disappointed cast were thus to go their separate ways, but only after the end of the tour had been marked with an exchange of presents. Damaris popped into Eastbourne town centre, where she purchased a dark green glass whisky decanter, which was presented to Margaret after the last performance, 'all prettily wrapped, on a silver salver'. Margaret bought presents for everyone: Damaris received a pair of pink plastic orchid earrings. Though not to her taste, Hayman felt she had to wear the earrings occasionally (and rather self-consciously) so as not to offend. Margaret was also in the habit of buying gifts from

Roman Catholic church shops, and Damaris still has a plastic Madonna figure, given to her in later years.

Margaret had described the tour as a delight, and much enjoyed the camaraderie of being part of a company – a reminder of her early days in rep. At the end of the production, she was left feeling very low. In fact, according to Damaris, 'She went into a complete gloom.'

During the ensuing months and years, Damaris became a regular visitor to the Old Hall and spent a great deal of time with the Davises, getting to know them intimately and even keeping house for them on occasions. She felt that they were clearly devoted to each other; whenever Margaret left the flat, Stringer would always watch her departure lovingly, blowing her a kiss. Damaris described the living room as light and cosy but neither bedroom (Margaret and Stringer had separate bedrooms) was particularly comfortable.

She and Margaret were both enthusiastic swimmers and often went to the women's pool in Hampstead Heath, where afterwards they would sunbathe stark naked. They also took bracing walks together on Hampstead Heath. Margaret was inquisitive and loved meeting new people and discovering their backgrounds and their stories. She was humorous but could be unpredictable and surprisingly direct. While Damaris never heard Margaret express an overtly political opinion, she realised that Margaret held strong moral beliefs and, though well mannered, wasn't afraid to speak her mind when she felt the situation demanded it.

Stringer and Margaret both enjoyed attending the theatre and loved the Australian play, *Summer of the Seventeenth Doll*, which had opened in London. In the summer of 1957, Margaret and Stringer threw a garden party for the cast and some close friends. Damaris recalled watching Robert Morley theatrically sweep into the flat, neighbour Rumer Godden, in the extensive lawn garden, help to serve cups of real turtle soup, which Stringer (in charge of the barbecue) described as 'rather different'.

That autumn, Margaret was invited by the Australian Elizabethan Theatre Trust to tour the country in various productions. The timing was perfect. Margaret had suffered a mini-breakdown at the end of the *Earnest* tour and needed something to lift her spirits. Escaping to the other side of the world in a new adventure seemed attractive. She was now in deep debt to the Inland Revenue and desperately required some income. Her plan was to avoid paying tax in the UK while earning tax-free income 'down under'. Unfortunately, in typical Rutherford fashion, her financial calculations were capricious: she stayed too long in Australia and ended up paying tax there too! She had also been under the impression that she would finally get her chance to play the Nurse in *Romeo and Juliet* whilst overseas. Sadly, the Trust decided not to do the Shakespeare play and Rutherford's hopes of playing that cherished part were dashed forever.

There was some advance publicity for the trip. On 3 October 1957 *The Stage* ran the headline 'Miss Rutherford Flies Out': 'Boarding a plane at London Airport to fly to Australia – she is to appear in several productions for the Australian Elizabethan Theatre Trust during the next six months. Meanwhile an Australian newspaper ran a story reporting that, 'England's most gorgeous old battle-axe is coming to Australia. Attired in a majestic clash of tinkling bangles, necklaces, furbelows, a swirling cloak, all preceded by her formidable U-shaped chin, Miss Rutherford is due to alight from an aircraft in Sydney this week – she detests the appellation of battle-axe.' Presumably describing her as 'a gorgeous old battle-axe' was okay.

Stringer loyally accompanied her, as usual. Describing their departure, journey and financial mismanagement, Margaret wrote, 'The first touches of autumn were in the air as we left London airport in a "whispering giant". In order to avoid consecutive days and nights in the air, which I dislike, we broke our journeys at Beirut and Singapore. In Beirut we went on a shopping spree and then saw wonderful ruins at Baalbek and the fine American college. At the

Raffles hotel in Singapore the manager most graciously allowed us to pay with an English cheque as we had overspent in Beirut.'

The tour started in Sydney with *The Happiest Days of Your Life*. The Davises had been given the use of a flat 'in a beautiful house and grounds at Point Piper, high on a hill outside Sydney with a wonderful view of the harbour'. An aunt of the actress lived in Sydney and helped settle the couple in. Margaret discovered that the Winter Garden cinema was showing *Aunt Clara*. She found the Australian public to be extremely friendly and kind, and thus felt immediately welcomed. One of her fans gave her a large stuffed orange kangaroo which she named Flora – after Flora Robson. 'I only name my stuffed animals after people I really like.'

Miss Rutherford also found performing with local actors stimulating. 'They have a joyousness, a certain carefree quality that we don't have in England. Even the audiences differ. I thought that the Sydney one was tough – I found I needed more voice and attack. But then it *was* during a heat wave. I don't think that they understood the humour quite the same way as an English audience, but the whole theatre glowed with warmth and humanity.' She also participated in a number of poetry readings, which were 'met with quite a heady response'. These included two nights on 31 October and 1 November 1957 at the National Gallery of New South Wales. All 700 seats had been sold for the first night and she was thus asked to repeat the performance the following day.

In between working the couple enjoyed some Christmas shopping. Margaret had picked out a pottery plaque of the Sydney Harbour Bridge, but Stringer convinced her that this was a mistake. 'The bridge girders aren't in the right place,' he explained. Margaret duly decided to purchase a little blue china bird in a golden cage and some earrings in the shape of Australia; Stringer chose a boomerang-styled tie. Margaret appreciated the Australians' love of the outdoor lifestyle and she and Stringer went swimming at every opportunity, particularly enjoying the surf at Bondi beach.

The tour moved to Tasmania in January and from there to Melbourne, where Rutherford appeared in a production of *Time Remembered*. The company took the play to Adelaide and then finally returned to Sydney. Margaret and Stringer had been away several months longer than anticipated but were in no hurry to return home, so decided to travel by sea. Their ship was due to leave Sydney on 4 June 1958 and the evening before they left, they hosted a ball on board for all their Australian friends. 'It was Stringer's birthday as well as a farewell party so we had a cake and champagne.' The ship docked at Melbourne and Perth, but Margaret found the heat unbearable and was convinced that the temperature in the Suez Canal would be too much for her. They decided to travel by air for the rest of the journey home and thus disembarked in Ceylon (Sri Lanka). They stayed at the Galle Face Hotel in Colombo, and arrived 'with our cloaks, coats, umbrellas, parcels, string bags and picnic things. After checking in, we made a regal procession to our room with the junior purser and Ceylonese servants trailing behind us, each servant carrying one of our belongings on his head!'

The rest of the trip involved visits to Karachi, Bahrain and Frankfurt, before finally returning to England. The couple stayed initially at a hotel in Windsor, as their Highgate flat had been let in their absence. Reflecting on their extended Antipodean experience, Margaret wrote: 'I had been very ill with a nervous breakdown before I went to Australia but at the end of the trip I had made a complete recovery – I never felt better in my life – thanks to Australia and its people.'

Soon after her return to the United Kingdom, Margaret was again invited to take part in *A Night of a Hundred Stars*, another midnight revue presented at the Palladium in aid of the Actors' Orphanage. The show took place on 28 June 1958, and Margaret appeared in the sketch 'Bubble Man' from the revue *Share My Lettuce*. She played an infuriated charwoman trying to clean up the mess made by the bubble-blowing of actor and singer Graham Payn, Noël Coward's partner. Other performers included Kirk Douglas and Burt Lancaster, Laurence

Olivier and Vivien Leigh, Alec Guinness, Rex Harrison, Frankie Howerd and Roger Moore.

Margaret's next piece of work came about in an interesting fashion. In late summer that same year, Adrian Brown (later to win an Emmy and be nominated for a BAFTA, but at that time a junior drama director for BBC television) found on his desk a large pile of scripts of former theatre successes, from which he had to choose one as his next project. Of them all, he liked only *The Noble Spaniard* by Somerset Maugham, and this because, in Brown's words, 'It was the sort of delicious soufflé that required a heightened acting style, giving a nod and a wink to the audience, so to speak, as if saying: "We all know this is nonsense, but please enjoy the joke with us."' The setting is a French seaside villa, rented for the summer by a wealthy English couple, Mr Justice Proudfoot and his more aristocratic wife, Lady Proudfoot, with their two nieces. In this setting a passionate Spanish grandee, there to 'take the waters', falls in love with one of the nieces, Marion, a young widow; and his impetuous Latin ardour causes myriad crises of mistaken purpose and intent.

Brown saw here an opportunity to work with Margaret Rutherford, an actress he had long adored so he sent the script to her and Stringer, offering them the roles of Mr Justice and Lady Proudfoot, as husband and wife a combination they had never played before. After some days, Margaret rang Adrian, only to say, 'You very kindly sent me the play, but I'm afraid I don't much care for it. I find it rather cruel to make fun of an ageing person who mistakenly thinks someone has fallen in love with her.' Adrian was disappointed, but could see there was some truth in this estimate of the play. The director was, of course, unaware that this particular storyline must have been somewhat resonant of Margaret's distressing relationship with the much younger Malcolm Troup. Margaret clearly felt that this part was too painful for her to contemplate.

However, half an hour later the telephone rang again, and this time it was Stringer Davis, to say, 'Thank you so much for sending me the script – I understand that my wife is reluctant, but I myself am rather keen on the part, and am ready to start rehearsals whenever you say.' Adrian knew that this was a much more substantial role than Stringer was usually offered, and one he would be chagrined to pass up, so he seized his chance, telling Stringer that so lightweight but stylish a comedy as this required particularly skilful players, and if he could not get together the cast he hoped for, he might have to look for an alternative play . . .

'Oh,' responded Stringer, in a thoughtful tone. 'May I ask you not to do anything hasty?' And he put the phone down.

Within fifteen minutes Adrian's telephone rang once more. 'Hello, this is Margaret Rutherford again. I've been thinking about the Maugham play and I suppose . . . if we saw it as a fantasy . . . if we made the audience realise it was all nonsense, then I don't suppose the play would cause offence . . . so if it's not too late . . .'

Adrian was delighted. 'Oh yes, I absolutely agree, Miss Rutherford, the play is a complete fantasy, a sort of fairy-tale, and no, actually it's not too late!' Stringer was clearly unheeding or oblivious of his wife's romantic sensibilities and had obviously persuaded her to accept the part. Thus Margaret and Stringer had the chance to play husband and wife together for the first time. Margaret may have been further convinced of the play's fantasy qualities when she discovered that Kenneth Williams was to be playing a romantic lead in the cast. However, Williams, who was appearing at the time in the classic radio comedy *Beyond Our Ken*, was rather acidulous about the play in his published diary entry for 2 September 1958: 'Read-thru in the afternoon of *The Noble Spaniard* – I can see it's a crock of shit.' Several weeks later came another tart entry, made shortly after the recording, 'Never more glad that anything was finished before in my life. Utterly sickening.'

If Williams was unhappy, either with his part or with the production process, he gave no sign of this at the time. And no one had forced him to take the role. On the contrary, Adrian Brown, who had been quite friendly with the actor for several years, had telephoned Kenneth at home to ask if he would like to be in 'a daft Victorian comedy, playing Captain Chalford of the Heavy Dragoons', a delicious prospect, and soon after receiving the script, Williams telephoned the director, also at home, to say he would love to do the play. Brown's retrospective opinion is that, 'Frankly I think he felt I did not maintain the friendship warmly enough and so he wrote these paranoid comments some time later. None of us felt the play was more than a pleasing trifle, to be performed with style and dash.' Adrian thought Williams was excellent in the play, 'its absurd plot requiring Captain Chalford, every time he entered a room, to find his lady-love clasped in the arms of a different man, always in perfect innocence'. In his autobiography, *Just Williams*, Kenneth wrote of his appearance in the 'BBC television play, *The Noble Spaniard*, which starred Margaret Rutherford, whom I can see in my mind's eye now with her knitting bag at rehearsals. "Pains," she would say. "It is all a question of taking pains," and when it came to the performance she was as delightfully eccentric as always.'

Other cast members included Robert Eddison as the ardent Spanish nobleman and Maxine Audley as the charming widow, while Lucy Griffiths, who was yet another of Margaret's adult foundlings, played the maid (at Margaret's request). Rehearsals were arranged for a church hall in Shepherd's Bush, and on the first day Mr and Mrs Stringer Davis arrived to set up camp in one corner with reclining chairs and a primus stove. Margaret however assured Adrian that she and Stringer would be ready to spring into action as soon as required: 'Don't worry about us making ourselves at home, just give us a shout and we'll be ready.' Soon, however, rehearsals had to be moved to a larger hall because Margaret and Stringer became confused by the overlapping markings on the floor, set out with tapes in different colours to suggest the layouts of several rooms.

During rehearsals Adrian overheard Stringer murmur to his wife: 'The wonderful thing about you, Margaret, is that you can be larger than life and yet remain completely real.' She replied, 'You can do it too, Tuft.' But poor Stringer knew that he could not. For instance, in one scene Stringer was required to enter a room, express surprise at the presence of a visitor and then advance to shake the character's hand. Stringer had some difficulty with this entrance: 'Sorry, old man, it can't be done,' He told Brown.

'Why not, old chap?' inquired the director.

'Ahh . . . well . . . the thing is . . . you see, when I enter I have to remove my hat.'

'Yes.'

'Well, it'll still be in my right hand.'

With a moment's thought, Adrian responded, 'Stringer, why not transfer the hat to your left hand on the way over?'

Stringer nodded pensively. 'Ah! Yes that would work. The trouble is now . . . should I lead off with my left foot or my right?'

After ten minutes of practice, Stringer had perfected his entrance.

Rehearsals and recording lasted for three weeks, and Margaret soon settled comfortably into her role. Adrian realised that she always felt much happier with her husband around. In general, actors with whom she felt at ease afforded her a sense of security that might otherwise be lacking. Adrian, in mid-twenties and a comparatively novice director, found it charming, if embarrassing, when Margaret and Stringer would address him as 'teacher'. 'Margaret was wonderful to work with. If she got the words muddled, or missed a cue, she readily admitted her mistake, saying, "I really must get hold of that, mustn't I?" The whole cast, including Williams got on very well, and the only moment of rehearsal tension arose when Maxine Audley – on the telephone to her agent about her next job – missed a cue. Margaret was very cross and erupted, stating that this play was difficult enough to get hold of for veterans like herself and Stringer, "So what makes these youngsters think they can be so casual?"' According to Adrian, 'Maxine – not as young as all that – didn't make the mistake again.'

In a bizarre radio trailer for the play, Margaret Rutherford was called on to play a mermaid with Kenneth Williams as a shipwrecked mariner. The short item had absolutely nothing to do with *The Noble Spaniard,* but was the brainwave of some BBC publicity wallah who evidently felt this comical scenario would entice potential viewers. Perhaps it was the same man who had written Margaret's *Desert Island Discs* script . . .

The Noble Spaniard was broadcast live from Lime Grove Studios on BBC television on Sunday 21 September. There occurred some unexplained incident at the studios the day before the play went out, for on 28 September, Margaret Rutherford wrote a letter to Michael Barry (BBC Head of Drama) in which she apologised for 'letting fly!' He replied: 'I was deeply concerned to find you had been put to such distress on Saturday. Please feel that the need to speak strongly was fully understood . . . discipline is required as an essential part of artistic achievement. I was as angry as you at the bear-garden behaviour you had to witness. I wish I had arrived earlier, but trust you were not further inconvenienced. The incident was a slur on the pleasure we all had at seeing you back in television.'

No one can now remember what this unfortunate episode might have been and, happily, it did not affect the performance. *The Noble Spaniard* was greeted with enthusiasm by the critics: 'Mr Adrian Brown's production went rattling by with a dashing assurance . . . Miss Margaret Rutherford managed to free the spectacle of ardour in old age from embarrassment . . . she added some passages of superbly comic indignation,' said one, while another stated that the production had 'stared improbability boldly in the face, and passed on'. All in all, the play was extremely successful and received excellent notices. Robert Morley telephoned Adrian next day to say, 'You are the only director I know to get a performance out of Stringer Davis.'

Adrian subsequently became great friends with Margaret and Stringer, spending a couple of Christmases with them as their guest. He grew extremely fond of Margaret, and was touched by her generosity: 'She was always raking people in and looking after them.'

On one festive occasion they had invited some Australian actors they'd met on tour, including Ray Barrett who, while Stringer carved the turkey, regaled the guests with stories of Margaret swimming on Bondi beach, her voluminous bathing costume barely covering large expanses of flesh. This meal had been late coming to the table and a flustered Rutherford appeared at the door to say, 'I'm having a little trouble with the Brandy Butter', although after the plum duff had been enjoyed she smoked a cheroot by way of relaxation. Another time, Adrian, driving his mother out in his first car, daringly decided to 'drop in' at the Old Hall. They arrived at the rather grand front door to be met by one of Margaret's resident 'waifs and strays', to whom Adrian introduced himself. Requesting they remain outside, the self-styled 'lackey' swept off, returning shortly to announce: 'Mr and Mrs Davis would be delighted if you would join them on the terrace for afternoon tea.' Padding over the lawn, under the cypress tree, towards one of the grandest views in London, the callers were served a most civilised tea and some lively conversation, during the course of which Margaret turned to Adrian's mother and discreetly murmured: 'You must be very proud of him, Mrs Brown!' Adrian recalls the conversation with great affection. 'Such moments are not readily forgotten.'

There were no further dramas for the BBC but Margaret was interviewed for several factual programmes for radio during this period. *This Is Britain* was recorded at her home in Highgate. She talked on the arts programme *In Town Tonight* and made an appearance on the *Today* programme which ruffled a few of 'Auntie's' feathers and generated a memo from the producer, Jocelyn Ferguson:

Re: Donald Milner's interview with Margaret Rutherford
I thought it didn't do justice to Margaret Rutherford herself. She sounded hesitant, sentimentally feminist, and her lack of intelligence seemed all too obvious – none of her ideas were new or even old ones well expressed. This may be true of her private character, but the entertainment value at her expense didn't seem to justify

letting her down in public. Nor did I think the interviewing was up to Donald Milner's usual standard – his questions seemed contrived and too long winded. But for the sake of those who liked the piece, I was glad it got into the reel.

In January 1959, Margaret appeared on *The 1959 Show*, Associated-Rediffusion's New Year television spectacular, starring Tommy Steele, Diana Dors and Peter Sellers. Rutherford read a Hans Christian Andersen story – the first time she had ever done such a reading on television.

Margaret's only film appearance during this time was as Aunt Dolly in the 1959 film, *I'm All Right Jack*, a satire on British industrial relations in the 1950s, produced by the Boulting brothers and filmed at Shepperton. Peter Sellers plays Fred Kite, the Stalinist shop steward with idealistic dreams of Russia: 'All them cornfields and ballet in the evenings.' Dennis Price manipulates his Woosterish nephew Stanley Windrush (Ian Carmichael) in an escalating labour dispute which gradually leads to a general strike. Sellers, an extraordinary parody complete with a Hitler moustache, exhibits the versatility of his acting while his daughter, the lovely Liz Fraser, a spindle polisher at the missile factory is Windrush's romantic interest. Terry-Thomas is factory manager Major Hitchcock and Dennis Price and Richard Attenborough are duplicitous munitions manufacturers. Stringer had a few lines as a newspaper reporter.

In a sort of White Queen cameo, Margaret Rutherford has a few scenes as the aristocratic and reactionary relative of Windrush. There is a lovely scene with Irene Handl's marvellous Mrs Kite, which is full of awkward silences, the juxtaposition of social order and wonderful comic timing. *I'm All Right Jack* is all about caricatures – the factory workers are truculent and lazy, the managers are double-dealing public schoolboys – and the politics are somewhat muddled. The ambiguity is highlighted in Margaret Rutherford's character's behaviour, as noted by Roger Lewis: 'I do not understand how dowager Aunt Dolly . . . all bosom and bustle and breathing fire, can witter about "one of those horrid unions" and yet then, when there is a General Strike, and people are waving banners and cheering, she's proud to announce, "What a nation we are once we are stirred!"'

West End theatre work had proved meagre for Margaret towards the end of the decade. James Stewart had talked of bringing *Harvey* to the London stage, and wanting Margaret to co-star, but unhappily this didn't come to fruition. In December 1958 she appeared in a short season of *Alice Through the Looking Glass* in Brighton, but it was not until January 1959 that she was approached to undertake a more substantial stage role.

Farewell, Farewell, Eugene began its provincial tour at the Grand Theatre, Leeds, on 30 March 1959. The play, which concerns the efforts of two sisters to visit a diamond-prospecting relative by writing Christmas card verses, transferred to the Garrick Theatre on 5 June 1959. The piece was adapted by Rodney Ackland from the American original by John Vari and was directed by William Chappell. Margaret played yet another eccentric, although she thought that the part was broad enough for her to portray a serious side to the character and not just provide comic relief. Margaret had agreed to do the play in New York, but only if it was initially produced in London. Peggy Mount played her sister, and the cast also featured Philip Lowrie, Avril Elgar, Frances Guthrie and Brook Williams. For once Stringer didn't have a part.

Reviews were mixed, with the *Manchester Guardian* calling the play, 'A desultory farce – the trouble is that although the joke does not collapse it does not develop either,' and *The Times* stating: 'Peculiarities are given a great deal of strongly individualised humour and pathos . . . for Miss Rutherford life is perpetually springtime. She finds a bottle of pale ale irresistible and, if not restrained, would go through a box of liqueur chocolates like a dipsomaniac. A vulgar party upstairs makes her feel like a tethered balloon.' The *Daily Telegraph* declared that, 'The play is hampered by monotony . . . it seemed like a recipe for a good play, and one left the Garrick wondering why it hadn't come off. As it is nothing much happened.' The *Observer* was more positive: 'Her rebellion against her vampire of a sister is intensely funny and in the clowning there is a touch of hysteria that is moving and almost frightening. Miss Rutherford – it's time to say it – is not only a great comic but a great actress. I know that she acts in a highly personal manner, yet what we see is not Margaret Rutherford, the actress, but a woman of the Margaret Rutherford type, and in real life there are women we can only describe by referring to her. If acting can be called creative, here surely is a high example.' The *Daily Mail's* critic was of the opinion that, 'The very sight of these actresses together reduced most of last night's audience to helpless laughter.'

Damaris Hayman was always invited to Margaret's first nights and remembers a delightful dinner at Prunier's afterwards. Although Margaret enjoyed better health while appearing in *Farewell, Farewell, Eugene*, there was one incident during the run when she suffered a minor fall, and was unusually belligerent following her arrival at the theatre. Damaris was contacted, and arranged for Margaret's doctor to go backstage and administer a sedative in the dressing room.

The show had already been in production for seven weeks when young actor Philip Lowrie, still at RADA and unable to believe his luck, joined the cast. Now with a long list of theatre and television credits, and probably best known as Dennis Tanner, Elsie's son, in *Coronation Street*, Lowrie was just beginning in the business when he found himself appearing on the West End stage in the company of Margaret Rutherford and Peggy Mount. Having seen the play before he started rehearsing and worked initially with the understudies, Lowrie then did a dress rehearsal with Mount and Rutherford. He was cast as a young, banjo-playing cockney and had about four scenes with Rutherford, including a raucous rendition of 'Knees Up Mother Brown'. Margaret actually revealed her bloomers during the dance sequence – which Peggy Mount didn't approve of, telling Lowrie, 'That's a very cheap way of getting a laugh.'

Lowrie described both character actresses as wonderfully kind. Peggy Mount used to bring in a selection of shrimps and crab to share each week with the cast. The young actor used to stand in the wings and watch 'Miss Rutherford'. 'She would always give her all and if she failed to get a laugh with one line she made sure that she got an extra laugh somewhere else in the play. The audience adored her. One night Prince Rainier and Princess Grace came to the play, which distracted the rest of us, although Margaret was wonderful as ever!'

Lowrie wasn't the first to describe Margaret Rutherford as 'a fresh air fiend'. By the time November came, her dressing room was often cold and draughty, as the window was constantly open whatever the weather. One evening the assistant director told Philip that, 'Miss Rutherford would like to see you in her dressing room.' At first, he was concerned that he was in trouble, but couldn't work out what he may have done to upset the actress. She occasionally invited him in for a Dubonnet before the show. Perhaps this was the answer – a pre-show aperitif. He would have to brave the freezing cold dressing room and would make sure he was well wrapped up. When he knocked on her door, he discovered one of the other cast members, Frances Guthrie, was already inside.

Miss Rutherford explained that she had a friend coming in to see that evening's performance who was rather deaf and unfortunately was to be seated at the back of the stalls. Margaret was worried about her friend missing some of the dialogue. She thus asked if Frances and Philip could 'raise your voices and deliver your lines a little louder than usual so that my friend will be able to hear everything clearly'. Philip later discovered that there had been some grumblings that Miss Guthrie had not been projecting enough and it was difficult to catch all her lines. Margaret had created this story of her friend in order to get the message across to the relatively inexperienced Guthrie while avoiding any note of criticism. She had asked for Philip to be there so that Miss Guthrie would not feel singled out.

While appearing in the production, Margaret would sometimes

walk from her home in Highgate to the theatre: luckily the route was mainly downhill. She caused quite a stir striding through the London streets in her favourite bottle green cloak and being greeted by passers-by at every opportunity. Stringer would meet her at the Garrick after the performance and accompany her home. Neither Stringer nor Margaret drove, but they kept an account with a cab firm.

Farewell, Farewell, Eugene ran for eight months, during which time Philip Lowrie and the rest of the cast enjoyed 'a wonderful time'. In the summer, the company were invited to Old Hall for garden parties. On one visit the guests were told that they were all going swimming – costumes and cars were provided and they were all whisked away to the Hampstead Heath Lido where Margaret Rutherford donned a floral swimsuit with frilly skirt and matching bathing cap. She happily took to the water with gay abandon and much splashing, completely disregarding the astonished looks from the assembled onlookers.

On the last night of the run, Philip and Margaret had finished their dance routine and had milked their customary applause, Rutherford gazed at her partner and, with eyes twinkling, announced, 'And one more time!' Much to Philip's amusement, they did indeed repeat the dance all over again. Margaret was invited by French dancer and choreographer Roland Petit to appear in a midnight gala for charity in aid of the victims of the Malpasset dam disaster in Fréjus, South of France. She immediately asked Philip if he would join her on stage in their 'Knees Up Mother Brown' routine, to which he readily agreed.

In April 1960, Margaret was contracted to appear in a BBC television play, *Day After Tomorrow*, written by her friend Frank Baker. Rutherford played Amy Carr, an ageing spinster, with Noël Purcell as Peter O'Connor. Joan Hickson (the landlady) and Stringer (clergyman) also featured. The play centres on Miss Carr, who lives in a bed-sitting room overlooking Primrose Hill in London. Her chief problem is the unhappy relationships she has with her landlady and her fellow lodger, who are conspiring to admit Amy into an old people's home. The sympathetic friendship which she strikes up with Peter

O'Connor, an old sailor, helps to reduce her loneliness. Critics generally felt that the play was mawkish and sentimental and only saved by Rutherford's performance as the lonely pensioner.

Margaret was also involved in a radio version of the play, produced by Charles Lefeaux. In a letter to her in June 1960, Lefeaux wrote to Rutherford, explaining that *Day After Tomorrow* had to be re-written. 'This means I'm afraid that the Clergyman which Stringer played is no longer on the cast. I know how disappointed you will both be but I fear it was inevitable in the new medium.' Mr Lefeaux had also corresponded with her earlier in the year: 'I am going to produce a rather stylish version of *The Way of the World* for the *Third Programme* with Dame Edith [Evans] and Sir John [Gielgud] and hope that you will be free and would like to play Lady Wishfort.' Margaret agreed, of course, and turned in a delicious performance.

ELEVEN

Of Arab Princes, Transsexuals and Hollywood Stars

'I didn't like the play. But I saw it under unfavourable circumstances – the curtain was up'

GROUCHO MARX

MARGARET RECEIVED AN unexpected visitor while appearing in *Farewell, Farewell, Eugene.* Prince Juan, a member of the Jordanian Royal family and the estranged brother of King Hussein, had, of course, in the time-honoured tradition of a 'Stage Door Johnny', initially presented his gold embossed card to the Garrick's amused stage door keeper, and was directed to Miss Rutherford's dressing room. She was extremely flattered that this fair-haired, handsome, blue-eyed Prince professed to be one of her greatest fans.

The friendship developed and the prince was a regular visitor backstage, occasionally bestowing gifts, such as 'a charming Victorian silver sweet dish'. He also dined at Old Hall, always immaculate in apparel and manners – he wore blue silk-lined opera cloaks and carried an ivory baton. Prince Juan would tell stories of glorious temples, desert secrets and boyish pranks at the royal palace. Damaris Hayman met him on a number of occasions and agreed that he was, indeed, a very pleasant young man – 'But something wasn't quite right and it was Margaret's Australian friends who were first suspicious of his motives'. The delightfully myopic Margaret and Stringer were totally oblivious of any possible skulduggery: 'If our friends began to put doubt in our minds about the authenticity of the prince, Stringer and I accepted him exactly as he was. The fact that as, a Moslem, he should not have eaten pork or drank alcohol, which he did, never disturbed us. It was not our business.'

Then, one day, the couple were unable to contact Juan about an arrangement, so Stringer telephoned the Jordanian Embassy to ask for his address. An official told him: 'There is no Prince Juan. He does not exist.' Even then Margaret refused to believe that her royal friend was an impostor, and considered whether the Prince could be a political exile. Even she and Stringer had to consider the truth when soon afterwards they received a letter from the prince, explaining that he was not exactly an Arab prince – he was, in reality, a Portobello Road antique dealer, who had spent time in prison on 'a false cheque' charge. He invited the Davises to lunch to explain himself and managed to convince them that his little fraudulent indiscretion 'was nothing to do with his imper-sonation of a prince' but merely because 'he loved beautiful silver'.

In regard to his royal deception that had so beguilingly disarmed them, Margaret and Stringer were utterly forgiving. 'He had played the fairy prince role so beautifully that we played it with him and did not ask ourselves. He had taken us on his magic carpet to lands and experiences that we would never have known about. If he had been genuine he could not have been more of a gentleman, behaved better or been more like a real prince. He brought us so much pleasure and happiness.' Damaris Hayman confirmed that, 'Margaret didn't care that the "Prince" was a charlatan. He was interesting, excellent company and she liked him very much.'

*

For the two months since the end of the London production of *Farewell, Farewell, Eugene* Margaret had been unemployed, so she and Stringer had plenty of time to busy themselves with preparations for the Broadway transfer. The play had enjoyed immense success in London and it was thus with great excitement that, on 11 August 1960, Margaret and Stringer climbed the gangplank in Southampton and boarded the *Queen Mary* for the five-day voyage to New York. Directed to their berth, they unpacked the usual paraphernalia. They needn't have bothered. Although there was no sign of Fred Kite, a genuine trade union dispute had unfolded and the ocean liner was prevented from sailing. While awaiting the outcome of the negotiations, the Davises spent a week at the Haven, a hotel in Sandbanks where Margaret autographed a number of wooden spoons, booby prizes for the darts team. Eventually, it was decided that Margaret and Stringer could wait no longer for the sea passage and they were directed to travel to New York by air.

On arrival in Manhattan, the couple rented an apartment in the Oliver Cromwell hotel on West 72nd Street. 'We had breathtaking views and looked down on twinkling lights below us – the first night we had our usual supper of eggs and bacon, but we did miss our ginger marmalade.' Margaret's initial task was not, in fact, to find a jar of the favoured preserve, but to locate a swimming pool. However, she and Stringer soon discovered Jones Beach, on the Atlantic coast, and despite the size of the Ocean's rollers the couple adopted the location as a favourite swimming haunt. This was the first time Margaret had returned to the city since the 1947 *Importance of Being Earnest* tour. She recalled her favourite walk – across the George Washington Bridge. Stringer's quest was more varied – before doing some reconnaissance on local jazz clubs, he was dispatched to purchase a pressure cooker.

In an interview with the *New Yorker* magazine, Rutherford introduced her collection of stuffed toys to the bemused journalist, including the brown fur rabbit, which sported a two piece velvet suit:

'That's Minnie. I've had her sixteen years.' When the subject of American sub-culture was raised unexpectedly, Margaret announced, 'I'd be proud to be a beatnik, if they'd have me. To me anything unusual is a joy. Your American beatniks behave in an individual way and they're vivid not dun coloured like most people.' She explained that she didn't like to spend more than six months in a play. Stringer, described in the article as 'white haired and pink faced', explained that this was because 'Margaret is such a dynamo. She has such electricity in her body – I gave her a watch last Christmas and it went all askew when she first wore it.'

In hindsight, Margaret didn't need to worry about spending more than six months in this particular production. At the commencement of rehearsals, she wrote: 'Mildred Dunnock, who had the smallest feet I have ever seen – like an Elizabethan child – greeted me warmly, "I am so happy to meet you – I am looking forward to working with you."' This was probably the highpoint of the process. The director of the play was relatively young and unpractised and there were immediate problems. According to Rutherford, 'Sparks flew and the whole cast demanded a new and experienced director.' Each member of the cast had different ideas about how to proceed and who should fill the director's shoes. Margaret's contribution was to call for phenobarbitone and take to her bed.

There was talk of postponing the opening, but the cast decided to persevere. The demanding rehearsal schedule, in combination with press demands and the stultifying humidity, caused Margaret some distress. Throughout most of her career, she had needed an afternoon sleep, and due to the circumstances, she was now afforded only a fifteen-minute nap.

It came as no surprise that when *Farewell, Farewell, Eugene* finally opened on 27 September 1960 at the Helen Hayes Theatre, the critics murdered the show, and it closed after just seven performances. *The Herald Tribune* called the production 'one of those comedies in which Eugene never appears, neither except for Miss Rutherford, does the comedy'. Howard Taubman in the *New York Times* wasn't sympathetic: 'Margaret Rutherford goes through an assortment of her comic routines – she runs the gamut of physical contortions, double takes and rubber-faced reactions – maybe she was finding the play hard to carry off?' An unnamed critic pronounced that, 'This is an entirely trivial play . . . Rutherford clowns and prances and with the aid of Mildred Dunnock serves to make the early scenes completely incomprehensible . . . over-acting galore.'

Rutherford proclaimed herself 'heartbroken', and felt she had let 'my American public down'. She and Stringer didn't return home, however, but remained in New York. She comforted herself with some poetry readings, including one at a school where she trotted out her old favourite, 'The Lady of Shalott'. She also appeared on Gloria Swanson's weekly radio show, and the couple spent time with Mildred Dunnock and her husband at their home in Connecticut. While in New York, recovering from one of her few theatrical flops, Margaret was contacted by Dorothy Mather, informing her that she had received better news. Margaret had been asked to do a film, *On the Double*, in Hollywood with Danny Kaye. This meant she had to stay a little longer in the city before flying out to California.

It was thus that Margaret, who presumably now had more time to hang out with the beatniks in Greenwich Village, encountered another extraordinary character who was to have a huge impact on her life and, indeed, even more of an impact on how she would be remembered after her death.

Gordon Langley Hall, a British writer living in New York, had sent Margaret a copy of his book, *Me Papoose Sitter*, about his life as a teacher on the Gull Bay Ojibways' 'First Nation' tribal reserve in Canada. Hall supposedly wanted Margaret to play a part in the proposed film of the book and arranged a meeting at the Helen Hayes Theatre. 'He came round to my dressing-room. He was such a good-looking manly gentleman, immaculately dressed with a nifty bow tie.'

Margaret's idea of manly seems different from the usual understanding: Gordon was definitely not 'manly' in the macho sense. In fact Damaris Hayman described him as 'a rather camp young man'. In any case, Margaret liked him straightaway and felt an instant rapport. At the time Gordon was living with Isabel Lydia Whitney, artist and muralist, in her expansive New York mansion, but he later moved to Charleston, South Carolina.

Gordon claimed that he had been born in Sussex in and that his father, Jack Copper, had been Vita Sackville-West's chauffeur. (These were the first of many deceptions: it subsequently came to light that he was born Gordon Kenneth Ticehurst in 1922.) He later wrote, 'When we met in 1960, Stringer and Margaret's hearts were touched by me and they asked me to join their family.' Although he was never legally adopted, he coyly referred to Stringer as 'Father' and Margaret as 'Mother Rutherford' from then on. There is no doubt, however, that there was an affectionate relationship between them, which was nourished by regular correspondence and Gordon's occasional visits to England.

Gordon had always professed that he had been born a girl and that at birth his clitoris was so swollen that the medical staff didn't know which gender to ascribe him. 'In Britain in those days, when in doubt, the child was automatically registered as a boy. Then when I was between twelve and fourteen there were irregular bleedings that were, close relatives told me, "to be bravely borne but in secret".' He maintained that after his move to South Carolina, 'Fate took a hand – I became violently ill with more bleeding and was rushed to hospital.' He documented that the nurse pulled back the sheet, whereupon she got the shock of her life – for there lay a beautiful woman! According to Langley Hall, he consulted a number of doctors who 'found that I was physically changing'.

Fortunately Margaret and Stringer were blissfully unaware of Gordon Langley Hall's physical traumas when they left New York and flew to Los Angeles for *On the Double*. They had asked the studio to provide accommodation near to the coast in order to satisfy Margaret's need for ocean air, and Paramount had dutifully arranged a room at the Shangri-La hotel in Santa Monica. The hotel in that period was an architectural gem and historic landmark – a beacon of Deco beauty that boasted Pacific Ocean views from every room. The couple loved staying in Santa Monica, and particularly enjoyed relaxing on the extensive beach and taking to the surf. A piece in *Life* magazine described the couple swimming backstroke in the sea and was accompanied by a priceless picture of Margaret kicking her legs energetically in the water. She was quoted as saying: 'Swimming is my only real exercise. Even if the water is shallow, you can roll around and feel fresh. When I come out I feel like a new woman.'

Margaret soon made her presence felt in the City of Angels. She and Stringer were collected from the Shangri-La at 6.30 a.m. on the first day's shooting by chauffeur-driven Cadillac. They didn't travel light – even to spend a day at the studio – and their accoutrements included hamper, suitcases, rugs, cushions, baskets and bags. Margaret remembered that, 'The suitcases were too tall for the shallow boot, the hamper didn't fit either, so all this had to be packed on the front seat. We then climbed in through the two front doors to the back seat. When we arrived at the studio gate the commissionaire had heard of us but was not sure whether we had been given a dressing-room. The embarrassed driver pulled up at a sidewalk and dumped us there with all our belongings while he went off to find out what was happening.'

It was not a terribly glamorous arrival in Hollywood, but typically Rutherfordian. 'We did feel a little foolish squatting on our piles of luggage.' But Margaret was soon greeted by a number of extras and studio employees who recognised her and greeted her like royalty. She and Stringer were helped to her accommodation, a cottage, which she described as having its own front door portico: 'There were ordinary street lamps and a stone-flagged pavement. Inside the front door was a sitting-room with a sofa, table and writing desk . . . behind this wall was a small changing room and then a bathroom and little kitchen with the inevitable fridge.'

She later wrote to Dorothy Mather: 'I am taking a breath before the real thing starts but have met Danny Kaye. He seems more like a carefree schoolboy than anything. He gave a welcoming tea party for me on our stage, no speechifying or anything like that, thank goodness. There was a large samovar and Danny did the pouring. Dana Wynter, seated on his other side, remarked suddenly: "It has an alarming kick." (Mr Kaye had amusingly added a little bourbon to the tea.)' He asked Margaret where she was staying in Los Angeles, and when she replied that she was at a hotel in Santa Monica so that she could go swimming every day, Kaye replied: 'Oh, you're too hearty for me.'

Margaret found film-making at Paramount much more serious than at the British studios that she had been used to. 'I have often been asked if there is much difference in the technique of making films in Britain and America. It was the extreme professionalism of Hollywood that impressed me. The first day on the floor there was scarcely any talk at all. Noise was cut down to a minimum while the crew found their way about.' She and Stringer were also fascinated by the fact that Paramount also had a permanent cowboy set which was used for their impressive output of Westerns over the years. She and Stringer took the opportunity to watch some filming and were particularly impressed by the behaviour of the horses: 'There came the call for "action" and I have never seen anything like it in animal life. One moment they had their noses right down . . . and then within a distance of no more than three yards both those horses were in action. They raised their heads and went into it with the cowboys. At full gallop they rode through the set with everyone waving, turned a corner and disappeared.'

Margaret adapted to studio life pretty well and enjoyed soaking up the atmosphere of the grand Hollywood tradition. 'During the midday break we ate at the restaurant and I was especially impressed by the way the memory of Cecil B. DeMille was honoured. The table where he always sat has been made into a permanent memorial with his picture and I think some props from one of his films. It is a kind of little shrine in his memory and no one ever sits there. I also liked the aura of tradition about Paramount Studios. After all, beautiful films have come out of Paramount all one's life.'

One day, Margaret was sitting in her cottage when she took a telephone call from Dorothy Mather about the television play, *The Two Wise Virgins of Hove*, which she had been offered on her return from America. She happened to look out of the window to see a figure she recognised immediately. When not on location in Nevada, Clark Gable had been filming studio scenes for *The Misfits*. Rutherford put the telephone down and went outside on the doorstep with Stringer, where they watched Gable walk away. For some reason, the actor turned around and, seeing the intrigued couple observing him, waved at them. Word had got around about the troubles on the set while filming *The Misfits*. Rutherford thought Gable looked tired and jaded: 'I suddenly got the impression that he was waving as if he was saying goodbye to films, goodbye to everything. It was a strange feeling . . . just a few months later he died from a heart attack.' Margaret returned to her telephone call to find an exasperated Dorothy Mather still hanging on.

Rutherford also claimed to have met Marilyn Monroe, another star of *The Misfits* – famously her last screen appearance. Rutherford recalled that, 'The dear waif-child, whom life and Hollywood were destined to destroy, came into my dressing room to lay her sad little face in my lap and was soon asleep.' It is impossible to authenticate the details of this particular rendezvous, but both Monroe and Rutherford were certainly at Paramount at the same time.

On the Double is a World War Two comedy (a spoof on the book *I Was Monty's Double*) in which an American GI (Danny Kaye) poses as a British General and hoodwinks the Nazis on the eve of D-Day. Rutherford played the General's bombastic aunt Lady Vivian, and she and Kaye team up to provide a shaky rendition of the Highland fling. The actress described Danny Kaye as one of the greatest comics in show business and claimed that they soon developed a mutual respect and rapport. There was some trouble on the set, however, when Margaret discovered that Kaye's working practices were very different from her own. Kaye liked the idea of spontaneity and wasn't keen on filming a scene repeatedly until it was absolutely right. He didn't strive for perfection in this manner – even if technically there were errors. This certainly didn't chime with Margaret's idea of working – every take of hers was different and she liked to feel her way into the part. Actor Alan Cuthbertson also remembered that, 'Margaret Rutherford had other problems with Danny Kaye. She wanted to speak in the broadest Scottish accent, but Danny told her no one could understand what she was saying. She didn't like that at all.'

The film was not particularly well received by critics. The *New York Times* described the piece as 'a melancholy dive into self plagiarism'. Nonetheless the whole sojourn had been hugely enjoyable overall and Rutherford wrote: 'Our farewell to Hollywood was just as efficiently organised as the entire production had been.' Tellingly she made special mention 'that everyone had worked to see that the tax figures and everything were in order – a most tiresome business for any actor'. She said her goodbyes to Danny Kaye and described 'a gay little crowd of studio officials who came to see us off'.

The quintessentially English couple had loved America but were pleased to be home again by the end of November. Margaret and Stringer had relinquished their 'Old Hall' flat when they went to the USA in the summer and so, on their return, went to stay at the Ethorpe Hotel in Gerrards Cross. They needed to recover from their Hollywood adventure, but also had to acquire permanent accommodation. While decamped in the hotel, they walked the Buckinghamshire country lanes of their early courtship, Margaret describing the country air as being 'like nectar'. One evening the couple stumbled across a house off the beaten track with a 'For Sale' notice outside. They made an offer the following day and before long were able to move in.

It later transpired that the property, at 66 Oak End, Gerrards Cross, was situated immediately next door to the town's unmanned fire station – a loud bell rang to warn the firemen to down tools' from their gainful employment jobs and come to the station. The bell sounded frequently during the summer and regular visitors to Oak End used to be driven to distraction by the noise. Somehow, Stringer and Margaret never seemed to notice the din . . .

The television play that Margaret had read while in Los Angeles was broadcast on 22 December 1960. *The Two Wise Virgins of Hove*, an ITV Television Playhouse, featured Margaret as Emily Bagnold and Martita Hunt as her friend Mabel. Following several unexplained visions, the elderly Emily and Mabel decide to leave Hove and rent a villa in Jerusalem. This production was not a happy experience for Margaret. Miss Hunt liked a drink and could be very difficult. In fact, everyone on the set was terrified of the one-time Miss Havisham – including Margaret, who did not approve of her fellow actress's behaviour and told her so.

Unfortunately Rutherford's next production was to prove even more miserable. *Dazzling Prospect*, in which Margaret reprised her role as Bijou Furze in a belated horse-racing sequel to *Spring Meeting*, was to be directed by an uncertain John Gielgud. Girlegud's diary entry on 27 March 1961, from *A Life in Letters*, stated: 'We start rehearsing the play today. I am not much looking forward to the next two months, unless the play turns out to be more than I anticipate.' His mood had picked up a month later: 'The Irish play is neat and funny. Margaret Rutherford is immense, in every way, and such a duck. I think it bodes admirably if the critics don't slash it as being snobbish and old fashioned. We have had very agreeable and unhurried rehearsals. I hope we are not over optimistic.'

Another member of the cast, Sarah Miles, had gone straight from RADA into the production, playing an upper-class beatnik called Aaron Fox Collier. Miss Miles explained in her autobiography, *A Right Royal Bastard*, that she respected Gielgud a great deal: 'Such dapper style and inborn good manners . . . but he did have a penchant for changing all our moves daily.' She described how he would come into almost every rehearsal and announce: 'Good morning, everyone, you're all going to have to be very patient with me today, I'm afraid, because I want to start again from scratch, I'm so terribly sorry.'

Miles very much enjoyed working with Rutherford and declared Margaret and Stringer a perfect couple: 'So much in love with each other. They'd have to be, because Stringer had the habit of reading poems out loud all the time, his own poems, naturally, and Stringer, bless his heart, was no poet.' She recalled one of Stringer's efforts:

> Poor little Robin Redbreast had a terrible cold.
> But robins don't get colds, not ever so I'm told.
> 'We do get colds, we do, we do!' I hear a robin cry,
> 'Eagles and lions get colds too, the same as you or I.'

The subject matter was close to Stringer's heart – or should I say head. Miles described poor Stringer's propensity to such infections. As he recited his latest verse to the cast he was often battling sniffles: 'He'd sometimes have to wipe his nose, at which point Margaret would nudge me and wink. Love, compassion, patience, and above all, humour sparkled in that wink.'

Before the London opening, scheduled for 1 June, the company first visited Dublin and then toured England. Wherever they visited, Margaret insisted on finding a suitable place to swim, enlisting the help of Miles, who became her swimming partner and whose job it was to discover the location of the local pool or appropriate stretch of water and ensure that she transported her elderly companion there every morning.

Sarah Miles wrote: 'She would insist on swimming every day, come hell or high weather and, believe me, it was damn near freezing on that tour. She wore a black utility swimsuit with little legs. Oddly enough, she wasn't as fat in the altogether as she seemed on stage. I can see her now, the furious wobble of her turkey bits as they hung beneath her clenched and stubborn jaw. How she'd grind her teeth and roll her eyes, around and around they went as she plucked up courage for the plunge! Some people are never old, even though their bodies seem to tell another story. Margaret's spirit on those early-morning swims filled me with sprightliness that I didn't think I had any more – and I was sweet seventeen.'

During the second act of a Hull performance, in the middle of the tour, Sarah realised that the Tannoy had gone strangely silent. Margaret was supposed to be on stage but had clearly missed her cue: 'I ran into her dressing room, to find her fast asleep in her chair. I gently woke her up.' Margaret was justifiably horrified. 'Oh, God, whatever next?' She grasped hold of Sarah Miles in a blind panic: 'Have I been missed, do you suppose?' The two of them rushed to the wings, where 'Margaret made a fine and hilarious entrance'.

In addition to her role as swimming companion, Miss Miles, from then on, was given the responsibility of ensuring Margaret's untimely slumber did not occur again. 'Fortunately it never did, nor would it even if I hadn't been there to play policeman, because Margaret was much too professional for that.' For the young actress, however, 'Things got steadily worse. *Dazzling Prospect* was turning decidedly dim, yet mum was the word. For it seems to be the done thing, when one is touring a new play round the provinces, never to utter home truths. One just keeps on saying how great everything is, even if the truth is that the play one is lugging around is an absolute crock of shit.'

It wasn't, however, the job of the critics to keep mum. On the final stage of the tour before its opening in London, the *Brighton Argus* reported: 'The humour varies from farce to farmhouse and is totally inadequate.' In the words of Sarah Miles, 'We all trundled our way like the mindless cattle to the Globe Theatre, Shaftesbury Avenue, slaughterhouse.' The opening night on 1 June was disastrous. 'By the interval my heart was in my boots. Why was the audience so uncannily quiet? I quickly went into Margaret's room, to take up my duty as a policeman to her dreams. No chance of her falling asleep that night, though – she was up and roaring, powdering not only her nose, but everything in sight.' Miles asked the veteran actress, 'Why is everything so strange out there?' Rutherford replied, 'If you think this is strange just wait for the curtain call.'

The two actresses were next to each other as the curtain call came, and braced themselves for the audience reaction. 'The curtains opened, the great wild beast bellowing, "Boo! Boo! Boo!" I was astonished at the fury emanating from everywhere . . . I could see the prompt corner nervously whispering, "Shall I bring the curtain down?"'

'No,' said Margaret. 'We'll stay here till they run out of ammunition.'

Noël Coward noted in his diaries: 'I went to the opening of *Dazzling Prospect* (by John Perry and Molly Keane). It was quite disastrous. Disgracefully directed by Johnny Gielgud. Booed wholeheartedly by the audience. Margaret Rutherford was funny at moments. Poor Joyce (Carey) struggled through a non-existent part. The whole thing was really shameful, and naturally enough got the most appalling reviews.'

It was true. The critics were merciless in their mauling. Bernard Levin, alluding to the play's racehorse connection, declared that the production was, 'Pitiful – you might say it is *Imbecility* out of *Staggering Incompetence* leading only to the horror of the denouement after 150 stupefying padded minutes.' Another wrote: 'Ye Gods what a terrible play – the failure was absolute – the production was as hopeless as the play – Miss Rutherford perambulated on stage like a vast pussy cat on wheels. As skilfully and hard as she works, the poverty of the authors' invention is a heavy handicap . . . outside of her performance there is nothing to enjoy.'

The play ran for just two weeks and the cast only discovered that they were coming off from an article in the *Evening Standard*. Sarah Miles was particularly upset about the effect it had on Margaret: 'I think she deserved better than that.' By all accounts, *Dazzling Prospect* should never have come under starter's orders.

TWELVE

And the Awards
Go to . . .

'Acting is an everlasting search for the truth.'

SIR LAURENCE OLIVIER

'Acting is merely the art of keeping a large group of people from coughing.'

SIR RALPH RICHARDSON

SEVERAL MONTHS AFTER the disappointment of *Dazzling Prospect*, Margaret Rutherford received an unexpected personal boost, confirming her position in the hierarchy of British theatre. In June 1961, Margaret's skill and dedication were recognized when she was awarded the Order of the British Empire by Her Majesty Queen Elizabeth, the honour given for her 'Outstanding Contributions to the Dramatic Arts'. She was delighted with the 'gong' and thrilled to be invited to the Palace.*

---

* Some years later, the Queen gave a reception for 400 guests to mark the 400th anniversary of Shakespeare's birth. A number of thespian dames including Flora Robson, Edith Evans and Sybil Thorndike were invited, as well as several theatrical knights (apart from Olivier, who was rehearsing for a National Theatre production of *Othello*). The Queen apparently informed Margaret: 'It is my husband's birthday

Margaret's only engagements that summer were in radio: in July, she featured in a Home Service broadcast, *How Pleasant to Know Mr Lear*, in which she read a selection of Edward Lear's verse. The actress wrote to the producer to say how pleased she was with the programme and that, 'My husband was quite enchanted.' She also recorded an appeal on behalf of the Hampstead Old People's Housing Trust. Fortunately, the autumn brought her some theatrical work, as well as an opportunity to travel abroad again – this time to Malta, to appear in a production entitled *Our Little Life*, described in its programme as: 'A study of the relationships between MEN and WOMEN – an unusual dramatic entertainment devised and directed by Basil Ashmore.' The programme of five one-act plays written by, among others, Strindberg and Chekhov was produced between 4 and 7 October at the Teatru Manoel, Valletta and also featured Jean Bloor, Margaret Whiting and Stringer.

Basil Ashmore's son, stage designer Elroy Ashmore, describes his father as a prolific director, producer and reviewer: 'He was also very good at taking the initiative. Being a near neighbour of Margaret Rutherford's, he felt able to ring her, totally out of the blue, and introduce himself. He also knew exactly how to push the right buttons.' Basil flattered Margaret by saying something along the lines of: 'You're a wonderful comic actress but I'm sure there's a great, serious actress in you trying to get out . . . come and work for me!' She was naturally flattered, not to mention tempted by the prospect of warm weather and dips in the Mediterranean. Elroy also suspects his father might have got the work in the first place by contacting the Manoel and saying, 'Employ me and I can get you Miss Margaret Rutherford.'

Margaret liked being on the island: 'How we loved Malta, the soft browns of the buildings of Valletta – the warmth of the people and

and you are going to sit next to him – so you can talk about the theatre.' Margaret also recounted that, 'I was asked to stay behind and have coffee with the royal family in their private sitting room. In came Princess Anne carrying a pile of her friends' autograph books for me to sign. Her Majesty was horrified, but of course I was delighted to plough my way through the books.'

joyousness of the people playing in the streets I found most endearing.' She described the Manoel Theatre, built in 1732 as 'one of the most beautiful that I have ever played in. Indeed, with the cleanest back stage that I have ever seen.' This apparent enthusiasm wasn't entirely genuine, as Elroy Ashmore remembers that she wasn't entirely happy with the Manoel's management, who she felt were doing everything on the cheap and not looking after her properly.

Rutherford felt the success of the production in Valletta was due to the fact that, in Malta, 'No one had such a rigid conception of the roles that I could play, whereas in England I was not accepted outside my usual medium of the eccentric lady.' Her words proved prophetic ten days later in London, when Croydon's Pembroke Theatre hosted a production of *Our Little Life*, in which she reprised her roles as the Marquise in *Indian Summer* by Alfred de Musset and Tante Katya in *Come Home My Children* by Margaret Turner. In an addition to the Valletta show, she also played Cora Tuft in a Henry James piece.

Milton Shulman's *Evening Standard* review was, as usual when it came to Margaret's work, quite vindictive: 'The production consists of six short plays whose chief merit is that they are mercifully short. Miss Margaret Rutherford occupies most of the evening and it is sad to see her floundering in dramatic waters too deep for her talents – she is a natural patron saint for the county set. But when she tries to be an aggressive American matron or flirtatious elderly Marquise, or an East European refugee, incongruity runs riot.'

Norman Shrapnel was somewhat more favourable: 'Miss Rutherford plunges into tragedy with all the verve and enthusiasm that she normally brings to lighter things – but with less splash.' He was less complimentary about Stringer Davis: 'His portrayal of Chekhov's little lecture on the harmfulness of tobacco made it seem like a circus performance.'

Margaret recognised that there were problems at the Pembroke – mainly due to the fact that the production was in the round. 'It wasn't helpful to the monologues and three of the first items were monologues. The audience just did not feel comfortable seeing the back of our heads or side views. One was desperately inclined to keep spinning like a top in order to accommodate all the viewers.'

Basil Ashmore's wife Barbara was also in the business – as a stage manager – and the Davises and Ashmores became very good friends. Elroy particularly remembers them celebrating the festive season together: 'Margaret Rutherford was quite an amazing person . . . and incredibly kind. On Christmas Day for about seven years in a row, when I was a teenager, Margaret would send a taxi to collect us and take us to the Ethorpe Hotel in Gerrards Cross for lunch.' Although mainly of a temperate nature, Elroy Ashmore recalled that if Margaret was upset by someone's ill-considered behaviour she wouldn't shrink from saying so. 'She couldn't stand people mucking about or not doing the right thing. During Christmas lunch, at the hotel, the diners always watched the Queen. Margaret was a staunch royalist and once, a couple at the next table were chattering throughout the Queen's speech. Margaret rounded on them quite fiercely. These people were quite taken aback, while cheerfully enjoying their plum pudding, when they suddenly found themselves being berated by the formidable Miss Rutherford!'

After lunch, they would all retire to Margaret and Stringer's for afternoon tea, served on Rockingham china from a large cosied teapot, before the car arrived to take the Ashmores home. Elroy remembers the house as an assortment of chintz, velvet curtains and lamp stands. Margaret's generosity wasn't, however, just for Christmas. As both Ashmores were employed in the theatre they weren't terribly well off. Margaret was well aware of this, and every month, for quite some time, Elroy's father was sent a bottle of whisky and his mother half a dozen bottles of wine. Elroy also believes that Rutherford secretly helped fund his attendance at art college.

In turn, Basil Ashmore also tried to help Stringer's career. Although he didn't think Stringer was a terribly good actor, the director sympathised with him having to live in Margaret's shadow. At one time, Basil telephoned to offer some work, but when Stringer found that Margaret wasn't in the play, he replied, 'Oh no . . . I couldn't possibly . . . not without Margaret!'

Towards the end of the year, Margaret Rutherford was invited to speak at the Women of the Year luncheon, in aid of the Greater London Fund for the Blind. The event was held at the Savoy Theatre, and the other special guest was balloonist and photographer, Rosemary Mudie. Margaret's final appearance of 1961 (also for charity: the *Evening News* 'Toy For A Sick Child Appeal') was on 22 December when she took part in the Royal Philharmonic Orchestra's Christmas concert of *The Toy Symphony*. Margaret attempted to play a tuba, 'bravely producing cuckoo sounds and managing a couple of feeble hiccups'. An unusual list of performers included Moira Lister, Edmundo Ros, Cliff Michelmore and Sir Len Hutton.

The New Year began with an exciting offer from John Gielgud to appear as Mrs Candour in *The School for Scandal*. It would mean a return to the West End and a chance to expunge the memories of *Dazzling Prospect*. The weekend before rehearsals began, Margaret and Stringer went down to Sussex to stay with Rumer Godden and her husband, James Haynes-Dixon, who had retired to the countryside. 'Margaret Rutherford loved the peace and quiet of the grounds and the tranquillity of the country house,' recalled Godden in a tape recording. Margaret needed to be back in London first thing on Monday morning to meet Gielgud and the rest of the cast but decided not to travel on the Sunday – instead opting for the 9 a.m. train from Hastings to London the following morning.

The four of them were up late on Sunday night attempting renditions of old music hall songs. Stringer, who played the piano for this impromptu entertainment, was particularly concerned that the quartet had failed to remember the lyrics of a number entitled '365 Days' and went to bed somewhat unsettled. On the Monday morning Rumer woke Stringer and Margaret at 6 a.m. with cups of tea, allowing them an ample period to prepare for the train journey, and left them to get ready. However, by 8 a.m. the couple had not appeared and time was pressing. The hostess went upstairs to find a helpless Margaret Rutherford, still in her dressing gown, belongings strewn around the floor, muttering, 'I mustn't be late.' Rumer got Margaret dressed, helped her pack and finally got her and Stringer and their belongings into the car when Stringer suddenly announced: 'Ah yes . . . I've got it. I remember the words to that song.' Stringer insisted they all get out of the car, return to the house, gather around the piano in the drawing room and listen to him patiently perform '365 Days'.

James Haynes-Dixon had to drive like a maniac to get to the station, where the train was about to depart. Going on ahead to warn the ticket collector, he managed to engage a porter, and an unhurried Rutherford strolled down the platform, still completely oblivious to the time. She thanked Rumer and her husband graciously for their hospitality, wished the porter farewell and shook hands with the station master.

'No one was irritated at the delay,' according to Rumer Godden. 'There were no banging of carriage doors or whistles being blown furiously. The passengers were, in fact, "entranced", and when the train finally left the platform, there was a smattering of applause from the commuters.' This was 'just typical of the great love that people gave and got from Margaret'.

Gielgud's production of *The School for Scandal*, Sheridan's comedy of manners which was first performed at Drury Lane in 1777, opened on 5 April at the Theatre Royal, Haymarket. The production cost £18,000, the most expensive H.M. Tennent had ever staged, and the cast was stellar, with Ralph Richardson and Anna Massey as Sir Peter and Lady Teazle, Daniel Massey as Charles Surface, Laurence Naismith as Sir Oliver Surface and Peter Barkworth as Sir Benjamin Backbite.

Despite the first week's takings, which were a box office record of £5,500, the critics were undecided regarding the production – though not about the talents of Miss Rutherford. *The Times*: 'Few sparks in all-star Sheridan . . . the tower is Miss Margaret Rutherford. Her Mrs Candour, wearing an immense headgear and dainty muff, perpetually engaged in what she would call 'double talk' and sucking up scandal like a fish sucking its way around a glass aquarium. And that is the quality that the greater part of the proceedings somehow lacks.' The reviewer in *Punch* wrote: 'Those parts of it that contained Margaret Rutherford's Mrs Candour and Laurence Naismith's Sir Oliver were very funny. Miss Rutherford's performance is right on the nail, a gobbling old turkey savouring every scrap of gossip, while hypo-critically denouncing scandal-bearers.' Caryl Brahms wrote: 'Margaret Rutherford is a National Theatre by herself. Certainly I cannot conceive of one without her. Because she does not merely get her laughs, she acts for them and can be (although it is not called for here) heartbreaking as well as so funny it hurts. Her Mrs Candour draws up scandal as the sun draws up the waters from the earth – strongly, naturally, inevitably. And her glee in sniffing the sweet incense of some wrecked reputation is equalled only by our own as we watch suspicions becoming certainties.'

The distinguished actress Anna Massey had been a neighbour of Rutherford when they both lived in Highgate and had often seen her around the village. 'She was marvellous – all tweeds and hooded hats,' said Massey, who was thrilled at the opportunity of working with the venerable performer she had long admired: 'Margaret Rutherford was a formidable talent – her blazing truth always came through and touched you. She could make you laugh and cry. She was always economical with her acting and never, never over the top. She always did less rather than more. A mistress of perfection.' She also recalled that Margaret suffered from terrible stage fright: 'She was terrified of forgetting her lines. She always came in early, got into make-up and sat in a darkened room with Stringer. I have seldom seen an actor so nervous before a performance. She never dried although if she did forget her lines she sometimes muddled them up or made them up, which created some difficulties with the other cast members. It's hard enough to play Sheridan when you have all your faculties and she battled bravely to say the right text. I felt for Margaret coping with such terror every evening.'

In her engaging autobiography, *Telling Tales*, Anna Massey admitted she 'found the play very demanding and felt somewhat at sea. Gielgud was an instinctive director, not a teacher, and sadly he lacked patience. I floundered and he could not help me. He also changed his mind all the time – we were forever incorporating his new ideas and when they didn't work he changed everything again.' Gielgud's style of direction can't have made it easy for Margaret to get hold of a part with which she was already struggling.

Another member of the cast with memories of Rutherford's performance is Benjamin Whitrow: 'She was very special as Mrs Candour. On her first entrance she would receive a round of applause, and her opening line, "Lady Sneerwell, how do you do today?," was accompanied by a curtsy. Then, very deftly, she turned and curtsied to the audience. Brilliant and charming. During the opening performances she was unsurpassed but she appeared to lose her confidence and timing as the run progressed.' The actor also confirmed that if necessary Margaret could be assertive. 'She was quite tough. One night on our way off after the final curtain someone turned the lights off too early. She roared out in the darkness. I was surprised by this unexpected show of anger.'

'Things were very hierarchical in those days,' recalls Whitrow. 'A party was given to celebrate Rutherford's seventieth birthday on stage after the show. Two trestles tables: one down stage for the cast, covered with a white tablecloth serving champagne and three-cornered sandwiches; the other way up stage with no tablecloth serving beer and four-cornered sandwiches for the crew. There seemed to be a vast divide between us. Before long, there was music. Margaret went straight up stage and grabbed the nearest stagehand, hauled him to the centre and started jiving with him. I have never forgotten this wonderful gesture. Soon others started to dance and the ice was broken.

Stringer liked to visit us in the dressing rooms and try out his card tricks. He was very nervous and would put his fag down still lit in the ashtray and light up another. We felt sorry for him. His devotion to her was absolute. I'm sure they were happy.'

Seven weeks into the run, Margaret recorded a television programme for the BBC: *Perspective Eccentricity*, in which she and poet John Betjeman were asked by Kenneth Kendall for their views on eccentricity and individualism. A few days later, on 28 May, she was taken ill and carried from her dressing room on a stretcher and taken to St Mary's Hospital. She received a get well letter from the BBC producer, who had read of her illness. She replied: 'I, myself, enjoyed the afternoon very much,' referring to the recent interview. 'It was a very high spot in the year's events and I am now recovered from a sharp attack of lumbago.'

It may well be that she experienced acute back pain, but, in a letter to Mark Whiston, Daniel Massey hinted at other possible causes: 'I adored her. She was sweet to me. She was probably ten years too late to play the part but she was a miracle and the timing, given the fact that she was on a pill to wake her and another to put her out, was miraculous.' Massey went on to praise the actress: 'It was a privilege – she made one feel special, partly through the exercise of her astonishing gift, but also because she gave so much to life. She knew exactly what she was doing. She had grace, a gentleness and a sense of wit and idiosyncrasies for the Gods. It was all too brief a meeting.'

The medication Massey referred to may also have contributed to Margaret's somnolent encounter with the infamous Haymarket ghost. The incident occurred when Margaret and Stringer were given permission to sleep in her dressing room at the theatre, because of threatened industrial action by train drivers due to take place the following day. Stringer was provided with a camp bed and Margaret occupied the comfortable sofa. She explained the experience in a BBC radio interview: 'It was in my dream, that I saw somebody in my dress cupboard. I saw a leg – the leg of a man. And of course there is a famous ghost who haunts the Haymarket, a former manager, called John Buckstone. And I felt he'd come to see me. I was really very pleased so I stroked his leg and I thanked him for coming.' Fortunately Stringer didn't wake to find Margaret sleepily stroking a strange man's thigh. However, the next morning, he confirmed that he'd heard Margaret calling out and, at the same time, 'had heard a door slam behind him'. But Rutherford explained: 'There was no door which could have opened. His was a waking experience of his presence and mine was a sleeping one, you see.' Fellow ghost-spotter Donald Sinden confirmed that, when he saw the apparition while playing at the theatre in the 1950s, he was definitely awake.

The School for Scandal played to packed houses for six months. On 13 October Rutherford was replaced by Gwen Ffrangcon-Davies and Geraldine McEwan took over from Anna Massey. Gielgud himself took over as Joseph Surface. According to the *Evening Standard* Margaret Rutherford left the show prematurely, due to 'prior commitments', but it is more likely that she was following her six-month rule and that the strain of playing the part was becoming too much for her. After London, the production toured the USA for sixteen weeks, including a seven-week season on Broadway at the Majestic Theatre.

Despite the trials and tribulations of a West End run, Margaret wasted no time in engaging herself in further work – this time courtesy of the cathode ray. On 17 October 1962, Margaret appeared in 'The Liar', a television episode in the series *Zero One*. She played the garrulous Mrs Pendenny, a passenger in a plane from Montreal to London, who accuses fellow passenger Robert Flemyng of murdering his wife, who has been found dead on the aircraft.

In another television play, *The Kidnapping of Mary Smith*, the following year, Margaret was a sweet old lady who witnesses a wages snatch in which a clerk is stabbed. The gang kidnap her but then have no idea what to do with her. The actress described her character as 'a woman of high principles . . . there must be atonement for offences committed and no half measures will do. It was something I particularly liked about the play. I do think it's important to know it's ethically sound in intent as well as having a delightful story.' The play was not a critical success but an unusually high number of viewers wrote to the *Radio Times* praising the play and her performance.

The Mouse on the Moon was a sequel to *The Mouse that Roared,* which starred Peter Sellers. He wasn't in the second film, but had recommended Margaret Rutherford to the director, Richard Lester. Lester's budget was restricted, but he was fortunate in that Cornel Wilde had just filmed *The Sword of Lancelot* at Pinewood, so Lester was able to make use of the existing sets. In *The Mouse on the Moon*, the plot follows an imaginary, Ruritania-type nation launching a space programme using local wine as rocket fuel. Rutherford receives top billing as Grand Duchess Gloriana XIII, ruler of the Duchy of Grand Fenwick. There is a bright start to the film in which she appears in full military regalia, astride a horse in a trooping the colour pastiche. Unfortunately the film gallops rapidly downhill after the opening scene. The script is weak and the story meanders. Despite her billing, Rutherford is not featured enough to keep the film interesting. The cast do their best: Ron Moody is as good as ever as a scheming prime minister, Terry-Thomas, sporting a red carnation and customary cigarette holder, is an inept MI5 agent. Frankie Howerd plays himself in a fleeting, rather peculiar appearance and British comedy stalwarts John Le Mesurier, Graham Stark and Clive Dunn are seen in cameo roles. An edition of *Time* magazine that summer described Margaret Rutherford as 'possibly the funniest woman alive'. Luckily the journalist couldn't have seen *The Mouse on the Moon.*

The film premiered at Cape Canaveral in Florida, just six years before the actual moon landing. Prior to the premiere, the studio arranged a press junket in New York to which astronauts and technical staff were also invited. When Margaret and Stringer initially arrived in the city, they were greeted by a stunt man adopting the role of Grand Fenwick's Ambassador, along with 'the Fenwickian military band': 'It was all very jolly but we were a little nervous. It seemed to be Hollywood hokum publicity and we wondered if we could keep it up.' On reaching Florida, Astronaut Scott Carpenter took Margaret and Stringer on a tour around the space center, and she also met fellow flyers Gordon Cooper and Walter Schirra. 'We got to know the astronauts informally when we went swimming in the hotel pool. They gave me a signed group photograph, which I cherish as one of my most unusual souvenirs.'

Following the Cape Canaveral extravaganza the couple flew to New York for another showing of the film, and stayed in a palatial suite in the celebrated Plaza Hotel. 'Our days were quite hectic,' wrote Margaret, 'as I never had fewer than three interview dates and often five, ranging from meeting top American journalists to appearing on the big television programmes including Johnny Carson's *Tonight Show*. Dinner with Hermione Baddeley at the Russian tea-room and a visit to the theatre to see Daniel Massey in the successful musical *She Loves Me* were the other bright spots. Before leaving New York the studio gave me a party at Sardi's. Then on to the beautiful plane home and who should be with us but 'Binkie' Beaumont and [theatre impresario] Prince Littler. Back to England indeed!'

Terence Rattigan came up with the idea for what turned out to be Margaret's next film when he was stranded at London Airport on his way to America to discuss a couple of Broadway projects. The airport had been closed temporarily and he was directed to the VIP lounge, where he observed the behaviour of the frustrated elite passengers. Rattigan developed a treatment and sold it to producer Anatole de Grunwald for nearly £40,000. The film's director, Anthony Asquith, whose professional relationship with Rutherford stretched back many years, asked Margaret to play the strident Duchess of Brighton. Initially, Margaret turned the role down, finding the character insubstantial. According to the actress, Rattigan rewrote the part, building it up, and, more significantly, also introduced a cameo role for Stringer.

Rehearsals for *The VIPs* began in December 1962 and the film was subsequently shot in six weeks at Boreham Wood Studios for MGM. The film features such a starry cast that Margaret Rutherford only receives billing after Richard Burton, Elizabeth Taylor, Louis Jourdan and Elsa Martinelli. Rutherford is an ageing aristocrat, reluctantly seeking a job in Florida to pay for the upkeep of her family seat in Sussex. Margaret remarked that she chose clothes that a duchess would ordinarily wear, 'So, along with my fur trimmed travelling coat, I chose a perfectly ordinary squashy green felt hat. I decided that the hat would make my part credible and be of some consequence.' Another prop from the wardrobe was a large bag in which she is constantly rootling around and trying to locate mislaid items. This 'bit of business' was based on Margaret's 'splendid crocodile bag in which things were inclined to get lost' and with which she always travelled. Her presence on screen is also always accompanied by jaunty background music.

The Duchess is a pill-popping eccentric: 'I've got two enormous purple things that apparently knock you out. I've also taken a couple of pep pills which have pepped me up all over. I'm flying already.' On the plane she refers to the stewardess (her old friend Joan Benham) as 'Conductress!' When asked to fasten her safety belt she looks horrified, 'But I haven't brought a seat belt. Have you?' she enquires of her fellow passenger. This line reprised her role in *Innocents in Paris*: she must have added it to the script. When the passengers disembark, Rutherford heads for the bar, where she orders a drink and climbs on to the bar stool, referring to flying as 'a ridiculous form of locomotion'. She swills her brandy like a vintage wine and inevitably the pills and alcohol combine radically so that she immediately becomes tipsy. Rutherford underplays this scene beautifully, when it would have been all too easy to ham it up.

Although she still doesn't have a huge amount to do in the film, Rutherford is quite wonderful. Despite the doughty nature of her character, she brings a touching vulnerability to the role: 'I'm Lady – not *a Mrs* – Brighton, although I sometimes wish I was,' she advises an airport official. In her first scene, when she checks in with airline employee Lance Percival, she is wearing the aforementioned green hat, which seems to have a life of its own. She refers to it as 'a brute' and has to keep tipping it back or jamming it on her head depending on its mood.

Stringer appears as an elderly waiter in the VIP lounge – there is a lovely little scene in which they discuss the Duchess of Brighton's home in Sussex. He suggests that the Duchess goes to bed, as she has fallen sleep in the lounge. She agrees but declares, 'On the bed not in the bed – otherwise the trumpet of doom wouldn't wake me.' Stringer gives her yet more pills, designed to keep her awake all night in case she misses her flight the following morning: 'I shall clearly arrive in Florida in an advanced state of drug addiction.' She throws her head back and, in a wonderfully comic moment, her hat inevitably falls off. They discuss her village in Sussex and she allows herself a moment of regret, describing her seat at Brighton and its daffodils. She recites from *The Winter's Tale*: 'Daffodils that come before the swallow dares, and take the winds of March with beauty.' This is all the more poignant, considering the resonances between character and actress. The Duchess's relative impoverishment mirrored Margaret's own financial plight, and Rutherford's increasing dependency on medication was all too similar to Her Grace's need for uppers and downers.

The principal storyline, however, is the love triangle between Burton, Jourdan and Taylor. This was supposedly based on an incident when Vivien Leigh had attempted to leave Laurence Olivier for Peter Finch – only to be thwarted by fog, which grounded their aeroplane. There are some nice moments for brash Australian businessman Rod Taylor, aided and finally rescued from financial ruin by his adoring and unconfident secretary Miss Mead (Maggie Smith, who was nominated for Golden Globe as Best Newcomer). Orson Welles plays a megalomaniac film mogul with tax problems, travelling with Italian starlet Elsa Martinelli.

Burton and Taylor were in the midst of a passionate affair, which created a huge amount of publicity for the film, and were paid a reported $3.2 million, which included a share in profits. According to Damaris Hayman, Liz Taylor had rather expansive requests in her studio accommodation: 'She apparently insisted on an extra large dressing room . . . in mauve. Two walls were knocked down to make a three-room suite, which included a queen-size bed.' In contrast, Margaret requested the provision of a baby Belling – a portable stove on which she and Stringer could make tea and her beloved bacon and eggs! Margaret wrote that she enjoyed acting with Elizabeth Taylor, although they didn't actually share a single scene. Stringer thought the future Mrs Burton much too grand. In a press interview at the time Margaret reiterated her desire to play the Egyptian Queen: 'I have always dreamed of playing Cleopatra but now I fear Miss Taylor has beaten me to it.' The film was mainly harangued by the critics as a sort of 'airport version of *Grand Hotel*'. However, it did extremely well at the box office and opened to record-breaking business.

Margaret Rutherford was recognised for her work in *The VIPs* when she won an Academy Award for the Best Actress in a Supporting Role. The 1963 category included her old cohort, Edith Evans, who was nominated for her role as Miss Western in *Tom Jones*. Margaret didn't attend the ceremony and the award was accepted on her behalf by Peter Ustinov. Although her performance merited an Oscar, many felt she had been overlooked in her previous role as Madame Arcati in *Blithe Spirit*, and that her exceptional work on the screen for nearly thirty years was deserving of such an honour. Margaret was absolutely thrilled to win the Oscar and it was always on display on her mantelpiece. She also won a Golden Globe and a Laurel Award for her performance as the Duchess of Brighton. In addition, at a Variety Club function at the Dorchester, Margaret was named Film Actress of the Year and received the gift of a silver heart.

It was also in 1963 that Margaret Rutherford had her portrait painted for the first time. Alex Portner's painting was exhibited at the London

Hilton in October, but at the unveiling Rutherford declared: 'I don't like it. I think it has an askance look – a quizzical expression. I know I'm no beauty. Perhaps it has an element of caricature. Still, it is as Mr Portner saw me.' Stringer was equally unimpressed: 'Mr Portner has presented my wife with a pale complexion which misses her lovely rose skin colour but it is a good likeness of Margaret in one mood.' There was a contradictory story in the *Daily Mail* in which Margaret publicly praised the painting: 'I think it's quite splendid!' The *Mail's* reporter wrote: 'Margaret Rutherford studied the portrait, attired in a grey and yellow floral dress, dangling gilt necklace and large brimmed straw hat. She said, somewhat quixotically, "The last time I wore this I was talking to Gordon Cooper, the astronaut."'

Portner later wrote to Margaret and Stringer from his Chelsea studio:

> I enclose a reproduction of the double portrait – it was shown for the first time at the Hilton Art Gallery, where it became the centre piece of the exhibition. It was quite surprising what affect the painting had on the facial expressions of people once they had caught sight of it. One moment before they had looked indifferent and pre-occupied, the next moment when seeing you, Margaret, their faces relaxed into smiles. To me, it was a wonderful experience seeing all those people expressing their love, devotion, and admiration for you and for the happiness you had given them.

In 1964 Margaret was asked to appear in a quirky American television documentary, *The Stately Ghosts of England*, based on the experiences of Tom Corbett, one of Britain's leading clairvoyants. She and Stringer are driven around in a Rolls-Royce Silver Ghost, visiting haunted houses with Mr Corbett. The locations were three of England's famous stately homes, Longleat, Salisbury and Beaulieu. Margaret acted as hostess at the various houses: 'I wore flowing gowns, my favourite green cape and a plethora of hats. Although the producers wanted me to play it for comedy, I decided to play it straight.' After the shoot, Tom Corbett threw a dinner party at his home in London and Margaret later discovered that there was a sound crew in the next room monitoring hidden microphones. 'The only metaphysical sound that they heard was my voice saying, "The Brussels sprouts are beautifully cooked."' Margaret later posed for a photograph, pretending to drive a vintage car, which was later produced as a picture postcard. *The Stately Ghosts of England* was shown on NBC in the USA in January 1965, but to my knowledge has never been broadcast in the UK.

Margaret's next vehicle also featured four wheels: *Solid Gold Cadillac,* written for Broadway by Howard Teichmann and George Kaufman, was a satire about crooked business practices. Margaret and her agent had lunch with American producer Arthur Lewis at the elegant Quo Vadis restaurant in Soho and persuaded him that she should be cast as Laura Partridge, the minor shareholder who asks awkward questions at a company's AGM and ends up with a job in the firm. The other principal was Sid James, but difficulties arose when it became clear that he wanted his name above the title. Rutherford and her agent were not happy about this, and after much discussion it was agreed that the two stars would share equal billing. Margaret liked Sid but certainly didn't approve of his womanising. Young actress Sheree Winton (Dale Winton's mother) played a glamorous blonde and was inevitably the target of Sid's amorous advances.

Rutherford wrote, 'After a chaotic dress rehearsal, the play opened in Birmingham in May. There were three highly complicated stage sets, which were mechanically moved in front of the audience. It was quite an experience for even the younger members of the cast, but Arthur Lewis, the producer, had assured me that if I stayed still I would end up in the right place.' Margaret would inevitably invite friends back to her hotel after the show and always managed to persuade the staff to re-open kitchen after midnight and cook everyone bacon and eggs.

The show transferred to London but opened at the Saville Theatre to poor reviews. Margaret's nemesis Milton Shulman was true to form.

'A creaky relic of some bygone days,' he wrote. 'It enables Margaret Rutherford, eyes popping, chins wagging, cheeks puffing, to repeat once again her familiar portraiture of an elderly female eccentric terrifying the hell out of a man too timid to defy her. The play is "obvious", trite, predictable and ponderous.' The *Daily Mail*'s critic called it 'Ghastly and unprofessional – Miss Rutherford mutters and twitches through the part, reducing it all to the same dull, damp level. A more preposterous piece of casting than Sid James I do not expect to see.' The critic in the *Daily Telegraph* was a little more appreciative: 'A Cinderella story and cheerful satire on "Big Business" . . . Cinderella is played by Margaret Rutherford, wearing some quite wonderful clothes and the air of enjoyment of an accredited witch whose magic has worked – she has a wonderful time.' *Plays and Players* decided that, 'A characterisation which depends largely on gargoyle imitations becomes rather thin when spread over an entire evening; and good supporting actress though Miss Rutherford may be, she cannot support a whole play. Sidney James is no Olivier . . . but is a tower of strength, amiably holding the play together.'

At the beginning of July, Margaret missed four days of the production due to 'overstrain and exhaustion' and was admitted to a nursing home. She returned to the stage, but remained a resident of the home. 'I was going through a very bad patch of ill health at the time with a doctor attending me at the theatre each night so that I could make my entrance. Once I got to the stage I was never nervous and enjoyed the production immensely. It was the getting on stage that was the effort. Each night after the show I would return to the nursing home to recharge myself for the next day's performance. As always it was a great help that Stringer was in the cast. He played the part of the company secretary.'

Margaret became depressed again at the end of the month and could no longer continue, leaving the play for good. On 27 July, the *Daily Mail*, under a headline which read, 'Star's Illness Closes Play', reported: 'Margaret Rutherford is out of the West End play for the second time through illness. The part will be undertaken by her understudy but the show will close on 4 September. She has a variation of her earlier illness.' The show's producer, Arthur Lewis said, 'Without her, the show's not there.'

Stringer was quoted in the press as saying, 'We think a bug has got her. Last week she was in fine form and went off for the weekend for electrical treatment, which she has been having since it was found she was suffering from depression. This week she was taken with a sudden dizziness and sickness and couldn't stand properly. Doctors tell us it's happening to people all around Gerrards Cross.' I can only assume that the he was referring to the sickness, and not suggesting the town's residents were all wired up.

The theatre scene had altered and *Solid Gold Cadillac* now seemed dated and out of time and place. Michael Billington summed up the change in sensibilities: 'In the early sixties, the chasm widened. If the previous decade was marked by generational division and conflict, the Sixties saw the young not merely rattling and shaking the culture but increasingly taking charge. Youth which had been knocking at the door in the previous decade finally attained the commanding heights in theatre, film, television, pop and fashion.'

Margaret Rutherford, always attracted by nonconformity, declared: 'I approve of long hair and colourful clothes for young men – as long as they wear them with distinction and are clean. Fashions have become ageless, too. There are fewer barriers between youth and age. I may not wear a mini skirt but I long to dangle myself with beads and fringes.'

The would-be flower child was sadly a couple of generations too old to embrace completely the 1960s zeitgeist of Mary Quant, Biba and *Barbarella*. She was definitely more Jane Marple than Jane Fonda.

THIRTEEN

A Stout-Hearted Sleuth

'I shall have your murderer for you in a few hours, Inspector.
Leave it to me.'

MARGARET RUTHERFORD AS MISS JANE MARPLE

MARGARET RUTHERFORD WAS first offered the part of Agatha
Christie's Miss Marple in December 1955 when she was sent
the script of *Death by Drowning* by BBC radio producer, H.B. Fortuin,
with an accompanying letter: 'I wonder whether you would see yourself
as Mrs Christie's intuitive spinster?' She didn't take up that offer and
even when the initial Miss Marple film was first mooted in December
1960, Rutherford wasn't too keen. 'I never wanted to play Miss Marple
in the Agatha Christie films. I didn't want to let my fans down by
involving myself in anything sordid. Murder, you see, is not the sort of
thing I could get close to. I don't like anything that tends to lower or
debase or degrade.' In light of her family background, it isn't surprising
that Margaret felt uneasy about the subject of murder. Although her
father's crime was not public knowledge, appearing on screen trying to
solve a number of killings – albeit in a light-hearted manner – was a
little too resonant.

However, Margaret discussed the offer with Dorothy Mather and then sought advice from her friend, the writer Alison Uttley, who persuaded the actress that, 'It is, in fact, a question of art, just as a murder in a morality play. It can be pleasing and entertaining and it does have a moral value of a sort. And one likes to throw one's weight on the side of good, doesn't one?' Rutherford said she was also encouraged to play the amateur detective by the director, George Pollock, who persuaded her that, 'Miss Marple was not so much concerned with crime, even though she was an indomitable sleuth always one stage ahead of the police, but that she was more involved in a game – like chess – a game of solving problems, rather than of murder.'

There was, though, a more pressing reason to take on the Miss Marple character, and one which had nothing to do with artistic integrity. Margaret and Stringer were broke, and had only just been rescued from bankruptcy with help from the Benns. Margaret admitted that she had always been quite hopeless with money: 'The only reason that I need or want it is so that I can enjoy it with my friends. At this period I was definitely not friendly with the income tax gentlemen . . . my financial worries had started some time before. I suddenly realised that I shouldn't have any income in the near future as the government were asking for every penny of it.'

Because of her inability to budget, Margaret owed a substantial amount in back taxes, which the authorities were now demanding. It wasn't that she didn't believe in paying taxes; it was just that she felt they were too high: 'I was determined that if they raised the taxes once again I would go to gaol. I would never have wanted to leave Britain and live abroad, as others have done, but I would have to make a stand before I let myself be driven out by the outrageous impositions of the tax authorities. I hoped that if necessary I would have the guts to go to gaol . . . I was quite prepared. Of course, I know it would have been uncomfortable, but I would have done it if it were the only way. Some of us have to draw the line somewhere!' Fortunately, with the income from the Miss Marple films, she managed to avoid becoming resident poet at Holloway and negotiated a compromise with the tax authorities, allowing her to pursue her career on the right side of the law.

Murder She Said, released in 1961, was filmed at the MGM Boreham Wood studios and based on Christie's book *4:50 from Paddington*. Rutherford received top billing as Jane Marple, who witnesses the strangulation of a woman on a train travelling alongside her own. However, when she informs Inspector Craddock (played in all four films by Charles Tingwell), Miss Marple is dismissed as an elderly crank. She duly decides to take on the investigation – with the assistance of librarian Jim Stringer. This character didn't appear in any of Agatha Christie's books, and was created especially for Stringer Davis. It was actually quite a large role for Stringer, although, of course, it is Rutherford who is hardly off the screen. This is hardly a blood-curdling murder story; Rutherford plays it for laughs and, although the script is not the wittiest, she is always amusing. Ron Goodwin's catchy music also adds to the playful feel of proceedings.

Rutherford first appears boarding the 4:50 from Paddington, and she is inevitably dressed in tweeds and sporting a floppy cloche-type hat, the first in a selection of alarming creations. 'Again, as with all my characters, I wanted my audiences to feel the credibility of Miss Marple so I carefully chose the kind of clothes that I myself would wear.' In order to convince the police of her story, Miss Marple needs to prove that the body was dumped from the train. She thus disguises herself as a platelayer, in forage cap and overalls, searching the Great Western Railway line. The scene was filmed at Gerrards Cross, and George Pollock assured Margaret that he had been very careful in checking that no trains would thunder through during the shooting. 'We had to do it very early in the morning and the one shot of us peering over the edge of the track even today is one of my favourite "stills". There I am with jittery Stringer crouching beside me with just his eye showing. Delicious fun!'

The intrepid sleuths' legwork eventually leads them to the Ackenthorpe family, whose members are all murder suspects. Marple poses as an elderly maid to the irascible, parsimonious and autocratic head of the family, James Robertson-Justice, who later proposes marriage to her (it must have been the French maid's outfit that set his pulses racing). Joan Hickson, who was later to undertake the role of Miss Marple for the long-running television series, is the cook, Mrs Kidder. Ronnie Raymond played Alexander, described by Miss Marple as 'a curious child', and is a precocious Kenneth Williams type, aged fourteen going on forty-five. Even more campery is provided by Thorley Walters in the role as Cedric Ackenthorpe, and Hollywood star Arthur Kennedy is an even more unlikely member of the cast.

Murder She Said was actor Richard Briers' first ever film, for which he was rewarded with a fee of £25. He was a year out of RADA and remembers catching the bus from Notting Hill Gate to the studios. Briers played the owner of a domestic agency and was very nervous – particularly about working with 'such a big name as Margaret Rutherford'. He described her as a brilliant actress with extraordinary diction: 'She didn't have the looks so she had to be better than most.' His scene with her was actually filmed on the last day of shooting, and he found her to be tired and a bit grumpy. Briers recalled that there had been some friction on the set during the day and that she was quite tense. 'She wasn't the jolly lady I'd been expecting. But I couldn't blame her – faced by a fresh-faced, thin, nervous student. She was probably thinking to herself, "Oh my God . . . what have I got here?" Stringer, who was very sweet, was hovering in the background, making sure she was okay.' The scene, which is quite wordy, was shot in only two takes. 'I expect she just wanted to say the lines and get home!'

The beautiful Shakespearean actress, Muriel Pavlow, probably best known for her role as Thelma Bader in *Reach for the Sky*, plays Emma Ackenthorpe and utters the immortal line, 'I think someone in the family may be a murderer!' Miss Pavlow described working on *Murder She Said* as, 'A very charming experience – most of my work was with Arthur Kennedy, so I didn't get to know Miss Rutherford very well, but she was always kind and helpful. A lovely lady, very sweet and with no airs or graces. A fine actress.'

The film critic, Alexander Walker, wrote: 'Margaret Rutherford fills the spinster's tweeds of her renowned detective Miss Marple splendidly. She is hugely enjoyable. With chin wagging like a windsock on an airfield and eyes that are deceptively guileless, she clumps her way through lines, situations and disguises that would bunker an actress of less imperial aplomb.' A.H. Weiler (*New York Times*) wrote: 'As the indomitable spinster with a beagle's nose for crime, Margaret Rutherford leads the chase and the cast with a flair for this school of genteel and restrained detection that would do credit to the great Holmes himself. . . it is Miss Rutherford's show. Dressed with all the chic of a scarecrow and her prognathous jaw jutting determinedly, Miss Rutherford dominates most of the scenes with a forceful characterization that enhances the humor of her lines and the suspense in this murder.' *The Times* asserted that it was an unambitious film, but still had 'the immense advantage of a plot written by an expert. Not vintage Christie, perhaps, but as ingenious as ever, with clues and red herrings abounding.'

The second in the series, *Murder at the Gallop*, began filming just after Christmas 1962 and was released the following year. It was based on another Christie novel, *After the Funeral*, which had actually featured Hercule Poirot and not Jane Marple. Miss Marple, who joins a riding academy in order to investigate the death of an elderly recluse, is again aided by Jim Stringer. Margaret Rutherford is even better in the role second time around, and wonderfully expressive, using that slightly crooked mouth and pursed lips to full comic effect. She brings a 'feisty determination' to the character and seems more relaxed; she is also surprisingly active – cycling and dancing her way through the film – although the scene in which she is seen riding a horse was performed by a stand-in. At a dance in the Gallop Hotel, Rutherford, bejewelled and resplendent in evening dress, with black gloves and velvet bow in her hair, ends up taking to the floor and doing the twist with Stringer. Rutherford is rather careful, but Stringer attacks the dance with some gusto. It's just a shame that *Strictly Come Dancing* came forty years too late for them.

The film is pretty formulaic and very similar to its precursor. Another unsavoury family is in the frame, with each member suspected of murder. There are further killings, although no one seems particularly perturbed. (This must have been Finlay Currie's briefest appearance ever – he only screams an elongated 'Aaargh!' as he falls dead down the stairs.) As in *Murder She Said*, Miss Marple sets herself up as bait for the killer and the mystery is solved. She also receives a marriage proposal – this time Rutherford's great friend Robert Morley is the suitor. Yet again, she declines graciously. The cast also included Flora Robson as Miss Milchrest, bearing an uncanny resemblance to the Queen. Miss Robson said of her time in the film: 'There is nothing actressy about Margaret. She took to the part of being the star of the piece – a movie star – as she did to anything, with gracious responsibility and concern for everyone else.'

Margaret was interviewed during filming at Church Farm, Aldenham, Hertfordshire. The journalist reported that, 'Miss Rutherford, lightly disguised as Miss Jane Marple, Miss Christie's intrepid sleuthing spinster, received me with her customary graciousness. The small room was suddenly and unnervingly invaded. The assistant director and a call-boy popped in to say, "Ready when you are, Miss Rutherford." A hairdresser pounced on the star and did things with a tail-comb. "Such a clever girl," said Miss Rutherford. "She makes my hair look as if it curls naturally." A make-up man ("A real artist, you know") put his hand under the well-known formidable chin, turned the serene face to the light and added a finishing touch.'

The interviewer asked Margaret about her rendition of the twist, especially as the dance had been condemned by so many older people as 'ugly and immoral'. Margaret was surprised: 'Oh, I think it is delightful when it's done by young people – they are so graceful, and they seem to communicate with one another in movement. Immoral – you mean suggestive? Well I suppose it *could* be – but it can just as well be romantic: it can be anything you like to make it. New dances are always frowned on to begin with: why, the waltz was considered most improper when it first came in. But there – everything falls into proper perspective in time.'

The actress went on to give her views of the young generation. 'I look at them rather with awe. They have so much to face that we did not – the restlessness of the age and the threat of annihilation when they have scarcely lived at all. Every generation differs from the one before and we must remember that these young men and women come from parents who suffered the neuroses of the war. We must bear that in mind.' She went on to say, 'I do not mean we should be sloppy with them. They must have discipline – everybody must have discipline – but we should try to understand and encourage them. My husband and I have found that if young people are given responsible jobs, they take a pride in doing them well. Take the call-boy on this picture – such a nice boy: he is proud of his job as anybody at the studios. He is most reliable, never late, always polite. He has discipline.'

Kenneth Williams' critique of the film was that it was 'charmingly old fashioned: some of the casting was ludicrous, but the old girl's charm won in the end. She was a unique blend of grave decency and twinkling humour.' *The Times* decided that 'the whole thing is happily calculated to convince foreigners yet again that everything they have been told about the English is absolutely true and only a trifle understated.' Agatha Christie herself thought the whole thing 'incredibly silly'.

Christie's *Mrs McGinty's Dead* inspired the third Miss Marple film, *Murder Most Foul*. Marple again replaced Poirot and, as with the other films, the script was written by David Pursall and Jack Seddon. Opening engagingly with a woman being strangled and then hanging in silhouette while the oblivious and hapless copper Terry Scott has a secret pint at the local, it is the most humorous film in the series.

Jury member Miss Marple is admonished by curmudgeonly judge Andrew Cruickshank for knitting throughout the proceedings of a murder trial. Rutherford imbibes sharp intakes of breath, rolling her tongue around her mouth and popping out her cheeks like a mischievous hamster. In a parody of *Twelve Angry Men*, Jane Marple is the only member of the jury who is convinced that the defendant is innocent, and after much deliberating a retrial is ordered. Suspecting the murderer to be a member of a theatrical company, Miss Marple applies to join the troupe. She auditions for a part in the impoverished company with a hilarious rendition of *The Shooting of Dan McGrew*, in which she is all twirls and over-the-top dramatic gestures. The repertory company is run by would-be playwright-actor-manager and ham H. Driffold Cosgood, superbly played by Ron Moody. Miss Marple's acting does not impress Cosgood but he immediately welcomes her into the company when she mentions that she is a woman of independent means. He declares: 'I can see you in Duchess parts . . . regal roles.'

Several members of the troupe are dispatched by the unknown killer before Miss Marple – yes, you've guessed it – sets herself up as bait for the murderer. Surprisingly, however, Ron Moody doesn't propose to her. The theatrical scenes were filmed at the Palace Theatre, Watford, which was threatened with closure at the time, and Margaret Rutherford subsequently became involved in a campaign 'to save this darling little theatre'.

Some years later Ron Moody recalled their work together: 'She was wonderful and a very gracious gentlewoman – a throwback to the day of gentility and good manners, qualities which made her work so unique – each performance a collector's piece. But behind the genteel image was a consummate professional actress, a solid old pro who knew her business better than anyone I know. She was in the studio every morning before anyone else, always ready on set to shoot before anyone else. My favourite memory of this dear, dear lady was afternoon tea in her dressing room on the set. Cucumber sandwiches, the very best crockery – it was as if Pinewood had reverted to an English country garden, with the lady of the house dispensing the goodies. She dignified everything and everybody she touched.'

*

Murder Ahoy, the last the last of the four Rutherford Miss Marple films, also released in 1964, is not based on a Christie book and has an original script by Pursall and Seddon. Miss Marple becomes a trustee of a Royal Navy training ship. Following the poisoning of a fellow committee member, the tweedy Jim Stringer arrives at Miss Marple's Milchester cottage (in reality the Denham home of actor John Mills) and announces: 'I'm at a loss to know what all this is about.' He finds her in defiant mood: 'Damn the torpedoes – full steam ahead, Mr Stringer!', and she soon ends up on board. Other members of the cast include Lionel Jeffries, Miles Malleson, Joan Benham and Nicholas Parsons, as a 'brisk' doctor who ends up examining several murder victims.

Actor Francis Matthews recalls that the ship's scenes were filmed at the Thames Estuary near a naval base. 'I'm afraid I didn't feature as much I would have liked. If I remember correctly, I was murdered aboard the ship. Run through with a sword and then hung from the mizzen yard. But I did meet Margaret Rutherford – she was very sweet and actually quite funny. Stringer was always on the set, looking after her. Nice man.'

Mr Stringer is himself suspected of murder, but Miss Marple, in order to trap the murderer, stays on board while the others go ashore. She calmly knits while awaiting the arrival of the killer. The denouement is a sword fight between Marple and the murderer, but she gives him fair warning before the duel begins: 'I was British ladies' fencing champion in 1931.' Rutherford had never even held a sword before in her life and so took fencing lessons for four weeks. 'I was most fortunate in having one of the world's best teachers in a former Olympic swordsman Rupert Evans. I always called him Rupert of Hentzau after the romantic hero.'

Despite such swashbuckling antics, the film is rather slow-paced and pretty dull. Agatha Christie was appalled by it. 'To have one's characters incorporated in somebody else's film seems to me monstrous

and highly unethical . . . they wrote their own script for the last one –
nothing to do with me at all. One of the silliest things you ever saw! It
got very bad reviews, I'm delighted to say.'

Margaret maintained a consistent routine while making the Miss Marple
films: 'We are called every morning at five o'clock and Stringer brings me
a cup of tea. We are at the studios by seven-thirty for hair-dressing,
make-up and costume, you know. We start work at nine, either at the
studios or on location and break for lunch at one o'clock. I never go to
the studio restaurant. I have a light lunch in my room – Ryvita, cheese
and milk, a salad or something like that – and then I rest for half an hour.
I am very lucky, I can sleep for a short set time and wake completely
refreshed. We begin shooting again at two p.m. and work until six. We
are usually home at about eight for dinner and in bed by ten.'

The pressures of live theatre during this period had become rather
too much of a strain, and, although the schedule outlined above sounds
punishing for a seventy-two-year-old, Rutherford found screen work
less onerous than the stage. 'I find filming much more restful than the
theatre,' she declared. 'Once you are in the studios the outside world is
shut away and you can concentrate in peace. Home life between jobs
is often much more trying – all sorts of silly little domestic matters crop
up unexpectedly and have to be dealt with. In the studios you fall into
a pattern and that, I think, is a good and satisfying thing.'

After her initial reservations, Margaret Rutherford became very
fond of the sleuth: 'I regard Miss Marple as an extremely capable
woman, able to turn her hand to anything – she is one of the most
striking characters Agatha Christie has ever created. I very much
admire her and am honoured to play her. She is not interested in crime
for its own sake and she is not an avenger. She believes in the sanctity
of human life. She is with the forces of Light against the forces of
Darkness – and it is in this spirit that she seeks to illuminate the
sombre mysteries upon which she stumbles. She is for truth – that is
why she is so important.'

She enjoyed being treated like royalty on the set and 'took a tremendous kick out of the part'. Any question of profiting from films which depicted violence was dismissed: 'Of course there was murder involved but there was no sensationalism or blood and the other actors were most pleasant to work with. I think the Miss Marple films did a great service in winning us friends all round the world.'

Perhaps she felt a certain affinity to the role because of the surprising number of echoes of her own life in the events of the films. In *Murder She Said*, she and Stringer drive off with a 'Just Married' sign attached to the back of the car. She recites her prison party piece, *The Shooting of Dan McGrew*, when auditioning for the repertory company in *Murder Most Foul*. And, in *Murder Ahoy*, she is concerned with the welfare of a group of recalcitrant borstal boys. Throughout the series, and perhaps most poignantly, we see Jim Stringer continually fussing over Miss Marple's health and well-being. At least no one is murdered with a chamber pot.

'Margaret Rutherford was the first embodiment of Miss Marple on the cinema screen,' wrote Marion Shaw and Sabine Vanacker in *Reflecting on Miss Marple*, 'and emphasized the dotty element in the character but in no way captured the quietness and sharpness that the novels suggest. Rutherford was also far more domineering and bossy than the Miss Marple of the novels.' As this quote shows, there is still much debate as to whether Margaret's characterisation lived up to Christie's original creation – particularly as there have now been a number of celebrated actresses playing Miss Marple in films for television. But it was not until some years later that Margaret Rutherford discovered that Agatha Christie felt she was not actually the right actress to play her beloved amateur sleuth. Christie was quoted by biographer Charles Osborne: 'I kept off films for years because I thought they'd give me too many heartaches. Then I sold the rights to MGM, hoping they'd use them for television. But they chose films. It was too awful! They did things like taking a Poirot and putting Miss Marple in it! And all the climaxes were so poor, you could see them coming! I get an unregenerate pleasure when I think they're not being a success.' The author's husband, Max Mallowan added: 'My wife was rather critical of some of the films based on her books. Margaret Rutherford was admired by my wife as a character actress but she was totally miscast as Miss Marple.'

These accusations brought an immediate response from the producer, George Brown. 'I am very surprised. Dame Agatha was very closely concerned with the picture. In our judgement Miss Marple in the book was nothing like so interesting a character as the character which we could provide for the screen. We had a marvellous performer in Miss Rutherford. Dame Agatha had no reservations about the casting of Margaret Rutherford – she was highly delighted, came down to the studio at Elstree and was photographed with Margaret Rutherford.'

There was clearly some ambivalence in Christie's criticism, as in 1963 she dedicated her novel *The Mirror Cracked from Side to Side* to Rutherford. This suggests she can't have been entirely unhappy with Rutherford's portrayal. There were plans for Rutherford to star in a fifth Miss Marple film, based on the *The Body in the Library*, but this never materialised due to Christie's increasing unhappiness at the way her characters were being treated and ensuing contractual difficulties. In 1965, *The Alphabet Murders* (also known as *The A.B.C. Murders*) Rutherford and Davis reprise their roles as Miss Marple and Mr Stringer in a fleeting encounter with Tony Randall's Hercule Poirot. Shaw and Vanacker stated that, 'The drift towards farce, and the eclipsing of a character in a novel by the personality of the actress who played her, came to a halt when the contract with MGM was terminated.'

Margaret Rutherford was one of the highest-earning British actresses working for MGM during this period, and was reputedly paid £16,000 for each film. Following her work in these lucrative films and the success of *The VIPs*, she and Stringer felt able to move from their modest Gerrards Cross home. Remaining within the town, they moved more centrally – to Elm Close, 85 Packhorse Road, near the station and opposite the Ethorpe Hotel. Despite Margaret's earnings, the

Davises still owed the Inland Revenue substantial back taxes. The couple were perhaps unwise to take out a larger mortgage in order to buy a more substantial property – but it seems there was some expectation an Oscar-winning actress should occupy something more impressive than a two-up-two-down house in the Buckinghamshire backstreets.

The *Evening Standard* reported the news: 'Margaret Rutherford is moving to a five-bedroom house in Gerrards Cross, saying she needed to accommodate some elderly relatives: "Must look after the old people you know!"' It is not quite clear who she was referring to although John Carroll, Margaret's poetry patron who often pleaded poverty, later moved in, rent-free, to the converted top floor of the Edwardian property. Rutherford was always munificent when it came to Carroll – she would arrange luxury hampers from Fortnum and Mason to be delivered to him, anonymously, wherever he was living. Lucy Griffiths, who played the maid in *The Noble Spaniard* was another who benefited from such kindness and was perceived, by Margaret's close friends, to have taken advantage of the couple's generosity. Rumer Godden felt that Margaret was too trusting with some people and just couldn't refuse any requests for help from 'the limpets and hangers-on'.

Margaret and Stringer took on a cleaner and hired an interior designer to refurbish their new home, which Stringer described as sturdy: 'It's the sort of house where you can slam the door without the tooth mugs falling off the shelf.' Despite the attentions of the designer, the new house was a cornucopia of styles – a mismatch of first-night gifts, trinkets, objets d'art collected on their travels and a few antiques inherited from Stringer's mother. The lounge described as 'resplendent in cretonne and orange', with William Morris wallpaper and, in the corner, a cabinet full of Hans Christian Andersen figures made from pipe cleaners. A *Daily Telegraph* columnist described the scene: 'We had ginger marmalade and drank coffee from large green coffee cups, sitting under a reproduction of the *Mona Lisa* [obtained from *Innocents in Paris*] while a log fire blazed in the inglenook.'

Stringer and Margaret enjoyed living in the Buckinghamshire town and, although there was no doubt that she liked being recognised by the locals, she was not the type to indulge her celebrity status. The local butcher referred to her as 'Mrs Davis', which she seemed to enjoy. Mrs Davis was also very friendly with the local vicar, whom she would invite for afternoon tea, and who was quoted in the press as having 'a special liking for her cream buns'.

Brenda Davies, grandmother to celebrity chef Antony Worrall Thompson, was a great friend of Margaret Rutherford's. A rather fearsome but glamorous 'colonial type', Mrs Davies was friendly with a number of actors including Anna Neagle, Flora Robson and John Gielgud and entertained them at her home in Shiplake-on-Thames. As a child, Antony used to spend summers with his grandmother, and Margaret Rutherford often stayed in a caravan in the grounds, insisting that, 'I'm absolutely fine there – I really don't need to stay in the house.' Worrall Thompson recalls those days with great fondness: 'Margaret Rutherford was very kind, affectionate and warm – quite different from my austere grandmother.' Margaret was shocked to discover the boy couldn't yet swim: 'Come on, young man, you must learn, living so near to the water!' She duly accompanied him to the river and taught him the necessary skills. 'She was very gung-ho and wore a voluminous swim suit. She would swim from the bank of the Thames to a central island and also launch herself off boats into the river. She was such great fun and quite unconcerned at the amazed boating fraternity who would snap away at her with their Box Brownies!'

In June 1963, Margaret and Stringer were interviewed by Marjorie Anderson in a piece called 'In Partnership' for BBC radio's *Woman's Hour*. Margaret stated that first impressions were always important to her, and the fact that Stringer was 'electric' was what attracted her initially. She was also fascinated by his name, which 'I took to be Springer, feeling he sprung everywhere, but in the end after about a week, I realised that I'd got one letter wrong.'

Anderson asked Stringer if it was a problem being the husband of a star, to which Stringer replied: 'Well it's my biggest and most rewarding and excluding problem, I think. I love it, it's my life's work and I enjoy doing it and I feel greatly honoured to be able to present Margaret Rutherford to the world and help her, and I regard that as my great service to the theatre which I love next.'

The interviewer asked if there was any ever any friction between the two of them. Margaret returned the question by asking, 'Could there be any partnership without friction?' Stringer denied there was ever any discord, and Marjorie Anderson declared: 'You create round you an atmosphere of tranquillity. I can feel it now just sitting here.' Margaret agreed that achieving a calm atmosphere was one of their chief aims in life: 'We don't feel that anything can be accomplished or achieved without an atmosphere of peace, because otherwise you don't hear the overtones and undertones which are surely all round us in the universe, I believe so much in rhythm – the rhythm of destiny.'

A calm atmosphere was usually maintained at Elm Close, although Robert Morley, a regular visitor, recalled that Sunday lunch in their Gerrards Cross home could be full of surprises. Occasionally, while still recovering from the after-affects of a robust treacle pudding, Margaret would suddenly announce that she needed Morley to drive her to Feltham, or some other institution of incarceration, where she had agreed to do a poetry reading. Other lunch guests would be expected to attend, and without further ado they would all be on their way.

Stringer and Margaret were ideally suited for each other – who else would have tolerated each other's idiosyncratic lifestyles? A number of their friends and colleagues confided that, although Stringer could be quite charming, he was also something of a bore. Sometimes he was opinionated and self-important, particularly in theatrical matters, such as his lengthy pontifications about the importance of his one line in a production or how his astute stage directions had saved the day. To Margaret, however, this tediousness didn't seem to matter at all. She was either oblivious to his shortcomings or paid them no heed, letting his twittering wash over her. He was of great support to her and, most importantly, really did adore her.

Private secretary, confidant and nursemaid to his beloved wife, there is no doubt that Stringer's ministrations helped her through many dramas, both personal and professional. He admitted: 'My philosophy about it is that I spent a lot of years on the stage as supporting actor and I gained a good idea of how the stars can be supported on and off the stage. And I didn't see why I shouldn't support a star offstage as well.' Margaret always maintained that he had given up his career for her. 'What a joy this man has brought into my life; he is one of God's great blessings. The way he has unselfishly stood aside in his own career so often to shield and care for me during my bad spells; all the parties, the first nights, the triumphs, the disappointments – he has been there. He is my own private Rock of Gibraltar.'

Although it has to be said that nearly all his work came as a result of Margaret's involvement, it can't have been easy being the husband of a celebrity, and he performed his role well. It is difficult to perceive Stringer as a character in his own right. He was always defined by his relationship to his wife and, although he was never referred to personally as 'Mr Margaret Rutherford', one can only imagine that he would have accepted the title with a sense of pride. Stringer was a househusband long before the term came into common use, and for this Margaret gave him an allowance when he wasn't working. Unlike most househusbands, however, he also had, as one of Margaret's close friends said, 'a talent for getting into the publicity shots'.

Following the completion of the Miss Marple films, Margaret Rutherford was interviewed by Wendy Jones on BBC radio and was asked, 'Now, you've made six films in the past three years – don't you find it awfully tiring?'

The actress replied: 'Well it's my job – and we expect our job to be tiring – otherwise it wouldn't be a job, would it really?' In response to a question about what age she thought a woman should give up her job, Margaret responded: 'I don't think you can generalise about a thing like that – it's entirely individual according to how you feel . . . what your physique is . . . how much work that will stand as you get older, you know.'

Miss Jones was brave enough to ask Margaret if she had any thoughts on retirement. Margaret sounded as if no one had ever dared ask her that before, and as if she had never given it a moment's thought. 'No, except that I should hate the thought.'

FOURTEEN

The Very Pineapple
of Politeness

'She's as headstrong as an allegory on the banks of the Nile.'

RICHARD BRINSLEY SHERIDAN, THE RIVALS

MARGARET RUTHERFORD METAMORPHOSED from Miss Marple to Mistress Quickly in her next film, *Chimes at Midnight*, 'a sombre comedy and a lament for Merrie England', directed by and starring Orson Welles. Originally a stage play, the piece was drawn from five Shakespeare plays featuring Sir John Falstaff, and the film had its world premiere in 1966. Welles gives an extraordinary performance as Falstaff, and exposes the 'Lord of Misrule's' shifting relationship with Prince Hal (Keith Baxter). The voiceover is provided by Ralph Richardson, himself hailed as a magnificent Falstaff nearly twenty years previously in an Old Vic production of *Henry IV*.

Simon Callow, in his biography of Orson Welles, *The Road to Xanadu*, describes the film as 'a dark masterpiece . . . often wondrous and nearly always chaotic'. He also outlines the similarities in personality between Welles and Falstaff – braggart, womaniser, charmer and trickster, traits which presumably drew Welles to the project in the first place. *Chimes at Midnight* is a fascinating watch – mainly due to the fine acting (John Gielgud as Henry IV, Jeanne Moreau as Doll Tearsheet, and Fernando Rey as Worcester), but also because the restricted budget creates a unique blend of varying film quality, cheap sets and poor sound.

Early on, Mistress Quickly, the inn's hostess, is given a playful smack on the bottom by Jack Falstaff, who accuses her of running 'a bawdy house', and she cackles at his tomfoolery. Rutherford, who was paid £8,000 for her work, is impressive in the role, particularly towards the end of the film when she delivers a moving account of Falstaff's death. It makes one wonders what she might have achieved in her career had she been entrusted with a wider range of serious roles.

'Orson Welles was splendid to work with, although he was always pressed for money and usually in poor health,' remembered John Gielgud in his autobiography, *An Actor and His Time*. 'He engaged a very fine company but he could not afford to keep us all permanently employed. I went over for a week's shooting in Spain, then Margaret Rutherford . . . and then Jeanne Moreau, and Orson, who was playing Falstaff, had still not done any of his own scenes. By the time he got round to them he was tired out and there was nobody left for him to act with.' Despite this apparent obstacle, Welles was nominated for a BAFTA as Best Foreign Actor.

Keith Baxter recalled that the cast had much fun during the filming: 'It was wonderful – hilarious. There were no dressing rooms and room for only one "star" caravan in the yard. Although this had been allocated to Jeanne Moreau in compliance with her contract, she insisted Margaret Rutherford should occupy it and insisted, too, that Margaret should never know. Outside Margaret's caravan the afternoon sun warmed a patch by the steps. Margaret sat there between shots with a woolly cardigan round her shoulders while Stringer read to her, poetry and Chaplin's autobiography. He held her hand as he read.'

Baxter described Rutherford as 'having the heart of a romantic – her work was always underpinned by a unique purity. She was aware that her looks made people laugh, but she never thought of herself as a clown. Orson Welles had the utmost respect for her.' In his book, Baxter wrote that her 'homely features masked a most moving and glowing femininity, and upon whom feyness sat as naturally as the rough Cornish cloak flying across her shoulders.'

At the end of her month in Spain, Rutherford invited the cast to a teatime party at the Palace Hotel in Madrid. In his autobiography, *My Sentiments Exactly*, Baxter described the scene: 'Margaret and Stringer dispensed tea and gin to the smiling elderly trio playing Franz Lehár compositions among the palms . . . Margaret loved to dance. Shyly she asked Welles if he would partner her. He bowed and suggested they might try a foxtrot. Both were wonderfully light on their toes, laughing together as we cheered them whirling with such astonishing grace around the floor. Margaret danced with all of us, and then it was time to go. As we looked back, Margaret was waltzing happily with the cellist, Stringer on the gilt sofa, shining with love.'

Rutherford was soon in demand from yet another Hollywood legend. 'When Dorothy Mather rang me to say that Charlie Chaplin wanted to meet me to discuss the possibility of working together, my heart almost stopped beating . . . Mr Chaplin invited us all to the Savoy for cocktails. We went into that impressive entrance and up the stairs to one of those elegant suites overlooking the river.' Chaplin, accompanied by his wife, Oona, soon put Margaret and Stringer at their ease, and explained that he wanted Margaret to play a small part in his film, *A Countess from Hong Kong*. 'Up he sprang,' recalled Rutherford, 'lithe and light, and began a one-man performance of the part he wanted me to play. The expressions flitted across his face, his small hands built whole scenes as he traced patterns in the air, that handsome grey head bobbled and swayed with animation. Here was the full genius of this great man. I couldn't wait to begin.'

Stringer had brought along a copy of the Chaplin autobiography, which Margaret had given him as a present, and asked Chaplin if he would autograph the book. Margaret's inscription to Stringer read: 'To my favourite "Clown", Guide and Counsellor, Friend and Husband with the everlasting love of Eternal Things.' Charlie Chaplin studied the dedication and then wrote underneath, 'May I endorse Margaret's statement. Chaplin.'

A Countess from Hong Kong was filmed at Pinewood for Universal in January 1966 and released the following year. Having written and directed the film, Chaplin also appeared briefly as an elderly ship's steward, in what was to be his swansong. If this wasn't enough, Chaplin also composed the theme music, 'This Is My Song', later recorded by Petula Clark, which saved the film from complete financial ruin. *A Countess from Hong Kong* is a romantic comedy revolving around Natascha, a White Russian countess (Sophia Loren) who is forced into prostitution in Hong Kong and stows away on a luxury liner. She finds her way into the stateroom of American diplomat Ogden Mears (Marlon Brando) and attempts to blackmail her way to a new life in the USA.

Despite the star names, the film is incredibly ponderous, with interminable sequences of Sophia Loren hiding in Brando's bathroom or wardrobe. The dialogue is decidedly clunky and there are too many silent sequences. Even Brando is remarkably wooden, and the whole thing is only enlivened by Rutherford's cameo – one brief scene where she appears as a bedridden old lady, Miss Gaulswallow, a hypochondriac wrapped in pink fluffy shawl and propped up by a huge number of multi-coloured cushions. The supporting cast also accommodates Chaplin's son Sydney in a minor role, Tippi Hedren as Ogden's cold wife and Patrick Cargill as the ultimate gentleman's gentleman. In his biography of Chaplin, John McCabe describes how a reporter from *Newsweek*, Joseph Morgenstern, was allowed on set and watched some of the filming: 'He was intrigued by Chaplin's boundless enthusiasm and creative energy at seventy-six. Confirming rumours about the film, Chaplin admitted it was old-fashioned, and he confessed to nostalgia.'

The poor reviews confirmed Chaplin's admission. The *New York Times* called the film 'A painfully antique bedroom farce – it is awful, numbingly archaic.' Chaplin was particularly upset by the critics' response. He had enjoyed making the film and was genuinely surprised by the disastrous reception it received. On the whole the cast got on well, although there was some tension between Loren and Brando, who slapped the Italian siren on the bottom. 'Don't ever do that again,' she said, grabbing his arm. 'I am not the sort of woman who is flattered by it.'

Although she was only briefly involved, Margaret Rutherford enjoyed her time at Pinewood greatly. 'The thing I remember most about Chaplin's direction was the infinite eye for detail,' she wrote. 'In his direction and handling of the cast Charlie Chaplin was always considerate, never raised his voice and was one of the most helpful people I have worked with.' She was equally enamoured with Sophia Loren: 'What a charming girl . . . not only has she a magnificent carriage and beauty but manners to equal. When she came on the set one day and saw me sunk irretrievably in bed, she immediately bounded over and begged the "stills" photographer to take a picture of us both.'

Rutherford's few days on Chaplin's film had come at a time when she described herself as 'tired and over-wrought'. But the promise of further salvation came in the form of a letter from John Clements, written on 28 December 1965.

Dearest Margaret,

As I expect you know, Larry (Laurence Olivier) gives up the direction of the theatre at Chichester at the end of this week when I officially take over from him. I cannot tell you what delight it would give me if I could persuade you to come and play in my first season. In fact what I would dearly love is that you should play in the opening play! It has just got to be something that starts the new regime on the right note, and the more I think of it the more sure I am that it should be an evening of gaiety and, above all, of style.

There is no-one to whom those two words apply more than they do to you! The question is, of course, what play? My first thought was *The Rivals*. And then I re-read *The Clandestine Marriage*. I had forgotten what a delicious play it is! If you will play Mrs. Heidelberg I shall settle, with happiness and excitement, for that!

Sir John Clements had directed Margaret in *The Way of the World* in 1956 and had actually appeared with her as an actor in *The Master Builder* at the Embassy Theatre in 1934. He was now artistic director at Chichester and invited Margaret and Stringer down to Brighton to discuss the part – to which she readily agreed. Clements had already recruited Alistair Sim to the part of ageing Lothario Lord Ogleby.

There were to be seven weeks of rehearsals, so Margaret and Stringer moved into the Beach Hotel at Littlehampton. She was collected each day by hired car and taken to the Festival Theatre. 'There was something so invigorating in being able to have a long walk by the sea before lunch, then our afternoon nap and a delicious afternoon tea sitting outside in the late spring sunshine before leaving for the theatre. It was like a holiday.'

There was a gala performance on 31 May 1966, although the official season of *The Clandestine Marriage* ran from 1 June to 21 July. The play, written by David Garrick, was directed by Desmond O'Donovan, and Margaret Rutherford described the opening night as nerve-racking but 'magical'. When John Clements and his wife Kay Hammond arrived to take their seats, Rutherford reported that, 'There was such a special atmosphere about these two people that as they swept up the aisle to their seats the theatre rose and gave them a tumultuous reception.'

Kay Hammond's son, John Standing, who played Sir John Melvil, has joyful memories of the production. 'Rehearsals were absolutely magic and it was great fun to be with Alastair Sim and Margaret Rutherford. Both were very humble and she never pulled rank despite her legendary status. She was naturally eccentric but it wasn't contrived. To her, it was completely normal – that's why she was so funny. There was no doubt, however, that there was also an element of playing up to her character. She was electrifying.' Standing confirmed that Margaret was word-perfect with her lines apart from one night. 'Throughout the performance she referred to my character, Sir John, as Sir Johnny, which was much more "theatrical than restoration". It became funnier and funnier each time she said, "Yes, Sir Johnny. No, Sir Johnny. Do sit down, Sir Johnny." She just seemed to get stuck!"

Reviews were mixed: Herbert Kretzmer in the *Daily Express* wrote, 'Margaret Rutherford is at her most mugwampish as the formidable Mrs Heidelberg . . . the play is very plain . . . it lacks a consistent standard of comic writing.' The *Evening News* commented on how Rutherford, 'queen-like, sank in deep curtsy to meet the applause at her first entrance. Here were theatrical manners belonging to a very different age from the modern open stage at Chichester.' The *Guardian* summarised: 'Broad fun and much spirit but doesn't add much to previous distractions. Margaret Rutherford manages to fire off some of her special salvos, and between them [she and Sim] successfully keep the play going.' The *Sunday Times* critic concluded: 'Margaret Rutherford, whose peculiar splendours hardly need description was, on the opening night, both her indomitable self and rather muted. She took to her role without in the least disrupting the fabric of the comedy.' Alan Brien in the *Sunday Telegraph* decided: 'The play would have made a flat conventional evening of pious antiquarianism without the presence of Alistair Sim as an ancient fop. Matching this baroque turkey cock is Margaret Rutherford's ambulating tea cosy, a mound of padded quilting with the sadly pouting face of a lovable dairy cow in a children's story book. On the first night, Miss Rutherford seemed understandably a little confused by the plot . . .'

Clive Swift, who appeared as Canton, companion to Lord Ogleby, wrote, 'I could hardly believe that these comic idols were walking amongst us, but they surely were. I don't think I have ever been on stage with such a charismatic audience puller as Mr Sim. He and Rutherford rehearsed in diametrically opposite ways. He in minute, calculating detail. She straightforwardly sincere and as amorous, nouveau-riche, Mrs Heidelberg.' Rutherford had nothing but praise for the production, 'It was a very energetic one for me, but playing with Alastair Sim again gave me great pleasure.'

Margaret was back on stage again that autumn – this time in

Sheridan's *The Rivals* at the Theatre Royal Haymarket. 'Sir Ralph Richardson is the most irresistible man in the world. When he asked me to play this role I couldn't say no, even if it was to be so demanding.' The role was Mrs Malaprop and Rutherford was dogged by lack of confidence from the very beginning, 'Mrs Malaprop, whose misuse of the English language is one of the most brilliant pieces of comedy ever written . . . I found that to assemble Mrs Malaprop's verbal confusions accurately was quite a feat. Right through the production I was haunted with the thought that I would dry up. I always dreaded that 186 word speech that begins, "Observe me, Sir Anthony. I would by no means wish a daughter of mine to be a progeny of learning . . .".'

Keith Baxter described a key rehearsal contribution from Rutherford in his autobiography. In a scene between Richardson and Rutherford, the director, Glen Byam Shaw, admitted that he had no idea how to proceed. 'They were both acting superbly but it was not amusing, and twenty minutes of the play had passed without a big laugh, and it was, after all, a comedy.' Margaret came to the rescue by suggesting she eat a slice of toast. Baxter wrote: 'She knew that as she munched the toast all her chins would waggle, the audience would laugh and that would be good for the production, but she never saw herself as a grotesque. In her soul she was a girlish, loving, romantic woman and it was those qualities that lent such unique pathos to her work.'

However, it was the opening scene with Richardson that caused Rutherford major problems. Concerns about her memory proved prescient. The scene contained many of the more famous Malapropisms, but she often forgot her responses to Richardson's lines, and he did his best to carry her through. Keith Baxter confirmed that it was extremely difficult for Richardson: 'He had little to do but listen as Margaret struggled to get through. Backstage, the stage manager stood in the wings ready to prompt; Stringer, who played two parts in the play, was below the window with the script in hand. As I ran down for my first entrance I passed Richardson on the stairs going back to his room. He looked at me bleakly, "Oh Cocky! It's nightmare tunnel!"'

Damaris Hayman attended the first night (6 October 1966) with Joan Hickson. 'She had such star quality and usually lit up the stage when she entered but sadly she now seemed like a tired old lady. She even dried on her first line.' Afterwards when the two actresses went backstage, they found Margaret in 'a crumpled heap in the dressing room. It was quite horrible to see her like that'.

Rutherford herself was aware of her failings. 'As in all comedy the timing had to be precise. Catch the split second and the laughs come. Miss two beats and they are gone. Sensing the timing in a period piece is always difficult, but combining a crop of Malapropisms with this was very wearying . . . my memory was not as good as it had been and if I couldn't remember what Mrs Malaprop had to say then I just made up the words. I wonder how many of the audience knew?'

Frith Banbury witnessed Margaret's difficulties in the production. 'She wasn't good at all and had all sorts of difficulties with the Malapropisms.' He felt that her mental state was affecting her performance: 'The melancholy showed through in her work as the eccentricity had shone before and, although she tried to act with her usual flourish, her work was strangely restrained. I felt for her – because the people who saw her at the end of her career didn't know what she was like in her prime.'

Rosemary Say, the *Sunday Telegraph* critic, agreed. 'Unbelievably Margaret Rutherford was ill at ease in the part for which she might have been tailored (or corseted). Submerged in outlandish headgear, she brought out her Malapropisms with painful mistiming and with little gusto. No bustling fussiness and chatty interference from her in the love affairs of the young. She was not interested, and left us stranded, unsmiling and perplexed.' The *Daily Telegraph*'s Eric Shorter wrote: 'But Margaret Rutherford isn't just allowed her Malapropisms; she is allowed to indulge them to the full and despite her ever wonderful multiplicity of chins, which might themselves explain her verbal confusions, she did not seem at all happily cast.' Adrian Brown recalls: 'I do remember her hesitating before all the Malapropisms and, evidently working out that she was supposed to get these words wrong, said to me, "I haven't found her, have I?" And, sadly, she had not. I was shocked by the change in her appearance. Flesh had fallen away and her face was now gaunt and tired.'

Despite this, Keith Baxter felt that she 'gave an unforgettable performance . . . mining the role for all its romance. She could bring the house down.' Some of the critics were also impressed by her work, especially the journalist from the *Sunday Express*: 'The great Margaret Rutherford is back in the West End, and we can all rejoice . . . in one of the great comic parts of all time, the redoubtable Miss Rutherford displays all of her linguistic absurdities like precious jewels, and revels in their dazzle. Really, the woman is extraordinary. Her painted face peers witheringly from under a monstrous bonnet while her jaw is given to biting the air like a ventriloquist's dummy.' The *Sunday Times* review stated: 'The verbal brilliance of Mrs Malaprop is taken by Margaret Rutherford with a naturalness that makes the familiar mispronouncements seem once again fresh and funny.'

'The dresses I wore were very special,' wrote Margaret of her costumes. 'My favourite was a cloud of a white fichu over layers of cyclamen and apricot silks. Topping this was the most marvellous piece of millinery that I have ever seen. My first entrance as I was carried across the stage in a Sedan chair was quite spectacular.' She admitted, though, to finding the role incredibly tiring. 'But Jessie, my devoted dresser, saw that I kept my strength up with little cups of tea and sandwiches and Bovril before I left for the long journey home to Gerrards Cross each night.'

Jessie Pearce, who had been Yvonne Arnaud's dresser before Margaret, was, like her predecessor, devoted to Margaret and incredibly protective of the actress. In an interview during the production Miss Pearce admitted: 'I'm a bit of a dragon but I've got to be or Dame Margaret would never get any peace. People come from all over the world to see her and she simply can't bear to turn anyone away. You're the person an actress is with most during a play and you must be very tactful and diplomatic. Some artists are so moody their dressers are afraid to speak to them. But I've never known an actress so loved as Miss Rutherford. She's always charming and not a bit temperamental. I arrive an hour before the curtain goes up to check the make-up table and do the flowers. In *The Rivals* she has a train nearly three yards in length and I was always in the wings to help her. She always holds my hand before going on. Stringer is always here – he tells her what the audience is like and gives her a kiss for luck. When I go to their house she waits on me instead of me waiting on her and Mr Davis says, "Now, none of this maid business, Jessie. You're more to us than anything." You'd think I was their daughter, really. Dame Margaret and I have a wonderful relationship. When my husband died she didn't fuss me. She just said, "You know my arms are always here to comfort you."'

Angela Thorne, who played Julia, later wrote: 'Acting in *The Rivals* was a very special experience. Margaret Rutherford was a frail Mrs Malaprop and was unwell a great deal of the time but the audience adored her and when she was feeling confident her talent for creating laughter through great sincerity and truth shone. She should have played Mrs Malaprop ten years before. I believe she would have been definitive. No one can replace her. She was one of my favourite actresses.'

Margaret was indeed suffering poor health during the run, and it soon led to another breakdown. Keith Baxter remembered: 'Unless the weather was really impossible, Margaret and her husband, Stringer Davis, would walk from Marylebone Station to the Haymarket. They would arrive early in mid-afternoon, in time for Margaret to have a good sleep before the performance. But the walk would have agitated her and she would have a pill to relax. When it was time to wake for a cup of tea before putting on her make-up she was still sleepy, so another pill was produced to stimulate her. But this sometimes proved too distracting and she would take a pill to calm her. By the time she came into the wings for her entrance she was often in a state of real confusion.' Margaret had also developed an addiction to an aspirin derivative which resulted in her afternoon naps becoming much deeper and harder to emerge from.

During the production, Margaret was forced to take time off work, and Damaris Hayman took her to a private hospital in Harrow-on-the-Hill for further electroconvulsive therapy. Representatives of H.M. Tennent asked the medical staff if the actress would be able to remember the lines after the treatment. The attending psychiatrist replied: 'I've no idea, I have never treated anyone appearing in a play before!'

Margaret returned to the production and initially her mental state seemed to have improved. Actress and voice coach Celia Bannerman, who played Lucy, recalls: 'Margaret Rutherford was always in good cheer. After her illness, she would return and would be amazing for a short while – she seemed to know everyone's lines.' Unfortunately the ECT was only a short-term fix and, as time went by, she found it harder and harder to grasp the text and became increasingly tormented.

Keith Baxter noted that, 'After a while it was whispered that she was about to give notice. Richardson was in despair. Though her failing memory unnerved him, he liked working with her, and he knew, too, that they made a formidable pair at the box office. Vivien Leigh came to the play. She had admired Margaret Rutherford and was praising her performance in my room when Richardson burst in. We should all go down to Margaret's room and beg her to stay. We went downstairs. Margaret was sitting at her table with Stringer beside her. She was clutching her head between her hands. Ralph spoke gently; Vivien with the greatest tact and affection. The tears started to flow down Margaret's face. "I can't," she wept. "Oh please! I can't."'

Margaret Rutherford celebrated her seventy-fifth birthday during the run of the play and Damaris Hayman visited Elm Close for the party. She found Margaret to be in a very distressed state. 'Margaret collapsed in tears and asked me to stay with her for a couple of nights. She was extraordinarily upset.'

Eventually, it was obvious to everyone that Margaret simply could not continue as Mrs Malaprop and she came out of the show, to be replaced by Isabel Jeans. Hayman contended that it was after this production that Margaret Rutherford started to suffer from long-term memory loss and had trouble remembering even the most significant events of her life. *The Rivals* proved to be Margaret Rutherford's last stage performance.

There was, however, one much more positive experience during the run. In the 1967 New Year Honour's list, Margaret Rutherford became a Dame of the British Empire. Margaret and Stringer spent the night of 6 February at the Rembrandt Hotel in Knightsbridge. The following day Jessie Pearce drove them to Buckingham Palace and, ever the professional, gave the actress a final check on her outfit. Margaret was absolutely thrilled to be honoured in this manner. 'It was a wonderful moment when you stand before your Queen and Sovereign. I was overawed by the dignity and graciousness of the Queen.' Her quote to the press was a little more phlegmatic: 'It might help me pull my socks up.'

Afterwards the couple, along with John Carroll and Jessie Pearce, took lunch at the Ritz. Among Margaret's other guests was Dorothy Vaisey, with whom she had remained close friends since their days at Raven's Croft school over sixty years earlier. Dorothy Vaisey had carved herself a distinguished career in charity work for old people, running the organisation, Friends of the Poor and Gentlefolk's Help (now Friends of the Elderly), and had herself received both an OBE and a Damehood (DCVO) at roughly the same time as her old friend – whom she still referred to as 'Peggy'. The two Dames had enjoyed a gentle rivalry about their respective achievements and stayed in contact until Dorothy Vaisey's death in 1969.

Following her departure from *The Rivals*, Margaret Rutherford was offered a small part in the film *Arabella* (1967) as Princes Ilaria, a wealthy dowager whose fortunes have dwindled. The comedy was a vehicle for Italian starlet Virna Lisi who turns to crime to pay her grandmother's debts: 'using her quick wits and stunning good looks to con a succession of gullible rich men into parting with their fortunes'. The film also starred James Fox and Terry-Thomas.

Before she travelled to Rome for the shoot, Margaret telephoned Damaris Hayman in a panic. She felt she needed an evening dress and was at a loss to find something suitable. Damaris went through her friend's wardrobe and found a plum-coloured silk dress that Margaret Rutherford had been given after she appeared in *I'm All Right Jack*. Damaris discovered how much weight Margaret had lost since then and had to make 'some serious alterations'. She helped Margaret and Stringer pack for the trip and had all their bags and clothes ready in the hallway before the taxi came to take them to the airport. Stringer had specially purchased an Italian phrase book, although the only thing he wanted to know was: 'How do you ask for bacon and eggs?'

The Davises stayed at the Villa Fiorio in the Frascati hills outside Rome. Margaret liked Virna Lisi, whom she described as 'a beautiful girl who treated me graciously'. One evening in Rome Margaret was given an award for her work in films by an Italian film society – a medal inscribed with 'A Life for the Cinema'. Rutherford also described another, less pleasant event in the holy city: 'Because I am easily recognisable I am a fair target for autograph hunters, or worse still, people who just want to meet me. I never mind this when I am not working, but after a day's hard film work it can be utterly tiresome. I remember one very hot day in Rome (I dislike heat intensely) I was just coming back to the hotel after a hard day's filming when I was cornered by one of those intrepid English-matrons-abroad types. She demanded to know what "dear Miss Rutherford really thought of the Coliseum". Normally I am well mannered, but with bores I crack down. In this case my only answer was "Very draughty" as I glared at her.'

Sadly the heat and the demanding English tourists were the least of Margaret's worries while working on *Arabella*. Towards the end of the filming she slipped on a rug in her hotel room and broke her hip (coincidentally on the very same day that Dame Agatha Christie suffered a similar injury). Margaret required immediate surgery but insisted on having the operation in England and was thus flown home and carried on and off the aeroplane on a stretcher.

On 7 November 1967 the *Daily Mirror* reported: 'Veteran actress Dame Margaret was in "great spirits" last night in a London hospital after an operation for a fractured thigh bone.' Three weeks later she was transferred to a Nuffield Nursing Home near her home where she was faced with a long period of convalescence.

FIFTEEN

Going Dark

'The play is done; the curtain drops,
Slow falling to the prompter's bell:
A moment yet the actor stops,
And looks around, to say farewell.
It is an irksome word and task:
And when he's laughed and said his say,
He shows, as he removes the mask,
A face that's anything but gay.'

WILLIAM MAKEPEACE THACKERAY, 'THE END OF THE PLAY'

WHILE MARGARET WAS recovering from her broken hip she received a rather unusual missive from her self-proclaimed adopted son, Gordon Langley Hall, explaining that he was shortly going to be . . . Margaret's 'adopted daughter'. Gordon was going into hospital for surgery and from now on was to be known, somewhat exotically, as Dawn Pepita Hall. In the letter, he also described his relationship with an African-American motor mechanic: 'For all of the two years I have had the love and devotion of Mr John-Paul Simmons of Charleston, without whose constant encouragement, I do not think that I could have encompassed such a change.'

Stringer and Margaret were naturally flabbergasted, but to their credit, they accepted the situation philosophically. Margaret wrote: 'Our dear Dawn, Stringer and I are utterly baffled by your letter. Our main instinct is to congratulate you upon having come through your great ordeal. It is miraculous and almost defeats imagination to realise what extremity of suffering you must have been through. Our love for you could never change; be assured of this.'

Dawn and John-Paul were married in January 1969 in Dawn's Charleston sitting room. She claimed that it was the first legal mixed marriage in the state of South Carolina and, because of race-hate reprisals, the house was later firebombed. The couple visited England later that year, where Stringer and Margaret arranged a special ceremony to mark the occasion. The following invitations were sent out:

> Mr. J. Stringer and Dame Margaret Rutherford Davis, O.B.E. request the honour of your presence at the blessing of the marriage of their adoptive daughter, Dawn Pepita Langley Hall, to Mr John-Paul Simmons at two thirty o'clock Sunday afternoon, November the ninth, St Clements Church, Hastings, Sussex and afterwards at the reception.

The Press were present in great numbers, and a reporter from *Time* magazine asked Margaret if she was happy about Dawn's marriage to John-Paul. She was supposed to have replied: 'Oh I don't mind Dawn marrying a black man but I do wish he wasn't marrying a Baptist.' Although amusing, this just doesn't sound like something Margaret would have said. She was the most broadminded of people, and sectarian prejudice would never have been something that concerned her.

Despite her poor health, Margaret was still keen to work, but since *Arabella* she had remained 'available'. Margaret had always wanted to play the Quaker prison reformer Elizabeth Fry, and there was talk of her undertaking the role in a play, based on a book by Janet Whitney. Adrian Brown was approached to prepare a script, but the biographer asserted that she owned the copyright to the research and she wished to write the play herself. Unfortunately, despite Mr Brown's best efforts, Ms Whitney couldn't come up with a serviceable script and the project never came to fruition.

Margaret did provide the voice for the eponymous principal character in *The Wacky World of Mother Goose*, a feature-length cartoon featuring well-loved nursery rhyme characters in Fairyland. Rutherford, who sounds remarkably youthful as Mother Goose, is caricatured affectionately. The film also stars voice artiste Bradley Bolke, who never actually met Margaret Rutherford – the two actors recorded their parts separately.

There were some radio appeals for such charities as St Luke's Nursing Home for the clergy, but no offer of gainful employment until March 1969 when Rutherford was approached by Ned Sherrin, who was producing a television programme to mark the centenary of the death of Charles Dickens. In *The Great Inimitable Mr Dickens*, Sherrin and Caryl Brahms were planning to trace the writer's life through dramatised scenes from his novels.

Ned Sherrin had lined up a marvellous cast, which included Anthony Hopkins as Dickens, Arthur Lowe, Stanley Holloway, and Dames Gladys Cooper and Sybil Thorndike. Sherrin wanted Margaret Rutherford to play Miss La Creevy, the miniaturist from *Nicholas Nickleby*. Stringer had been instrumental in encouraging Margaret to undertake the part, feeling that a small role could be therapeutic. She received the script some weeks before the recording and Stringer went over the lines with her every day. Having heard that Margaret Rutherford was suffering from lapses of memory, Sherrin decided that, before rehearsals began, he should check that she had been able to learn the scene.

The producer asked Anthony Hopkins to accompany him and the two of them visited Margaret at Elm Close. Damaris Hayman had been staying and had also been rehearsing the lines in preparation. Unfortunately when Sherrin and Hopkins arrived, Margaret was actually having her afternoon nap and Stringer had to get her out of bed. She was thus a little drowsy and not at her best. Hayman remembers that Margaret had been word-perfect in the readings, but now had trouble recalling the lines. The actress was also thwarted by her false teeth, which kept slipping, making a performance even more difficult.

Sherrin wrote: 'Time after time she forgot the lines and each mistake added to her distress. We were as encouraging and admiring as we could be. Tony especially struck up a rapport with her, but it became agonising to watch. She was too ill and tired. The more she failed, the more determined to try again she became and the more tearfully disappointed. Our difficulty was to release her without allowing her to feel that she had let us down. We left at last with heavy hearts on Stringer's optimistic prophecy that her return to acting would perhaps be best judged in a large role in the theatre.' Damaris Hayman confirmed that Sherrin and Hopkins were 'incredibly sweet and patient' with Margaret – but she just couldn't sustain a performance.

In the summer, Margaret's mobility was still seriously restricted and she could only hobble around with the aid of two walking sticks. She had, however, been engaged to play the part of the bedridden grandmother in a film version of D.H. Lawrence's *The Virgin and the Gypsy*. The role of the deaf and crotchety old woman was relatively minor, but could have been amusing and was a part she would have nailed immediately in ordinary circumstances. But again Margaret simply could not remember her lines, and her scenes had to be shot and reshot. Unfortunately the film was being made on a very tight schedule, and it was decided that another actress would have to be engaged. Fay Compton was later hired to replace her.

Her poor memory caused further frustration and misery when she was asked to appear in the film *Song of Norway* with her old friend Robert Morley. There was an incident when she was needed on the set but was taking her afternoon nap and refused to move until she was ready. Despite much pleading, she wouldn't budge, so that eventually it was decided her services were no longer required. This was so unlike Margaret, always the professional, that Damaris Hayman even suggested that she deliberately sabotaged the job. Did she know she was just not up to working any longer and choose to avoid being embarrassed during the filming? *Song of Norway* was the last acting project for which Rutherford was contracted, and this unhappy dismissal proved to be a very sad end to her career.

During 1969 and 1970, the writer Gwen Robyns spent six months with Margaret and Stringer while researching Margaret's autobiography, which she was to 'ghost' two years later. The experienced author wrote to Dawn Langley Simmons that, 'Margaret was a very saddened woman. The depressiveness which she had fought so gallantly all her life had taken over and she sat the days away in her own twilight world. It was only at meal times that a twinkle came back into her eyes. It took some time to get her seated at the table and then Stringer would disappear into the kitchen to serve his meal. Margaret would sit very quiet like a small child. Firstly tucking her table napkin round her and then quietly watching the door of the dining room for Stringer's appearance.'

Margaret and Stringer had employed a daily help in the shape of would-be opera singer Violet Lang-Davis (no relation), but Stringer still prepared all the food. Margaret was quite particular about her meals and hated her plate to be piled up with food. Gwen Robyns related that while in Sydney on the 1957 Australian tour Margaret had made other hotel guests jump when an osso buco was placed before her and she trumpeted: 'Take it away – it looks like a graveyard!'

Stringer also bought the groceries and liked to be noticed around town. 'I am filled with admiration when Stringer goes shopping in Gerrards Cross in the summer in his Panama hat, flowered sports shirt and Bermuda shorts,' Margaret was quoted as saying at the time. Their fare was simple: steak pies brought from a local bakery were always served with a tin of tomato soup as a sauce; sausages were another favourite. Gwen Robyns recalled: 'The biggest treat was various flavoured blancmange from a packet always placed in the form of a crouched mouse. Margaret would always go through the same ritual: "Who is going to have mousie's head and who is going to eat mousie's tail?" Her little joke never failed and we all giggled like children.'

Despite Margaret's frailties, she was still determined to take to the water. 'It was a perishing early November day when she looked up at me and said, "Dear heart, could we go swimming? Wouldn't it be nice?",' recalled Ms Robyns. 'I protested that no public pool would still be open. She replied, "Oh I'm sure if you try you'll find somewhere." I telephoned the nearby swimming baths where it was explained to me that this was the very day they planned to drain the pool for the winter. But when they heard who was coming, they agreed to delay the operation until the afternoon.'

Robyns declared that living with Margaret and Stringer was like being centre stage in one of Rutherford's films. 'They were the most lovable eccentrics. Every morning I was wakened at seven a.m. by a light shining into my face. It was from a miner's lamp on a helmet that Stringer wore with his old dressing gown to make the morning tea.' She also found that Stringer was a stickler for routines – particularly when it came to washing up, 'He used to get furious with me when I put the silver in the wrong glass jars. There was a jam jar for spoons, another for forks another for knives and they could not be muddled.' She described Stringer as 'very peppery' and was forced to control her temper on occasions.

The task of researching Margaret's autobiography proved extremely troublesome: 'Gosh that book was difficult,' concluded Robyns. Not only was the actress's memory impaired, but her agent, Dorothy Mather, only spoke to the author on one occasion, and then only for an hour. Stringer forbade any mention of the Benn murder and wouldn't let Gwen into the bedroom where the archive material was kept. Damaris Hayman stayed in Gerrards Cross on occasions to help the process and verify certain facts, but felt that the 'autobiography', which was finally published in March 1972, was 'wildly astray in parts'.

In 1970 Margaret had her portrait painted for a second time – this time by one of Britain's most prestigious artists. Michael Noakes has painted most members of the royal family, including the Queen, as well as Frank Sinatra, Margaret Thatcher (twice) and President Clinton. Margaret Rutherford was unable to travel to Mr Noakes' London studio, so her sittings were done at Elm Close. The artist recalls that Margaret was much smaller than he had envisaged and also 'much prettier with a wonderful complexion'. Physically frail and easily tired, she was nevertheless always charming and polite. 'Margaret was mentally rather fragile and sometimes withdrawn. I tried to draw her out in conversation. I pointed at the Oscar on the mantelpiece, asking her when she acquired the statue. Miss Rutherford replied, "What dear?" I asked her again about the award: "When did you get it?" She looked at it and said, "Oh I don't know. Thursday, I think."'

Noakes remembers that although she wasn't very mobile, Stringer, who 'clucked around her like a hen', would take Margaret for a short walk around the garden after lunch, making sure she was well wrapped up 'in a splendid cape'. The painting was finished in September 1970 and it was shown at the 76th Annual Exhibition of the Royal Society of Portrait Painters. 'When Stringer and Margaret came to Trafalgar Square see the exhibition,' recalled Noakes, 'the sergeant on the desk and I had to put her in a wheelchair and struggled to transport her in a lift.'

The oil study of Margaret captures her beautifully. She is seen draped in a scarlet cloak, sitting in her favourite wing-backed chair. She loved the painting, and Stringer went even further, declaring, 'This is the happiest day of our lives.' Michael Noakes was delighted and touched by their reaction. During this period he also completed a drawing of Margaret, which is in London's National Portrait Gallery. Stringer had specifically asked that the portrait be given to the Globe Theatre, once H.M. Tennent's headquarters. The theatre changed its name in the mid-1990s to the Gielgud Theatre, and the painting can now be seen above the dress circle bar.

In 1971 Margaret suffered another fall, fractured her other hip and was admitted to Chalfonts and Gerrards Cross Hospital. During her six-month stay she was visited by Prime Minister Edward Heath who, by chance, had been invited to unveil a plaque. When he discovered that Margaret and Stringer were still in dire financial straits, he apparently made £2,000 available to her, as a special gift from the public purse.

While Margaret was hospitalised, Stringer took the decision to sell the expansive Elm Close and move to more suitable accommodation for Margaret's needs. 'Margaret Rutherford and Stringer Davis have sold their house in Packhorse Road for just under £20,000 freehold,' reported London's *Evening Standard* on 30 September. 'The house, built at the beginning of this century, has five bedrooms, three reception rooms, a lounge hall, bathroom and oil central heating. The property also has nearly an acre in land. The couple have bought a smaller property in Chalfont St Peter one quarter of the size and without stairs.' Stringer was quoted as saying, 'We move in there halfway through October and I hope to have it ready for my wife when she comes out of hospital.'

By the time Margaret was discharged from hospital to her new home, 'Hatfield', a bungalow situated in Joiners Lane, Chalfont St Peter, she was ailing. The Davises' new neighbour, John Luya, remembers Stringer manipulating a very frail Margaret, dressed in her favourite capes and long white socks and protected against the cold by several blankets, around in a wheelchair.

Margaret's health deteriorated rapidly over the winter and by the spring of 1972 Stringer could no longer manage caring for his incontinent and immobile wife. Assistance was provided by district nurses, who called on a daily basis to assist with basic requirements. A hoist to lift her in and out of bed was provided, but there was an accident and poor Margaret cracked a rib.

Damaris Hayman, who usually celebrated Margaret's birthday with her, was unable to do so that year as she was engaged to appear in a Les Dawson show in Leeds. She thus visited Margaret at Hatfield in the first week of May and found Margaret bedbound, 'a shell of her former self and semi-conscious'. Stringer was at his wit's end and knew that Margaret was dying. He asked Damaris to 'kiss my darling goodbye'. Damaris did as Stringer bid, and, as she 'bent down to say farewell, I saw that Margaret recognised me for a moment'.

A few days later, Margaret, now requiring twenty-four-hour nursing care, was admitted to hospital. One of her last visits was from Robert Morley, who recalled, 'She was strangely troubled and unhappy and naturally didn't have any idea who I was. She was for a long time the safest box office bet in the business and she knew it, the dear old bird.'

Margaret Rutherford died on 22 May 1972 at Chalfonts and Gerrards Cross Hospital, Chalfont St Peter. The causes of death were listed as bilateral bronchopneumonia, fractured left femoral neck and cerebral atherosclerosis. The funeral took place just three days later at St James Church, Gerrards Cross, with the Reverend J. Gordon Harrison officiating. It was a short, simple and traditionally religious ceremony, including the hymns 'Love Divine All Loves Excelling' and 'Now Thank We All Our God' and a reading of the 23rd Psalm. Robert Morley gave an address, and actor Robert Eddison read 'They Are All Gone into the World of Light' by Henry Vaughan.

A Service of Thanksgiving on 21 July 1972, arranged by H.M. Tennent, was held at the Actors' Church, St Paul's, Covent Garden, where there is still a plaque commemorating her life. There was a large turnout from the Benn family and close friends. Theatrical colleagues in attendance included Sir John Gielgud, Dame Flora Robson, Sir Ralph Richardson, Joyce Grenfell and Binkie Beaumont. The funeral hymns were reprised, while 'Ode to Joy' from Beethoven's Ninth Symphony was played on the organ. Keith Baxter recited 'The Scribe' by Walter de la Mare. He remembers that it was a quite a difficult poem and ambiguous in its content. A friend suggested that he read something else, but 'Margaret had left strict instructions that she wanted this particular poem to be recited and so I was determined to respect her wishes. I wanted to get it absolutely right and sought advice from Richard Burton.' Sir Ralph Richardson read an extract from the book of Revelation (chapter 7, verses 9–12), and there was a tribute by Dame Sybil Thorndike, in her ninetieth year, who insisted that there was nothing melancholic in goodbyes or farewells. She recalled an occasion when she and other artistes were gossiping about fellow actors and pulling them to pieces: 'And then Margaret was speaking suddenly and saying wonderful things. She never said anything horrid about anybody. She was a great actress and one whom we all loved most dearly. She was such a darling.' She ended by reading 'Farewell' by Walter de la Mare.

There were immediate tributes from family and fellow theatricals, but also from political figures. Prime Minister Edward Heath wrote: 'Dame Margaret made an outstanding contribution to the theatre. There must be millions of people who are today remembering her inimitable performances in the theatre, in films and on television and the enjoyment and pleasure which she gave. Harold Wilson added: 'For so many years she epitomised all that was best in British theatre. Her warmth and her talent delighted my wife and me, and countless others, throughout her career.' (Margaret was, herself, a fan of Mary Wilson's poetry.)

Noël Coward said he was 'terribly sad to hear of the death of my old friend – she created one of the funniest characters I ever wrote'. Laurence Olivier was unequivocal in his praise: 'Dame Margaret was one of the sweetest, warm and gentle ladies it could have ever been anyone's happiness to know. Her unique talent exercised itself with eccentric comedy but it could well have endowed more so-called serious work' Robert Morley concluded that her 'long-lined face with a huge jutting chin that seemed to twitch of its own volition . . . and a body of such uneven bulk it gave the impression of being on the point of toppling over – endowed her with grace and an odd charm. She was a marvellous woman . . . a good woman.' Dorothy Mather stated: 'She was a wonderful person and had the most gracious manners. She was never "funny funny". Everything arose out of the character she was playing.'

Margaret's idiosyncrasies were a godsend to critics and, although she sometimes dismissed the idea that she was an eccentric, there were times when she did nothing to dispel the notion. The *Daily Mirror*'s Donald Zec reported: 'If you paid her a compliment she would reply, "I am so very fortunate indeed, Donald, to have secured your affections." I once asked her if it was true that she slept with an east wind blowing over her face. She replied, "Naturally, dear boy, although I must confess I always have a favourite silk handkerchief draped over whichever ear is uppermost."' Stringer received numerous letters of condolence. Tony Benn wrote, 'I hope that the fact that the whole world is sharing your bereavement will be a comfort at the moment,' and Dame Sybil Thorndike lamented Margaret's passing: 'God rest her, darling woman – oh, Stringer, I wonder where they are – our beloveds – are they near us? I hope so.'

Margaret Rutherford's work has been sadly neglected in terms of media accolades: a season of her films appeared at the National Film Theatre in 2003, while a 1975 Radio 4 documentary, *The Art of Margaret Rutherford*, written and presented by her friend John Carroll, is an affectionate tribute. *For One Night Only*, written by Tony Bilbow, is a suitably idiosyncratic television film, and was broadcast on Channel 4 in October 1993. Timothy Spall is imaginatively cast as the ghost of Margaret Rutherford, who talks about her life and career. Producer/director Jane Oliver explained, 'This was an attempt to break away from the conventions of television. We wanted Timothy to play her because if it had been by a woman, people would have expected an impersonation. I think Margaret would have approved – she was a very free spirit.'

It is indeed an extremely affectionate and poignant portrayal by Timothy Spall, who doesn't attempt an imitation but does reproduce

Rutherford's perfect diction. Filmed in a small theatre with an invited audience, Rutherford is introduced sitting on a red throne in her chintzy dressing room, complete with standard lamp – a mini Elm Close – surrounded by photos and cards. A Madame Arcati-style crystal ball is used as a device to reveal characters and tell the story in flashback.

Rutherford announces her adoration of Ivor Novello (Michael Praed): 'What we had was propinquity without passion.' There is a jolly sequence of the two of them, swimming while singing, 'We'll Gather Lilacs'. Simon Ward does a rather good impersonation of Stringer, and, in a candid bedroom scene, Stringer and Margaret are portrayed as complete innocents, Margaret protesting to her husband, 'No, Stringer, that's my belly button!'

Other members of the cast include Nickolas Grace as Noël Coward and Liz Smith as Rutherford's housekeeper Elizabeth Orphin. At the end of her performance, Rutherford entreats the audience to join her in a meal, and a number of waiters appear in the audience with plates of bacon and eggs. What else?

Rutherford's legacy has also been recognised in other ways. Drama college students compete for theatrical awards named in her honour. Visitors to the Bridge Hotel in Northamptonshire can relax in the 'Margaret Rutherford Lounge'. Letter-writers in the Dominican Republic were once able to affix an image of Rutherford peering through a pair of curtains, as part of a series of stamps celebrating famous sleuths. Visitors to the Victoria and Albert Museum's theatre archive can see two of Rutherford's 'Miss Marple' capes, and intrepid fans can search out a 2002 blue plaque in Margaret's memory, unveiled at her Aunt Bessie's house at 4 Berkeley Place, Wimbledon, SW19.

Margaret Rutherford lived her life under a shroud of mystery, deception and secrecy, and it is ironic that the person who revealed her wretched family background was herself a charlatan. The enigmatic Dawn Langley Simmons, who died in September 2000 in Charleston, South Carolina, is the subject of Edward Ball's fascinating book,

Peninsula of Lies. Ball interviewed her husband, John-Paul Simmons, and exposed the truth of her fantasy life. Gordon had always maintained that he had already had his sex change when he met John-Paul – in fact the two of them lived together on and off before Gordon announced that he was going to undergo surgery.

Dawn's surgeon also confirmed that there was no evidence of Gordon having been born with female genitalia and that he was a transsexual. Incredibly, Dawn attempted to take the illusion even further. From the beginning of 1971, she pretended to be pregnant, and later claimed that she had given birth to a daughter, Natasha. In fact John-Paul had been carrying on a secret affair with another woman, who had become pregnant. Dawn paid the woman $1,000 to falsify the certificate showing her to be the baby's natural mother.

Dawn later claimed that Margaret Rutherford came to her in dreams when she was planning a biography of the actress. 'Mother Rutherford' told her to search for a trunk in the bungalow at Chalfont St Peter, where, on contacting the new owners, Dawn discovered a large coffer filled with archive material. It was in Dawn's biography of the actress, *A Blithe Spirit*, that Margaret's family background was revealed. Tony Benn remembers the week in 1983 when the book was published. 'It was all over the *News of the World*. They'd hired a genealogist to research the Benn ancestry and identified my connection with Peggy Rutherford and Julius Benn, to imply that I had a streak of inherited madness. I was worried that it would be politically embarrassing, but the only person who ever referred to it was a cab driver, who said, "Sorry to hear about your uncle," as if it had happened last week.'

Epilogue

Why must the show go on?
The rule is surely not immutable,
It might be wiser and more suitable
Just to close
If you are in the throes of
Personal grief and private woes.

NOËL COWARD

T OWARDS THE END of 2008, the Director of Public Prosecutions released a file, under the Freedom of Information Act, which gave some insight into the last year of Stringer Davis's life and solved yet another Rutherford mystery.

Stringer and Margaret had first met over forty years before Margaret's death, and the couple had been inseparable since their marriage in 1945. Now alone, Stringer set about responding to some of the letters of condolence he had received. On 15 July 1972, using Margaret's headed notepaper, he wrote to Joe Mitcheson and Raymond Mander: 'Thank you for your dear letter. I am taking consolation and companionship answering them. She was much loved. I don't know what I'm going to do . . .'

Work might have been a welcome distraction for Stringer, but this was hard to come by without Margaret. He made one television appearance in *The Museum Attendant*, an episode of the *Thirty-Minute Theatre* series, but no other offers were forthcoming. Stringer was distraught. Not only had he lost his life's companion, but his main role, over many years, of supporting and ultimately nursing his wife, had ended with Margaret's death. Vulnerable and lonely, he formed a relationship with the couple's housekeeper Violet Lang-Davis, who remained living at Hatfield. Mrs Lang-Davis, who had described herself as 'aide and lady's companion to actress Dame Margaret Rutherford', had trained at the Guildhall School of Music and made a living as a singer until 1965, when her husband was killed in a car crash.

Within a very short time after Margaret's death, Stringer asked Violet to marry him. The couple went to see Mrs Lang-Davis's parish priest in Hammersmith, Father Joseph Williams. 'They told me they were to be married and that they were looking for a house in Hammersmith.'

The wedding never took place. On 29 August 1973, Stringer Davis died peacefully in his sleep at home. Dawn Langley Simmons claimed that a treasured letter from Sir John Gielgud, Stringer's favourite actor, was found in his pyjama pocket. A few close friends attended the funeral at St James Church, Gerrards Cross, but there was no memorial service.

Six weeks after Stringer's death, Violet Lang-Davis visited Father Joseph and gave him Stringer's will, in which the priest was named as executor. The priest reported: 'The will had been opened and was placed in another envelope addressed to me. There was also a note written by Mrs Lang-Davis asking me to forward the will to Stringer's solicitors.'

On 9 June 1974 the *Sunday Telegraph* reported: 'Thieves have stolen an Oscar belonging to the late Margaret Rutherford from her former home at Chalfont St Peter.' Following a police investigation, on 9 October 1975, Violet Victoria Lang-Davis, aged sixty-five, was arrested and charged with forgery, criminal deception and theft. She appeared at Beaconsfield Magistrates Court, where she was remanded in custody to appear at the same court the following week.

The list of charges was 'that she on a day unknown between the 1st day of October 1973 and the 5th day of June 1974, at Chalfont St Peter in the county of Buckingham, stole an "Oscar", 4 fruit bowls, 6 plates of blue glass, a globe, a Copeland Doulton dinner service, part of a Minton service, two matching pairs of solid silver candlesticks, a pair of Sheffield silver plate candlesticks, a teapot and sugar basin of solid silver, a silver tureen dish, a silver meat cover, a solid silver canteen of cutlery and a bottle of Courvoisier, assorted furniture, a Meissen vase and assorted pictures, together with a value of £1,031 approx, the property of the estate of the late James Buckley Stringer Davis, with the intent permanently to deprive the said estate of the said property'.

There had been no burglary. It had been staged by Violet, who had also forged Stringer's will in order to become sole beneficiary. John Carroll told the police that he had become well acquainted with the handwriting of Stringer Davis and knew his signature extremely well. He testified that the copy of a will, purporting to have been signed by Stringer Davis, was a forgery.

Margaret's Oscar and Golden Globe, which were supposedly also stolen in the 'burglary', were discovered on sale at a Fulham antique shop. The owner, John Harvey, had bought them in good faith from Violet along with the items listed above and had subsequently sold the other articles. Violet also offered to sell him the house itself for £12,000. Margaret's Dame Commander's badge and breast star in silver with gilt enamels and her Variety Club Award were all later discovered for auction at Sotheby's.

Violet Lang-Davies spent one night in Holloway prison before she was granted bail. She failed to appear in court to stand trial and disappeared. A warrant for her arrest was issued but, for some reason, not followed up. A note in the 1985 DPP file states: 'Lang-Davis, it would appear, never stood trial and is still at large.'

Margaret and Stringer both died before Dawn Langley Simmons' book was published. Thankfully they were also unaware of Violet Lang-Davis's criminal activity. In death, as in life, Mr and Mrs Davis remain blissfully ignorant of the deception of their confidantes. They share a final resting place alongside each other in the inner circle of St James Church in Gerrards Cross.

The gravestone is marked:

TO
THE LOVED MEMORY OF
MARGARET RUTHERFORD D.B.E.
ACTRESS
MAY 11TH 1892 – MAY 22ND 1972
(Dear Wife of J.B. STRINGER DAVIS)
AND
JAMES BUCKLEY
STRINGER DAVIS
JUNE 4TH 1899 – AUGUST 29TH 1973

And at the foot of the memorial is a special inscription for Margaret Rutherford. It reads:

A BLITHE SPIRIT

Performance Credits

The following list of Margaret Rutherford's appearances is as full as possible, but by no means exhaustive. However, in an acting career that spanned over forty years there are likely to be some omissions. Her poetry readings and numerous charitable appearances are not included.

Theatre
September 1925 to May 1926: **The Old Vic School**
The Merchant of Venice (Attendant on Portia); *The Taming of the Shrew* (Bridesmaid); *Measure for Measure* (Citizen); *Antony and Cleopatra* (Slave); *Harlequin Jack Horner and the Enchanted Pie* (The Fairy with the Long Nose); *The Child in Flanders* (Gabriel); *The Merry Wives of Windsor* (Merrymaker); *Julius Caesar* (Citizen); *The Shoemaker's Holiday* (Citizen); *Romeo and Juliet* (Lady Capulet); *The Old Vic Follies* (*Shakespeare Birthday Programme*); *Much Ado about Nothing* (Guest)

November 1928: *A Hundred Years Old*, Lyric Theatre, Hammersmith (understudy for, Margaret Everest and Winifred Evans; played Dona Filomena as understudy to Mabel-Terry-Lewis)

April to December 1929: **Season with English Repertory Players, Grand Theatre, Fulham**
Trilby (Madame Vinard); *What Happened To Jones* (Alvina

Starlight); *David Garrick* (Selina Sowerberry); *Thark* (Lady Benbow); *A Tale of Two Cities* (La Vengeance); *The Passing of the Third Floor Back* (Mrs Shape); *Baby Mine* (Maggie); *Dr. Jekyll and Mr. Hyde* (Lady Hilda Holden); *Our Flat* (Madame Volant); *The Land Of Promise* (Agnes Pringle); *Tarnish*(Aggie); *Compromising Daphne* (Julia Ponsonby); *Lord Richard in the Pantry* (Lady Violet Elliot); *A Cuckoo in the Nest* (Mrs Spoker); *The Ringer* (Mrs Hackitt); *Jane* (Mrs Chadwick); *Moths* (Lady Dolly Vanderdecken); *The Green Beetle* (Chi Li); *A Little Bit of Fluff* (Aunt Hannah); *The Ware Case* (Rate); *The Three Musketeers* (Eustasia); *A Week-end* (Mrs Beckett); *The Liars* (Mrs Crespin); *Within The Law* (Helen Morris); *The Speckled Band* (Mrs Staunton); *Facing the Music* (Mrs Ponting); *Loose Ends* (Sarah Britt)

Little Theatre, Epsom
October 1930: *Dear Brutus* (Mrs Coade); December 1930: *The Sport of Kings* (Mrs Purdie)

November 1930 to March 1931: Rep at the Oxford Playhouse
Thark (Mrs Frush); *March Hares* (Mrs Janet Rodney); *On Approval* (Mrs Wislack); *If Four Walls Told* (Mrs Sturgis); *The Romantic Young Lady* (Doña Barbarita); *French Leave* (Madame Denaux); *The First Year* (Mrs Fred Livingstone); *The Unfair Sex* (Mrs Delisse); *The Importance of Being Earnest* (Lady Bracknell); *Interference* (Florence Rooke); *Mary Rose* (Mrs Morland); *The Ghost Train* (Miss Bourne); *Rookery Nook* (Mrs Leverett); *The Last of Mrs Cheney* (Mrs Ebley); *Ambrose Applejohn's Adventure* (Agatha Whatcombe)

1931: Repertory at the Greyhound Theatre (Croydon)
Hedda Gabler (Miss Tesman); *The Constant Wife* (Mrs Culver); *The Man With A Load Of Mischief* (The Innkeeper's Wife); *The Master Builder* (Aline Solness); *Sweet Lavender* (Mrs Gilfillian); *Lord Richard in the Pantry* (Lady Violet Elliot); *Loaves and Fishes*

(Mrs Railing); *Conflict* (Mrs Robinson); *Quinneys* (Susan Quinney); *The Laughing Lady* (minor character); *The Saving Grace* (Ada Parsons); *The Queen Was In the Parlour* (Miss Phipps); *The Laughter of Fools* (Elizabeth); *The Unfair Sex* (Pinker); *A Hundred Years Old* (Doña Filomena); *If Four Walls Told* (Mrs Sturgis); *Home and Beauty* (Miss Montmorency); *Trifles* (Mrs Peters)

1932: Season with Greater London Players
The Sacred Flame (Mrs Tabret); *Autumn Crocus* (Miss Mayne); *London Wall* (Miss Willesden)

April 1933: *Wild Justice* (Mrs Read) Lyric Theatre, Hammersmith, transferred to Vaudeville Theatre
February 1934: *Birthday* (understudy to Jean Cadell and Muriel Aked) Cambridge Theatre
April 1934: *The Master Builder* (Aline Solness) Embassy Theatre, Swiss Cottage
May 1935: *Hervey House* (Lady Nancy) His Majesty's Theatre
November 1935: *Short Story* (Miss Flower) Queen's Theatre
September 1936: *Farewell Performance* (Mrs Palmai) Lyric Theatre, Hammersmith
February 1937: *Tavern in the Town* (Aunt Bella) Embassy Theatre, Swiss Cottage
July 1937: *Up the Garden Path* (Emily Deveral) Embassy Theatre, Swiss Cottage
January 1938: *The Melody That Got Lost* (The Mother) Phoenix Theatre
May 1938: *Spring Meeting* (Bijou Furze) Ambassador's Theatre
August 1939: *The Importance of Being Earnest* (Miss Prism) Globe Theatre
April 1940: *Rebecca* (Mrs Danvers) Queen's Theatre
July 1941: *Blithe Spirit* (Madame Arcati) Piccadilly Theatre
28 September 1941: Concert in aid of the orphans fund of the Fire

Service Benevolent Fund (playlet: *Life and Mrs Muttlewell* with Rex Harrision and Lili Palmer)

September 1944: E.N.S.A. Tour of France and Belgium

December 1944: *Alice In Wonderland* (Queen of Hearts and White Queen) Palace Theatre

April 1945: *Perchance To Dream* (Lady Charlotte Fayre) Hippodrome, Golders Green

April 1946: *The Importance Of Being Earnest* (Miss Prism) Haymarket Theatre

March 1947: *The Importance of Being Earnest* (Lady Bracknell) Royale Theatre, New York

March 1948: *The Happiest Days of Your Life* (Miss Evelyn) Apollo Theatre

January 1950: *Ring Round the Moon* (Madame Desmortes) Globe Theatre

July 1952: *Miss Hargreaves* (Miss Hargreaves) Royal Court (later transferred to New Theatre)

February 1953: *The Way of the World* (Lady Wishfort) Lyric Theatre, Hammersmith

February 1954: *Alice through the Looking Glass* (White Queen) Prince's Theatre

18 March 1954: *Midnight Cavalcade* (Mrs Ackroyd-Smith) London Palladium, charity performance

December 1954: *Times Remembered* (Duchess of Pont-au-Bronc) Lyric Theatre, Hammersmith (later transferred to New Theatre)

March 1956: *A Likely Tale* (Mirabelle Petersham) Globe Theatre

June 1956: *Night of a 100 Stars* – sketch: 'Progress in Work', London Palladium, charity performance

December 1956: *The Way of the World* (Lady Wishfort) Saville Theatre

Spring 1957: Tour of *The Importance of Being Earnest* Lady Bracknell (Dublin, Limerick, Belfast, Edinburgh, Leeds, Liverpool, Eastbourne, Bournemouth)

September 1957: *The Happiest Days of your Life, Time Remembered* Elizabethan Trust tour of Australia

June 1958: *Bubble Man*, sketch in charity performance in aid of the Actors Orphanage at the London Palladium

March 1959: *Farewell, Farewell Eugene* (Minerva Goody (Povis)) Garrick Theatre

September 1960: *Farewell, Farewell Eugene* (Minerva Goody (Povis)) Helen Hayes Theatre, New York

June 1961: *Dazzling Prospect* (Bijou Furze) Globe Theatre

October 1961: *Our Little Life* (The Marquise, Tante Katya) Manoel Theatre, Valletta, Malta; Pembroke Theatre, Croydon

April 1962: *The School for Scandal* (Mrs Candour) Theatre Royal, Haymarket

May 1965: *The Solid Gold Cadillac* (Laura Partridge) Saville Theatre

May 1966: *The Clandestine Marriage* (Mrs Heidelberg) Chichester Festival Theatre

October 1966: *The Rivals* (Mrs Malaprop) Theatre Royal, Haymarket

FILM

1936: *Dusty Ermine* (Evelyn Summers aka Miss Butterby); *Talk of the Devil* (Housekeeper)

1937: *Beauty and the Barge* (Mrs Baldwin); *Big Fella* (Nanny (uncredited)); *Catch As Catch Can* (Maggie Carberry); *Missing, Believed Married* (Lady Parke)

1941: *Quiet Wedding* (Magistrate); *Spring Meeting* (Aunt Bijou)

1943: *The Demi-Paradise* (Rowena Ventnor); *Yellow Canary* (Mrs Towcester)

1944: *English Without Tears* (Lady Christabel Beauclerk)

1945: *Blithe Spirit* (Madame Arcati)

1947: *Meet Me at Dawn* (Madame Vernorel); *While the Sun Shines* (Dr Winifred Frye)

1948: *Miranda* (Nurse Carey)

1949: *Passport to Pimlico* (Professor Hatton-Jones)

1950: *The Happiest Days of Your Life* (Muriel Whitchurch);
Her Favorite Husband (Mrs Dotherington)

1952: *The Magic Box* (Lady Pond); *Curtain Up* (Catherine
Beckwith/Jeremy St. Claire); *Castle in the Air* (Miss Nicholson);
Miss Robin Hood (Miss Honey); *The Importance of Being Earnest*
(Miss Letitia Prism)

1953: *Innocents in Paris* (Gwladys Inglott); *The Runa way Bus*
(Miss Cynthia Beeston); *Trouble in Store* (Miss Bacon)

1954: *Aunt Clara* (Clara Hilton); *Mad About Men* (Nurse Carey)

1955: *An Alligator Named Daisy* (Prudence Croquet)

1957: *Just My Luck* (Mrs Dooley); *The Smallest Show on Earth*
(Mrs Fazackalee)

1959: *I'm All Right Jack* (Aunt Dolly)

1961: *Murder, She Said* (Miss Jane Marple); *On the Double* (Lady
Vivian)

1963: *The Mouse on the Moon* (Grand Duchess Gloriana XIII);
Murder at the Gallop (Miss Marple); *The VIPs* (The Duchess of
Brighton)

1964: *Murder Most Foul* (Miss Marple); *Murder Ahoy* (Miss Marple)

1965: *The Alphabet Murders* (Miss Marple (uncredited)); *Chimes at
Midnight* (Mistress Quickly)

1967: *A Countess from Hong Kong* (Miss Gaulswallow); *Wacky World
of Mother Goose* (Mother Goose (voice)); *Arabella* (Princess Ilaria)

TELEVISION

1938: *Have You Brought Your Music?*

1946: *The Importance of Being Earnest*

1950: *Miss Hargreaves* ("BBC Sunday-Night Theatre" 2 episodes)

1953: *Kaleidoscope*

1957: *At Home Sketch* (Carmichael's Night Out); *Place the Face*; *Dick
and the Duchess* (1 episode)

1958: *The Frankie Howerd Show* (ITV); *The Noble Spaniard*

1960: *Day After Tomorrow*; *The Two Wise Virgins of Hove* (ITV
   Television Playhouse, 1 episode)
1962: *Wednesday Magazine* (interviewee); *Film Profile* (interviewee);
   The Liar; *'Perspective Eccentricity'*
1963: *Tonight*; *Ivor Novello Series*; *The Kidnapping of Mary Smith*
   (ITV Play of the Week 1 episode)
1964: *The Stately Ghosts of England*
February 1966: *Jackanory* (5 episodes) – 'The Tale of Little Pig
   Robinson'; 'The Tale of Mrs Tiggy-Winkle'; 'The Tale of Johnny
   Town-Mouse'; 'The Tale of Mr. Tod'; 'The Tale of Beatrix Potter'
1966: *Late Night Line-Up* (interviewee)

RADIO
August 1938: *She Stoops To Conquer*
September 1938: *Detectives In Fiction*; *The Missing Kitten*
December 1938: *Newsreel and Empire* (Variety theatre);
   The Snow Man
February 1939: *The Importance of Being Earnest* (extract)
May 1944: *Miss Elizabeth Bennet*
July 1944: *Miss Duveen*
December 1944: *The Magic Red Knob* (Children's Hour Broadcasting
   Live, Parts 1-3)
October 1947: *Worzel Gummidge at the Treasure Ship* (Home
   Service)
November 1947: *Picture Paradise*
May 1948: Talk, 'It's Never Too Late To Be Happy' –
   Woman's Hour
May 1950: *Filmtime* (The Home Service interview)
May 1951: *Miss Hargreaves*
December 1951: *Meet the Buskers* (Light programme)
January 1952: *Desert Island Discs*, *Film Time*
August 1952: *This is Britain* (interview, Royal Court)
October 1953: *Dickens by the Fire*

November 1953: *The Frankie Howard Show* (Light Programme)
February 1957: *The Laughtermakers*
July 1958: *This is Britain* (recorded at Old Hall)
September 1959: *Today Programme* (interview)
October 1959: *In Town Tonight* (interview)
March 1960: *The Way of the World* (Third programme)
August 1960: *Day After Tomorrow*
July 1961: *How pleasant to know Mr Lear*
June 1963: *Woman's Hour* (with Stringer Davis)

Select Bibliography

Annakin, K (2001) *So You Wanna Be a Director?* (Tomahawk Press)

Attenborough, R (2008) *Entirely Up to You, Darling* (Hutchinson)

Ball, E (2004) *Peninsula of Lies* (Simon and Schuster)

Baxter, K (1998) *My Sentiments Exactly* (Oberon)

Benn, T (2004) *Dare to Be a Daniel* (Hutchinson)

Billington, M (2007) *State of the Nation* (Faber)

Bloom, C (1982) *Limelight and After: the Education of an Actress* (Penguin)

Brook, P (1998) *Threads of Time: A Memoir* (Methuen)

Callow, S (1995) *The Road to Xanadu* (Jonathan Cape)

Croall, J (2008) *Sybil Thorndike: A Star of Life* (Haus)

Day, B (ed) (2007) *Letters of Noel Coward (Diaries, Letters and Essays)* (A&C Black)

Falk, Q (2004) *Anthony Hopkins: The Authorised Biography* (Virgin)

Forbes, B (1977) *Ned's Girl – The Life of Edith Evans* (Elm Tree Books/Hamish Hamilton)

Forbes, B (1980) *That Despicable Race: A History of the British Acting Tradition* (Hamish Hamilton)

Freedland, M (1985) *The Secret Life of Danny Kaye* (WH Allen)

Garland, P (1998) *The Incomparable Rex (Harrison)* (Macmillan)

Gartside, MR (1999) *For All Seasons: The Story of Constance Cummings* (Wessex)

Gielgud, J (1979) *An Actor and His Time* (Sidgwick and Jackson)

Gielgud, J & Mangan, R (2005) *Sir John Gielgud – A Life in Letters* (Arcade)

Gottfried, M (1994) *Nobody's Fool – The Lives of Danny Kaye* (Simon & Schuster)

Guthrie, T (1960) *A Life in the Theatre* (Hamish Hamilton)

Harding, J (1987) *Ivor Novello – Man of the Theatre* (WH Allen)

Haymann, CD (1995) *Liz: An Intimate Biography of Elizabeth Taylor* (Heinemann)

Hoare, P (1992) *Serious Pleasures: Life of Stephen Tennant* (Penguin)

Hoare, P (1995) *A Talent to Amuse: Noel Coward: A Biography* (Reed)

Hogg, J with Sellers, R & Watson, H (2008) *James Robertson Justice What's The Bleeding-Time?* (Tomahawk Press)

Keown, E (1956) *Margaret Rutherford – An Illustrated Study of her Work* (Rockliff Publishing)

Lewis, R (1995) *The Life and Death of Peter Sellers* (Arrow Books)

Lewisohn, M (1998) *Radio Times Guide to TV Comedy* (BBC Worldwide)

Masset, A (2006) *Telling Some Tales* (Hutchinson)

McCabe, J (1978) *Charlie Chaplin* (Robson Books)

McCann, G (2005) *Frankie Howerd – Stand Up Comic* (Harper)

McCann, G (2008) *Bounder! The Biography of Terry-Thomas* (Aurum)

Miles, S (1993) *A Right Royal Bastard* (Macmillan)

Miller, J (1995) *Ralph Richardson – The Authorised Biography* (Sidgwick & Jackson)

Morley, M (1979) *Larger than Life – A Biography of Robert Morley* (Robson Books)

Morley, R & Stokes, S (1966) *A Reluctant Autobiography* (Simon and Schuster)

Morley, S (2002) *Asking for Trouble: The Memoirs of Sheridan Morley* (Hodder & Stoughton)

Morley, S (1983) *The Noel Coward Diaries* (Macmillan)

O'Connor, G (2002) *Paul Scofield – The Biography* (Sidgwick & Jackson)

Phillips, L (2006) *Hello – The Autobiography* (Orion)

Ross, R (2000) *The Complete Sid James* (Reynolds & Hearne)

Ross, R (2001) *The Complete Frankie Howerd* (Reynolds & Hearne)

Rutherford, M (1972) *Margaret Rutherford: an Autobiography as told to Gwen Robyns* (WH Allen)

Shaw, M & Vanacker, S (1991)*Reflecting on Miss Marple* (Routledge)

Sherrin, N (1991) *Ned Sherrin's Theatrical Anecdotes* (Virgin)

Sherrin, N (2005) *The Autobiography* (Little Brown)

Simmons, DL (1983) *Margaret Rutherford: A Blithe Spirit* (McGraw-Hill)

Simpson, M (2008) *Alastair Sim: The Star of Scrooge and The Real Belle of St Trinian's* (The History Press)

Strachan, A (2005) *Michael Redgrave: A Biography* (Orion)

Sweet, M (2005) *Shepperton Babylon, The Lost Worlds of British Cinema* (Faber)

Thompson, AW (2003) *Raw – My Autobiography* (Bantam)

Thomson, D (1996) *Rosebud – The Story of Orson Welles* (Abacus)

Tomlinson, D (1990) *Luckier than Most* (Hodder & Stoughton)

Tynan, K (1984) *A View of the English Stage 1944–1965* (Methuen)

Williams, H (1953) *Old Vic Saga* (Winchester Publications)

Williams, H (1938) *The Work of Lilian Bayliss* (Cobden Sanderson)

Williams, K (1985) *Just Williams – An Autobiography* (JM Dent & Sons)

Williams, K (ed Davies, R) (1994) *The Kenneth Williams Diaries* (Harper Collins)

Wisdom, N (2003) *My Turn – An Autobiography* (Arrow)

Acknowledgements

A VERY SPECIAL THANK you to Margaret's great friend Damaris Hayman, for sharing her memories with me.

I am much indebted to Rod Clare, Kelly Wooten and Richenel Ansano, Special Collections, Duke University, Malcolm Troup, Adrian Brown, Trish Hayes (BBC Written Archive Centre, Caversham Park, Reading), Mark Cardale, Mark Stevens, Senior Archivist, Berkshire Record Office, Kelly Jones (Wimbledon High School) and Mark Whiston. Their encouragement and enthusiastic participation have provided me with a wealth of information.

I am also grateful to the late Ken Annakin, Elroy Ashmore, the late Frith Banbury, Keith Baxter, David Benn, Melissa Benn, Tony Benn, Bradley Bolke, Celia Bannerman, Claire Bloom, Richard Briers, Peter Brook, Adrian Brown, Jess Campbell, Scott Carpenter, Petula Clark, Anna Evans (Chichester Festival Theatre), Irene Garland (Anglo-Norse Society) Geoffrey Green, Noel Hess, James Hogg, Mark Jones, Tessa Kulik, Ruth Leon, Roger Lewis, Philip Lowrie, Anna Massey, Francis Matthews, Virginia McKenna, Michael Noakes, Judy Parfitt, Nicholas Parsons, Muriel Pavlow, Ian Payne, Dan Peat, Josette Portelli (Manoel Theatre), Robert Ross, Rosy Runciman (Archivist, Cameron Mackintosh Ltd), Peter Sallis, Lyn Scrimshaw, Shirley Segal, Donald Sinden, Nina Soufy, John Standing, Sarah Stead, Clive Swift, Antony Worrall Thompson, Angela Thorne, Alan Travis, John Stuart-Webb, Benjamin Whitrow and Terry Young.

Thanks to the Staff at the V&A Theatre Archive, the BFI National Archive, Kristy Davis, Archive Officer, Mander and Mitchenson Theatre Collection, Gerry McArdle, Historical Disclosures, Army Personnel Centre and Sandra, Hilary and Lai-ming at Alexandra Park Library.

A particular mention must go to Daniel Merriman for his various contributions to the book and much appreciation to all the Merriman clan for allowing Miss Rutherford to join our household for a year.

Last, to Graham Coster, Dan Steward and Lydia Harley for their help and guidance.

Index